The
LONG LIFE
COOKBOOK

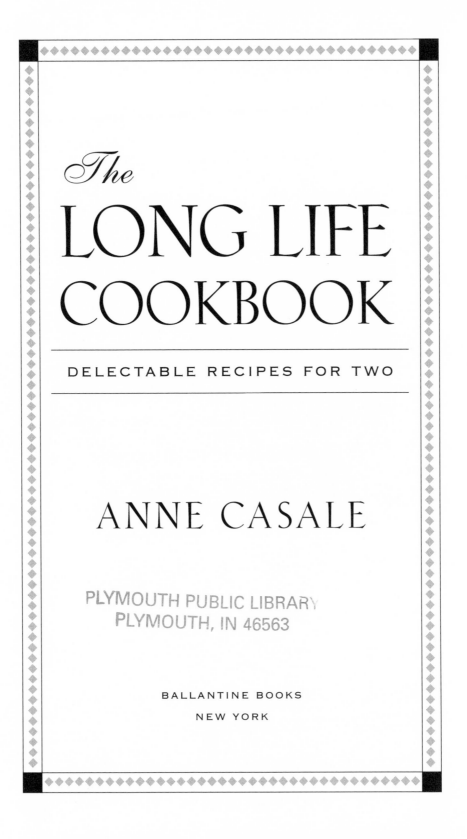

The

LONG LIFE
COOKBOOK

DELECTABLE RECIPES FOR TWO

ANNE CASALE

BALLANTINE BOOKS

NEW YORK

A Ballantine Book
Published by The Ballantine Publishing Group

Copyright © 1987 by Anne Casale
Revised and expanded edition copyright © 2002 by Anne Casale
"Nutrition Information" copyright © 2002 by Lynne S. Hill, M.S., R.D.

www.ballantinebooks.com

LIBRARY OF CONGRESS CATALOGING-IN-PUBLICATION DATA
is available from the publisher upon request.

ISBN 0-345-45176-7

Text design by Debbie Glasserman

Manufactured in the United States of America

First Revised Edition: February 2002

10 9 8 7 6 5 4 3 2 1

THE LONG LIFE COOKBOOK
is dedicated to
my four grandchildren,

Sarah and Denton Savage,
John Paul and Colin Edward Murphy.

The greatest legacy I can offer is a heart filled with love and the
wherewithal to lead a happy and healthy life.

Contents

Acknowledgments

My personal gratitude to David Wald, a very dear friend, for the many hours spent helping me put my thoughts into words.

The
LONG LIFE
COOKBOOK

Introduction: Cooking and Eating the Long Life Way

It's amazing what you can learn about people while walking up and down the aisles of a supermarket. One's taste, style of eating, and values are on public display to the well-trained eye. I have a terrible habit of looking into other people's shopping carts while marketing or at the checkout counter. When I see some of the so-called convenient frozen, premixed, precooked, processed fast foods loaded with fats and additives, I have to restrain myself from pulling those products out of carts. How I would love to take these people by the hand and offer a minicourse while walking through the supermarket. I would guide them up and down the aisles, introducing wholesome products and helping them to restructure old, unhealthy eating habits and discover enjoyable, healthy new ones.

My first lecture would be on reading labels. The majority of packages on supermarket shelves today provide nutritional information, and all have ingredients listed. A quick glance at those food labels reveals extraordinary amounts of fat, salt, and preservatives.

The course would include brief visits to the dairy, meat, poultry, and seafood sections, where I would offer suggestions for making the best selections. The produce area would be scrutinized at length as we took in nature's bountiful array of fresh fruits, vegetables, and herbs. We would continue along the aisle offering an array of imported pastas made from semolina flour, and then move into the aisle filled with assorted flours and such grains as rice, bulgur, and barley. Our last stop would be the condiment aisle, overflowing with dried herbs, spices, oils, and vinegars. As the grand tour ended, we would return all the convenient frozen, premixed, precooked, processed fast foods loaded with fats and additives to the shelves and start shopping again . . . *sensibly*.

As I would guide those people through the supermarket, allow me to guide you through these pages. Let me share with you a practical, nutritional approach to food selection and preparation—a style I call "long life cooking."

In my quest for an appealing, healthful way of cooking, I've tried to be creative in my use of ingredients. Pure olive, extra virgin olive, corn, and canola oils as well as unsalted butter are used in very limited quantities. In seasoning, salt has been reduced or replaced by such ingredients as fresh lemon juice, a dash of wine, herbs, and spices. Cream has been replaced with lighter enrichments of part-skim ricotta cheese and low-fat yogurt. Foods are sweetened naturally, not with artificial sweeteners, but with small amounts of sugar and/or sweet vegetables and fruits. Long life cooking does not mean sacrificing the excitement and appeal of the foods you love. These recipes are both healthy *and* delicious. I believe that food is at its best when we guard its natural flavors. Each dish should have its own identity—one that is not camouflaged by heavy sauces and thickeners.

Although most of the recipes in this book utilize foods that can be purchased in small quantities to serve two, many adapt themselves to cooking for one simply by halving the given amounts. Recipes can easily be increased if entertaining, and some (for example, soups, yeast breads, quick breads, and muffins) already have larger yields; all of these freeze well.

The recipes have been designed in a simple step-by-step style for efficiency and ease. Ingredients are listed in the order in which they are to be used. The nutritional analysis is listed at the end of each recipe.

All the recipes have been kitchen- and taste-tested to make sure that even an inexperienced cook can successfully complete them with the utmost confidence. With today's lifestyles, no one wants to spend hours in the kitchen preparing meals. *The Long Life Cookbook* offers a wide range of delectable, imaginative recipes that can be prepared in a limited amount of time; in fact, many can be on your table in less than an hour.

The Long Life Cookbook is more than a collection of recipes. It is a modern, sensible, and satisfying approach to food with an emphasis on freshness and simplicity, dedicated to your good health.

ANNE L. CASALE

Glossary: Ingredients

When it comes to ingredients, it is impossible to overstate the virtue of using the finest products possible. Their value is not measured in cost but in excellence of taste, quality, and freshness.

BREAD CRUMBS, DRY AND FRESH

Dry. Arrange slices of bread in a single layer on a cookie sheet. Preheat oven to 250 degrees and toast bread until crisp and golden, about 30 minutes. Break into 1-inch chunks and whirl in food processor fitted with metal blade until finely ground. Place crumbs in fine mesh strainer and sift into larger bowl. Discard any large crumbs or whirl again in food processor. Place in jars and keep in cool, dry place until needed. Store in the refrigerator during summer months.

Fresh. Cut up fresh or day-old bread, including crust, or tear it gently with fingers. Place in food processor fitted with metal blade. Run machine until bread is reduced to coarse crumb consistency.

CAPERS

These are the flower buds from a low, trailing, thorny shrub that thrives in the hot, dry Mediterranean climate. After harvesting, the unopened buds are dried in the open air, then pickled in casks of salted vinegar or dry-cured in coarse salt. Capers should always be thoroughly rinsed and drained before being added to any dish or sauce. For recipes in this book, I suggest you buy the tiny variety called "nonpareil," which are pickled in salted vinegar. Experts say this variety has more flavor than the larger buds. Spoon capers out of jar with a small spoon and place in a small strainer set over a cup. Pour strained vinegar from cup back into jar. (Jar can be refrigerated indefinitely without fear of spoilage if capers are covered with vinegar.) Then rinse the measured capers thoroughly under running water, and drain.

EGGS

Sizes are specified with each recipe. If they are to be separated, use eggs taken directly from refrigerator. A cold egg breaks cleanly and the yolk is less likely to rupture than one at room temperature. It is critical that no egg yolk find its way into the whites, for even a trace of yolk will prevent them from reaching full volume when beaten. If part of the yolk should fall into the white, use the shell to scoop it out. If beaten egg whites are used in desserts, these recipes specify that cream of tartar be added to stabilize them.

FLOUR

Recipes in this book call for different varieties of flour. Read labels and recipes carefully. Spoon the flour lightly into the measuring cup; do not shake the cup or pack or press the flour. Level lightly with the back of a knife. (Bread flour may not be available in some parts of the country.)

Unbleached All-purpose Flour. This type of flour is made from a blend of high-gluten hard wheat and low-gluten soft wheat. It is suitable for baking a complete range of products, including cakes, biscuits, muffins, and quick breads. If bread flour is unavailable, this type of flour is also recommended for yeast breads. Unbleached flour should be stored in an airtight container at room temperature and should be used within six months of purchase.

Bread Flour. This type of flour is milled from hard wheat, which has a high gluten content. The high-gluten protein in bread flour gives risen breads a light, fluffy texture. Bread flour should be stored in an airtight container at room temperature and should be used within six months of purchase.

Whole Wheat Flour. The entire kernel of whole wheat flour, also called graham flour, is milled from hard wheat, which has a high content of germ and bran. Place in an airtight container and store in the refrigerator. (The natural germ in the flour may turn rancid if stored at room temperature.) Before using it in any recipe, the amount needed should be allowed to come to room temperature.

Wondra Flour. For coating, I recommend Gold Medal Wondra, an instant, all-purpose flour that pours like salt. It will give a much lighter coating for sautéing.

LEMONS

An indispensable flavoring in many of my dishes. Try to pick smooth-skinned lemons; they have more juice. The juice can be substituted for vinegar in salad dressing. Use only freshly squeezed juice, never the re-constituted type, which leaves a bitter aftertaste. Make sure you scrub the lemon's outer skin well to remove any coating before using the rind in any dish.

OILS

Olive Oil. For recipes that specify olive oil, look for the word "pure" on the label and purchase the best quality you can afford. When extra virgin olive oil is listed, it is recommended for its fruity accent and enticing aroma, which come from the first pressing of the finest olives picked. It delivers a powerful olive color and distinctive flavoring for that particular dish, so a small amount goes a long way. In choosing either a pure or ex-tra virgin olive oil, purchase small bottles at first, before deciding which you prefer. Your palate will tell you which flavor suits you best. If you are going to purchase only one type of olive oil, I recommend that you buy the extra virgin and use it for all recipes listing olive oil. Olive oil does not have to be kept in the refrigerator, but it should be sealed and stored in a cool, dark place.

Vegetable Oil and Cooking Sprays. Only small amounts of vegetable oil, such as corn and canola oil, are used for recipes in this book, primarily for stir-frying and baking. There are many aerosol cooking sprays avail-able at the market, from corn oil to olive oil. You can also purchase a stainless steel mister and fill it with corn, canola, or olive oil whenever cooking sprays are recommended for cooking or for greasing pans.

THE ONION FAMILY

The strong-flavored members of the onion family, including chives, gar-lic, leeks, red onion, scallions, shallots, and yellow onion, are used as sea-sonings. They offer a variety of interesting tastes of different intensities. Although many can be used interchangeably, each type has a particular use and all share a starring role in the kitchen.

Chives. Thin, dark green, tubular chive leaves are the mildest flavoring in the onion family. They add wonderful seasoning to salads and baked potatoes, and may also be used as an attractive garnish.

Garlic. Buy bulbs that are tightly closed, with unwrinkled skins of white, pink to purple, or white with purple streaks. Store in a cool, dark place.

For easy peeling, place a clove under the broad side of a chef's knife. Thump the blade to split the garlic's clinging skin; it will then slip off easily. It is better to chop or mince garlic with a knife than to mash through a press.

Leeks. Buy leeks with crisp, green, unwithered tops and clean, white bottoms. Leeks should be straight and cylindrical. If the ends are very bulbous, the leeks will probably be tough and woody. To clean, trim roots and a portion of the fibrous leaf tops. Cut the stalks in half lengthwise and wash thoroughly under running water, holding the layers apart, until no sand remains.

Red Onion. This type of onion is also called Spanish onion. It is relatively mild and sweeter tasting than the yellow onion. Red onions can be used for the same purpose as yellow onions in cooking, or eaten raw in salads. Store in a cool, dry place.

Scallions. Select those with crisp, green, unwithered tops and clean, white bottoms. Try to pick scallions with large, bulbous ends. Trim roots and any brown or limp tops. Wash thoroughly and blot dry with paper towel. Wrap in paper towel and store in sealed plastic bag in refrigerator. Use within four or five days.

Shallots. These slender, pear-shaped bulbs are about the size of walnuts and are more perishable than onions. They should be stored in a cool, dark place. The shallot's flavor is more delicate than onion and it's more easily digested. To use, divide the cloves. Cut off tops and tails of the shallots. Peel with a small paring knife, pulling away the first layer of flesh with the skin that is usually firmly attached to it.

Yellow Onion. Yellow onions are considered to be the most pungent of all the globe onions. Look for ones with no trace of moisture at the base or the neck and with no growth of light greenery at the top—a sign that they have begun to sprout. Select smaller globe onions rather than the larger specimens; once cut, they do not keep well. Store in a cool, dark place.

PARMESAN CHEESE

This rich, nutty, flavorful cheese is essential to many pasta dishes in this book. Parmesan cheese should be grated just before using so that flavor is at its best. The production of imported Parmesan cheese labeled "Parmigiano Reggiano" is very strictly controlled. Ask to see the wheel and make sure it is stamped "Reggiano." To store, wrap in a thin layer of dampened cheesecloth, then in plastic wrap. Place in a plastic bag and seal tightly. Store in refrigerator. It must be stored in this manner because it dries out much more quickly than other cheeses. When freshly cut and moist, Parmesan is also an excellent table cheese with grapes or sliced Bosc pears.

PART-SKIM RICOTTA CHEESE

A soft, moist, snow-white cheese made from part-skim milk and whole milk, ricotta is very perishable. Always check the expiration date before purchasing. Some brands of part-skim ricotta cheese tend to be a little watery. If there is a thin layer of liquid on top of the cheese, drain it before using. Line a fine mesh strainer with a double thickness of dampened cheesecloth. Spoon ricotta into lined strainer set over a bowl. Place, uncovered, in refrigerator to drain thoroughly for at least 3 hours.

When ricotta is whipped in a blender or food processor, it has the dairy-rich flavor and smooth, creamy texture of thick whipped cream. To make whipped ricotta, empty a 15-ounce container of fresh part-skim ricotta into blender or food processor fitted with metal blade. Process until the graininess disappears and ricotta is the consistency of thick whipped cream: about 30 seconds. Stop machine once and scrape down inside blender or work bowl with plastic spatula. Spoon cheese back into container in which it was purchased and store in refrigerator.

Whipped ricotta is so versatile that I always have some on hand in the refrigerator. Its smooth texture blends well with dishes ranging from pasta to desserts. For breakfast, whipped ricotta is excellent spread thinly on toasted muffins or whole wheat bread. A delightful addition to ricotta-covered toast is a layer of sliced fresh fruit or a little cinnamon-sugar. One of my favorite breakfasts is bite-sized shredded wheat drizzled with a little orange blossom honey and topped with 1 heaping tablespoon whipped ricotta. It reminds me of the Italian pastry *sfogliatelle*. For a quick dessert, spoon 1 tablespoon whipped ricotta sweetened with 2 teaspoons of your favorite liqueur (Grand Marnier is my favorite) per serving over cut fresh fruit.

Whipped ricotta may be used for any recipe in this book using ricotta.

SALT

I recommend using coarse salt (Diamond Crystal or Morton brand) for seasoning because it is pure, contains no additives, and requires smaller amounts for flavoring. For baking, use common table salt.

VINEGAR

Balsamic Vinegar. This aromatic, concentrated vinegar is a specialty of Modena. Balsamic vinegar takes several years of aging to produce the best quality. It's worth investing in the real thing. Make sure the label confirms that it is balsamic vinegar of Modena. One of my favorite brands is Fini.

Red Wine Vinegar. Choose one that has a clear, deep red color. The flavor should be sharp but clean. My choice for a good domestic brand is Heinz.

White Wine Vinegar. This is similar to red wine vinegar but not as complex in flavor. There are many different brands to choose from. Both domestic and imported are excellent. My favorite is the white balsamic, which is now available in many supermarkets and specialty shops.

LOW-FAT YOGURT

Plain low-fat yogurt is a culture made from pasteurized milk, skim milk, and nonfat milk solids. Always check the expiration date on the container before purchasing. Many of the low-fat yogurts tend to be watery and should be drained thoroughly before using. Line a fine mesh strainer with a double thickness of dampened cheesecloth. Spoon a 16-ounce container of yogurt into the lined strainer set over a bowl. Place, uncovered, in refrigerator to drain for at least 3 hours. Yogurt will exude as much as ½ cup of liquid; discard liquid. After draining, yogurt will have the consistency of lightly whipped heavy cream. Spoon back into container in which it was purchased and store in refrigerator until needed. It can be used as a spread on toast, as a topping for baked potatoes, or just mixed with cut fresh fruit for a simple dessert. I also use yogurt for yeast breads, quick breads, salad dressings, and in other dessert recipes.

HERBS

One of the joys of the summer months is to look out my kitchen window at my herb garden. My daughters, Joanne and Amy, plant my herb garden every year as a gift for Mother's Day. Use fresh herbs whenever possible. Many supermarkets now carry fresh herbs year-round. If fresh herbs are not available, use the dried variety for many recipes. I provide both fresh and dry measurements. A general rule of thumb: 1 tablespoon of minced or chopped fresh herbs is equivalent to 1 teaspoon crumbled dried. When buying dried herbs, always look for those that are green rather than pale or powdered; the latter usually have less flavor. Buy herbs in glass jars so that you can see the color and judge the freshness.

Store jars away from sunlight and heat. For full flavor, rub the herb between your palms.

Basil. The most common basil of the more than a hundred different varieties available worldwide is sweet basil. These whole, bright green leaves are deliciously aromatic. This herb is best when the fresh leaf is available. (Many supermarkets now stock fresh basil year-round.) Pluck off the tender leaves just before you use them so that they won't bruise or go limp. Wash in cold water, drain well, and blot dry between two layers of paper towel. Basil marries perfectly with tomato, whether in salads or sauces. It also has a great affinity with sautéed eggplant or zucchini and is an indispensable flavoring for Basil Ricotta Pesto Sauce (page 55). I often use this fresh herb in place of lettuce in a sandwich. Try it just once, and you'll be hooked!

Bay Leaf. Fresh or dried, use bay leaf sparingly, for it has a strong flavor. If purchasing dry, always buy whole leaf, never crumbled or powdered. Look for leaves that are still tinged with green; if they are more than a year old, they will have lost their flavor as well as their color. Used sparingly, bay leaf adds a wonderful, subtle flavoring to roast pork, beef soup, and stews.

Dill. The pungent flavor of this herb is excellent either fresh or dried. If purchasing dried, I prefer the type labeled "dillweed," the dried fronds rather than dill seed. Use either fresh or dried for soups, salads, salad dressings, poultry, and especially fish. It also adds wonderful zest to either baked or boiled white potatoes.

Fennel. This whole seed has a licorice taste and should be crushed before being added to any dish. To crush fennel seeds, use a mortar and pestle. Alternatively, place fennel seeds in a mound on cutting board and give them a good thump with the broad side of a chef's knife to crush partially, then finely chop with knife. Fennel is excellent when sprinkled on top of broiled fish, roast pork, or cooked peas that are dressed with a little olive oil.

Marjoram. Use this strong, sweet, sagelike herb sparingly. Either fresh or dried marjoram adds distinct flavor in marinades for fish or poultry.

Mint. There are many varieties of this herb. Besides peppermint and spearmint, there are also pineapple, apple, and orange mints that can be used in fruit salads or as a garnish in cold summer drinks. Use peppermint or spearmint for the recipes in this book. Mint, which may be used fresh or dried, is very easy to grow and dry. Collect the leaves on a hot, sunny day, preferably just before flowering time. Wipe them with a damp cloth and dry on paper towel for a couple of days. Mint is a wonderful flavoring with roast lamb and broiled fish, or in salad dressings.

Oregano. Always use oregano sparingly because of the herb's strong, spicy flavoring, which is sharper than marjoram. Try to buy whole bunches of the dried plant; they hold their flavor longer in storage. The best quality comes from Italy, Greece, and Mexico. Oregano is an indispensable flavoring for marinara sauce, and marvelous on a tomato salad simply dressed with extra virgin olive oil, a pinch of sugar, and freshly milled black pepper.

Parsley. Parsley is a refreshing and versatile herb. It can be used with almost any meat, fowl, fish, or vegetable; finely minced, it will dress up any dish. The flat-leaf variety known as Italian parsley is more pungent in taste than the curly leaf. Use curly leaf for garnishing; use Italian parsley for flavor. Stems can be wrapped in bundles, frozen, and saved for soup. To store parsley leaves, wash and air dry on paper towel or spin dry in a salad spinner. Put in a jar and place a folded piece of paper towel on top to absorb additional moisture. Cover tightly and refrigerate. Parsley stored in this manner will stay green and fresh up to one week in the refrigerator.

Rosemary. Rosemary's powerful flavor is traditionally used with lamb, but it is equally good with chicken. The spiky dried leaves retain their flavor well.

Sage. Sage has velvety, grayish green leaves with a slightly musky taste. This herb must be used sparingly, especially fresh sage, a hardy perennial very easy to grow in a sunny garden. Fresh or dried, sage adds zesty flavor to chicken or pork.

Savory. A robust and very aromatic herb that tastes similar to thyme. There are two varieties of this herb: Summer savory is an annual with a mild, sweet taste; winter savory is a perennial species with a more robust flavor. Both summer and winter savory have a pleasant, piquant quality especially suited to poultry.

Tarragon. This herb has a slight hint of anise. Fresh tarragon, available through the summer months, harmonizes wonderfully with chicken and adds great flavor to zucchini and carrots. You might also want to try some snipped in your tossed green salad.

Thyme. A tiny-leaved herb with a warm, earthy smell, thyme is a hardy plant, easy to grow. Leaf thyme or common thyme is used for the recipes in this book. To dry, just hang in bunches in a warm, dry place, then rub the leaves off and store in a jar. If it is available, use lemon thyme, which has a faint citrus tang and is excellent on broiled chicken, lamb, or fish.

SPICES
Purchase all your spices in glass jars and store away from sunlight and heat.

Allspice. Allspice tastes like a blend of cinnamon and nutmeg, but is actually a single spice ground from the underripe berry of a tropical evergreen tree. The ground variety is recommended for all recipes in this book.

Cinnamon. Both whole-stick cinnamon and good imported ground cinnamon should be kept on hand. The whole stick can be ground with a mortar and pestle.

Ginger. Ginger comes from the root of the ginger plant. For all recipes in this book, freshly grated gingerroot is used.

Nutmeg. Select whole nutmegs and grate with a small grater whenever needed. You will find their flavor much better than the powdered variety.

Pepper. Pepper, both black and white, is probably the most widely used of all spices. The whole peppercorns are the dried berries of the tropical pepper vine. The black come from underripe berries that have been dried and cured; the white from dried, ripe berries whose dark outer shell has been removed. The two varieties of black peppercorns I use are Tellicherry, which comes from India, and Java, which is imported from the East Indies. Best when freshly ground, both black and white pepper enhance all savory dishes. White pepper is used in light-colored sauces, some salad dressings, and mayonnaise.

Nutrition Information

The following information will help you to understand the nutrition analyses found in this book.

CALORIES

(cal.) are a measure of energy in foods. It is recommended that you eat the number of calories that allow you to maintain your "ideal body weight." Thus, appropriate daily caloric intake will vary from person to person.

How to Figure Percentage of Calories from Fat. Take the number of grams *(gm)* of fat in your food. Multiply by **9** (each gram of fat has 9 calories) to determine the number of fat calories that food has. Take the number of calories from your food. Divide the fat calories by the total number of calories in your food source to obtain the percentage of calories from fat.

FAT

consumed in excess is thought to lead to many serious diseases. Current recommendations are to limit your fat calories in a day (not in any one particular food) to 30 percent. To find out how many grams of fat you may safely eat in a day, multiply your total caloric intake by **.3** and then divide by **9**. For example, if you eat 1,800 calories a day: 1,800 (calories) × .3 = 540 (calories from fat), and 540 (calories from fat) ÷ 9 (calories in a gram of fat) = 60 (grams of fat) or, the total you can eat in a day.

CARBOHYDRATES

(Carb.) are found in foods as simple sugars and complex carbohydrates, and they are a source of energy for the body. It is recommended that complex carbohydrates from fruits, vegetables, grains, and legumes be

increased in the diet and that simple sugars be decreased. Complex carbohydrates contain fiber that is beneficial. Carbohydrates contain 4 calories per gram.

CHOLESTEROL
(Chol.) is found in foods from animal sources—meat, poultry, seafood, eggs, and dairy products. It is wise to keep your daily intake to 250 to 300 milligrams.

PROTEIN
(Prot.) is known as the building block of the body. It is made up of amino acids and has 4 calories per gram. Protein is needed for growth, repair, and maintenance of cells, enzymes, and antibodies.

SODIUM
(Sod.) is found naturally in most foods. When eaten in excess, it can contribute to heart disease, high blood pressure, stroke, and kidney disease. Current recommendations limit a day's intake to 2,400 milligrams. Salt is the most common contributor to high sodium levels: 1 teaspoon has about 2,200 milligrams.

GRAM AND MILLIGRAM
(g and *mg)* are measures of weight. Nutrients eaten in large amounts, such as carbohydrates, protein, and fat, are reported in grams. Nutrients eaten in small amounts, such as sodium and cholesterol, are reported in milligrams. There are 1,000 milligrams in 1 gram.

All analyses have been rounded to the nearest whole number. When the analysis is less than 1, the decimal fraction has been given. Please note that percentage of calories from fat has been calculated before rounding off fat grams to a whole number.

LYNNE S. HILL, M.S., R.D.

SOUPS

BEEF BROTH   22

CHICKEN BROTH   24

ASPARAGUS SOUP   25

BROCCOLI SOUP   26

CAULIFLOWER SOUP WITH PARSLEY   27

CHICKEN SOUP WITH HERBS   28

CHILLED CUCUMBER SOUP   29

COLD MELON SOUP   30

LEFTOVER SOUP   31

LENTIL AND BROWN RICE SOUP   32

MINESTRONE SOUP   33

RAW MUSHROOM SOUP   34

BUTTERNUT SQUASH AND APPLE SOUP   35

GRATED POTATO SOUP   36

CHILLED TOMATO MINT SOUP   37

VEGETABLE BARLEY SOUP   38

JULIENNED VEGETABLE SOUP   39

My love for soup comes from my childhood. During the Depression years, soup was a staple in our home. My mother served it almost daily for lunch, especially during the winter months, and at least once a week for the main meal year-round.

I can remember being sent to the butcher shop to purchase meat for soup. At that time, beef hind shank or boneless chuck cost twelve cents a pound. The butcher would always ask, "Is your mother making soup today?" and throw in extra bones when I nodded yes.

Whenever I teach soup classes, my students ask, "Can I use bouillon cubes or canned broth?" My answer is, "I would not recommend bouillon cubes because they contain too much salt." If you do not have the time to make broth, you may substitute a low-sodium canned broth, which is significantly less salty than either regular or reduced-sodium canned broth. There are many brands of low-sodium broths available today at your local supermarket.

Broths are easy to make and will keep in the freezer for months. Rich broths are also the foundation for sauces, braised dishes, and stews. Do not be disturbed by the long simmering time that it takes to make broths. I usually choose to make my supply when I will be home all day to keep an eye on things. There is no need to watch the pot as long as there is sufficient liquid covering the ingredients. During the first 45 minutes of cooking, I check the broth frequently, adjusting the heat, if necessary, to prevent the broth from boiling too vigorously. I place a 16-inch wooden spoon across one side of the stockpot and tilt the lid on the spoon to partially cover the pan. This will prevent steam from building up and overheating the broth. Once the broth has settled to a slow simmer, I know it will tend itself, leaving me free to do other chores around the house.

SUGGESTIONS FOR MAKING AND STORING BROTHS

- Bring broth to a very slow boil over low heat without stirring. It will take 45 minutes to 1 hour to come to a slow boil, and during that time the fat and albuminious, grayish scum will rise to the surface of the pot.

- Grayish scum must be skimmed from broth several times; this ensures that the finished product will be clear.
- Garlic should be added to broth unpeeled. Peeled garlic will fall apart as it cooks, and tends to make broth cloudy.
- Simmering broth slowly over low heat brings out its full flavor. To extract even more flavor, allow the broth to rest for at least two hours before straining.
- Always strain the broth through a fine mesh strainer lined with a double thickness of dampened cheesecloth. Dampening the cloth will prevent it from sliding around in strainer, and a damp cloth also strains out more of the fat than a dry cloth. (If you don't have cheesecloth, you can substitute a dampened piece of muslin or thin linen tea towel.)
- If using broth within one week, transfer cooled broth to widemouthed jars and store in refrigerator. (Storing in a widemouthed jar will make it easier to spoon off and discard any solidified surface fat later.) For freezing, transfer broth to 1½-pint plastic containers, leaving 1½ inches of headspace to allow for expansion. Storing in this type and size container will simplify removal when ready to use. Run the bottom of the container under a little warm water, and frozen broth will pop right out into a saucepan. You can easily scrape off any frozen surface fat with a small paring knife before defrosting. After defrosting, you will have approximately two cups of broth per container.
- Freeze some broth in ice cube trays for sauces, braised dishes, and stews. To do this, transfer 2½ cups broth to a 1-quart glass measure or small pitcher. Carefully pour into the sections of a plastic ice cube tray. Freeze overnight. If you have difficulty removing frozen cubes (especially beef broth cubes), run the bottom of the tray briefly under warm water before popping. Using a small paring knife, scrape any frozen, solidified fat from cubes, then transfer them to a plastic bag, seal tightly, and place in freezer. Broth can be kept frozen up to four months. I recommend using Rubbermaid plastic ice cube trays for freezing broth cubes. This type tray has 16 sections and each section holds 2 tablespoons. If a recipe calls for ¼ cup of broth, all you need do is remove 2 frozen cubes from the plastic bag, defrost, and add to ingredients.

Soup is so versatile! It can be a delicate first course of Julienned Vegetable (page 39) or Chilled Cucumber (page 29) to sharpen the appetite, or a satisfying, hearty one-course meal of Lentil and Brown Rice (page 32) or Minestrone (page 33) to serve during the crisp, cold days of fall and winter.

There is one thing that all soups have in common: Friends and family find them irresistible.

◆ BEEF BROTH

Initial browning in the oven will caramelize the vegetables and intensify the flavor of the meat juices. This broth is the essential foundation for many of the soups in this book, and may also be used to add richness and body to sauces, braised dishes, and stews. The meat from stock may be reserved for sandwiches; remove any fat or sinew and slice meat thin. It is delicious served on whole wheat toast thinly spread with horseradish and mustard and topped off with slices of red onion.

YIELDS 2½ QUARTS

2 medium-sized yellow onions (12 ounces), peeled, halved, and cut into 1-inch wedges

4 medium-sized carrots (10 ounces), trimmed, scrubbed, and cut into 2-inch pieces

3 large celery ribs (6 ounces), trimmed, scrubbed, and cut into 2-inch pieces

2 medium-sized parsnips (6 ounces), trimmed, scrubbed, and cut into 2-inch pieces

2½ pounds beef hind shank, cut into 3 crosscuts; or boneless chuck roast, cut into 3 pieces

1½ pounds beef bones

1 cup water

1 teaspoon whole black peppercorns

3 large cloves garlic, unpeeled

1 large bay leaf

2 sprigs fresh thyme or ½ teaspoon dried thyme

10 parsley stems or sprigs

3½ quarts cold water, approximately

1 cup canned whole peeled tomatoes, coarsely chopped, juice included

1. Adjust rack to center of oven and preheat to 475 degrees.

2. Place onions, carrots, celery, and parsnips in an even layer in a deep 14-inch ovenproof skillet or small roasting pan. Arrange meat pieces on top of vegetables and put bones between pieces of meat. Place pan in preheated oven. Roast the meat and bones until well browned on both sides, turning once, about 30 minutes on each side. Transfer meat and bones to a 10-quart stockpot, leaving vegetables in the pan.

3. Add 1 cup water to skillet or roasting pan. Bring to a boil over high heat, scraping any fragments of meat and vegetables that cling to bottom and sides of pan with wooden spoon. Transfer vegetable mixture to stock pot. Add peppercorns, garlic, bay leaf, thyme, and parsley.

4. Add 3½ quarts of cold water to stockpot (or enough water to cover meat and vegetable mixture by 2 inches). Bring to a boil very

slowly, partially covered, over medium-low heat. It will take approximately 45 minutes to bring the broth to a boil.

5. Using a skimmer or small strainer, remove all the grayish scum as it collects on the surface while the water comes to a boil. Repeat skimming 3 or 4 times, until there is no scum visible. Turn heat down to low and simmer, partially covered, for 3½ hours. Add chopped tomatoes and cook for an additional 30 minutes. (The addition of chopped tomatoes during the last 30 minutes of cooking time will give the broth a beautiful amber color.) Turn heat off, cover pot, and let broth rest for at least 2 hours before straining.

6. Using a pair of tongs, transfer meat to a platter and reserve for sandwiches. Remove bones and discard. Strain broth through a fine mesh strainer lined with a double thickness of dampened cheesecloth into another pot. Squeeze cheesecloth after straining broth, to extract as much liquid as possible. Discard remaining solids. Cool broth to room temperature and pour into jars with tight-fitting lids. Broth may be kept in refrigerator for 1 week, or it may be frozen in plastic containers and ice cube trays for up to 4 months. (See pages 19–20 for storing method.) When ready to use, discard solidified fat from surface.

PER CUP:	CAL. 23 (2% FROM FAT)	FAT .05 G	SOD. 87 MG
	PROT. 3 G	CARB. 2 G	CHOL. 0 MG

◆ CHICKEN BROTH

This rich golden broth is not only fundamental for many soups in this book but equally essential to enhance the flavorings of numerous sauces and braised dishes.

YIELDS 2½ QUARTS

3½ pounds chicken parts such as necks, backs, wings, thoroughly washed in cold water

3½ quarts cold water, approximately

1 medium-sized yellow onion (6 ounces), peeled and halved

3 large celery ribs with leaves (6 ounces), trimmed, scrubbed, and cut into 2-inch pieces

2 medium-sized carrots (5 ounces), trimmed, scrubbed, and cut into 2-inch pieces

2 medium-sized parsnips (6 ounces), trimmed, scrubbed, and cut into 2-inch pieces

10 parsley stems or sprigs

3 large cloves garlic, unpeeled

½ teaspoon whole black peppercorns

1. Place chicken parts in a 10-quart stockpot. Add 3½ quarts of cold water to stockpot (or enough water to cover chicken parts by 3 inches). Slowly bring to a boil, partially covered, over low heat. Using skimmer or small strainer, remove all the grayish scum as it collects on the surface while the water comes to a boil. Repeat skimming 2 or 3 times, until there is no more scum on the surface, and only a little white froth left floating on top. Add remaining ingredients and continue simmering, partially covered, over low heat for 2 hours. Turn off heat, cover pot, and let broth rest for at least 2 hours before straining.

2. Strain broth through a fine mesh strainer lined with a double thickness of dampened cheesecloth into another pot. Squeeze cheesecloth after straining broth, to extract as much liquid as possible. Discard the solids. Cool broth to room temperature and pour into jars with tight-fitting lids. Broth may be kept in refrigerator for 1 week, or it may be frozen in plastic containers and ice cube trays for up to 4 months. (See pages 19–20 for storing method.) When ready to use, discard solidified fat from surface.

PER CUP:	CAL. 34 (.28% FROM FAT)	FAT .01 G	SOD. 59 MG
	PROT. 6 G	CARB. 3 G	CHOL. 0 MG

◆ ASPARAGUS SOUP

A very refreshing first course in early spring, when asparagus are abundant.

YIELDS 2½ CUPS
SERVES 2

1 pound asparagus (about 12 large spears)
2 teaspoons unsalted butter
½ cup thinly sliced scallions
2 cups chicken broth, preferably homemade
(page 24) or low-sodium canned
⅛ teaspoon coarse salt
⅛ teaspoon freshly milled black pepper

1. Wash asparagus several times in cold water to get rid of sand. Using a sharp knife, cut off tough part at base of spear. With a vegetable peeler, peel spears up from the base of each, leaving tips intact. Cut off tips and reserve. Slice each stalk in half lengthwise and then cut crosswise into ½-inch pieces.

2. In a 2½-quart saucepan, melt butter over low heat. Add scallions and sauté, stirring frequently, until slightly softened, about 3 minutes. Add asparagus stalks and broth. Turn heat to high and bring to a boil. As soon as soup reaches a boil, turn heat down to low and simmer, covered, until stalks are extremely soft, about 30 minutes (test by pressing a piece against side of pan with a fork).

3. While soup is simmering, cook asparagus tips in 1½ cups boiling water until crisp tender when tested with the tip of a knife, about 3 minutes. Drain in strainer and reserve.

4. Ladle half of the soup into a blender or food processor fitted with metal blade. Run machine nonstop until you have a smooth purée. Transfer soup to a clean pot; purée remaining soup. Season with salt and pepper.

5. When ready to serve, reheat, covered, over low heat. Place asparagus tips in soup bowls, ladle hot soup into bowls, and serve immediately.

PER SERVING:	CAL. 122 (33% FROM FAT)	FAT 5 G	SOD. 160 MG
	PROT. 12 G	CARB. 11 G	CHOL. 0 MG

◆ BROCCOLI SOUP

A fresh-tasting soup, lovely as a first course, satisfying as the mainstay of a luncheon, and very simple to make with the aid of a food processor. Vegetables, cut into 1-inch chunks, can be chopped in the processor fitted with metal blade.

YIELDS 1½ QUARTS
SERVES 4

1 medium-sized bunch broccoli (about 1¼ pounds)
1 quart chicken broth, preferably homemade (page 24) or low-sodium canned
1 large leek (6 ounces), trimmed, split in half, thoroughly washed, and finely chopped
1 large celery rib (2 ounces), strings removed, finely chopped
1 large carrot (4 ounces), peeled and finely chopped
1 tablespoon cornstarch
¼ cup cold water
¼ teaspoon coarse salt
¼ teaspoon freshly milled black pepper

1. Remove broccoli florets, including approximately ½ inch of stem. Cut or break florets into ½-inch pieces. Wash in cold water, drain, and set aside. Remove and discard the coarse leaves from stems and cut off about ½ inch of tough lower part of stalks. Wash thoroughly and peel stalks with vegetable peeler. Chop fine.

2. Place chicken broth, chopped broccoli stems, leek, celery, and carrot in a 5-quart saucepan. Turn heat to high and bring to a boil. As soon as soup reaches a boil, turn heat down to low and simmer, covered, until vegetables are cooked, about 20 minutes. Add broccoli florets and continue cooking, covered, for an additional 10 minutes.

3. In a small cup, dissolve cornstarch in cold water. Stir into soup and cook over low heat, stirring constantly, until thickened, about 5 minutes. Remove from heat and let soup rest for 1 hour so that the flavors meld together.

4. Ladle half of the soup into a blender or food processor fitted with metal blade. Run machine nonstop until you have a smooth purée. Transfer soup to a clean pot; purée remaining soup. Season with salt and pepper.

5. When ready to serve, reheat, covered, over low heat, stirring once or twice with wooden spoon. Ladle into individual bowls and serve immediately.

NOTE: Soup freezes very well and can be kept frozen up to 2 months.

PER SERVING:	CAL. 90 (4% FROM FAT)	FAT .4 G	SOD. 108 MG
	PROT. 9 G	CARB. 14 G	CHOL. 0 MG

◆ CAULIFLOWER SOUP WITH PARSLEY

The crisp-tender texture of the cauliflower florets is a perfect contrast to this velvety smooth puréed soup. A delicious first course, or it can be served for lunch with Corn Muffins (page 207).

YIELDS 1½ QUARTS

SERVES 4

1 large head cauliflower (about 1¾ pounds)
1 tablespoon unsalted butter
1 medium-sized yellow onion (6 ounces), finely chopped
2 large celery ribs (4 ounces), strings removed, finely chopped
2 tablespoons flour
1 quart chicken broth, preferably homemade

(page 24) or low-sodium canned, heated
¼ teaspoon freshly grated nutmeg
¼ teaspoon coarse salt
¼ teaspoon freshly milled white pepper
¼ cup minced Italian parsley leaves, well packed

1. Remove cauliflower florets, including about ¼ inch of stem. Cut or break florets into ½-inch pieces. Wash thoroughly in lukewarm water and drain in colander. Cook cauliflower in 1 quart boiling water until barely tender (test by tasting), about 6 minutes. Drain well in colander and refresh briefly under cold water. Transfer 1 cup florets to a small bowl and reserve.

2. In a 5-quart saucepan, melt butter over low heat. Add onion and celery; sauté, stirring frequently, until vegetables are slightly softened, about 3 minutes.

3. Using a whisk, stir in flour and ¼ cup of the heated broth. Cook, whisking constantly, until vegetable mixture is smooth, about 1 minute. Slowly whisk in remaining heated broth (whisking broth in slowly will prevent any lumps from forming). Add florets, turn heat to high, and bring to a boil. Turn heat to low, cover pot, and simmer, stirring occasionally, for 30 minutes. Remove from heat and let soup cool to almost room temperature.

4. Ladle half of the soup into a blender or food processor fitted with

metal blade. Run machine nonstop until you have a smooth purée. Transfer soup to a clean pot; purée remaining soup.

5. Add reserved florets to puréed soup. Add nutmeg; season with salt and pepper.

6. When ready to serve, reheat, covered, over low heat, stirring once or twice with wooden spoon. Remove from heat and stir in parsley. Ladle into individual bowls and serve immediately.

PER SERVING:	CAL. 117 (24% FROM FAT)	FAT 3 G	SOD. 102 MG
	PROT. 9 G	CARB. 14 G	CHOL. 8 MG

◆ CHICKEN SOUP WITH HERBS

An excellent soup to make when you have any leftover chicken.

YIELDS 1 QUART
SERVES 4

1 tablespoon olive oil
¼ cup finely chopped yellow onion
¼ cup peeled, finely chopped
   carrots
¼ cup finely chopped celery,
   strings removed
1 small zucchini (4 ounces),
   washed, trimmed, and thinly
   sliced
2½ cups chicken broth,
   preferably homemade
   (page 24) or defatted low-
   sodium canned
1 cup cooked chicken, skinned,

boned, and cut into ½-inch
   cubes
1 teaspoon fresh lemon juice
2 teaspoons snipped fresh chives
   or thinly sliced scallions (green
   part only)
1 scant teaspoon minced fresh
   tarragon or ¼ teaspoon
   crumbled dried tarragon
2 teaspoons minced Italian parsley
   leaves
¼ teaspoon coarse salt
¼ teaspoon freshly milled black
   pepper

1. In a 2½-quart saucepan, heat olive oil over medium-low heat. Add onion, carrots, and celery; cover pan and cook, stirring occasionally, until soft, about 10 minutes. Add zucchini and cook, partially covered, until barely crisp tender, about 1 minute. Add broth and chicken and simmer, partially covered, for 10 minutes. Stir in lemon juice, chives or scallions,

tarragon, and parsley. Season with salt and pepper. Ladle into bowls and serve immediately.

PER SERVING:	CAL. 131 (42% FROM FAT)	FAT 6 G	SOD. 221 MG
	PROT. 14 G	CARB. 4 G	CHOL. 31 MG

◆ CHILLED CUCUMBER SOUP

A particular favorite of mine during the summer months. This soup must be prepared and chilled at least 4 hours or overnight before serving to allow the flavors to blend.

YIELDS 3 CUPS
SERVES 2

2 cucumbers (about 1¼ pounds)
¼ cup thinly sliced scallions
1½ cups chicken broth, preferably homemade (page 24) or low-sodium canned
1 teaspoon fresh lemon juice
½ teaspoon minced fresh dill or

⅛ teaspoon crumbled dried dillweed
¼ cup low-fat yogurt
⅛ teaspoon coarse salt
⅛ teaspoon freshly milled white pepper

1. Slice one cucumber in half, wrap exposed end with plastic wrap, and reserve in refrigerator. Peel, halve lengthwise, seed, and coarsely chop remaining 1½ cucumbers. (You can cut cucumbers into 1-inch pieces and chop them in a food processor fitted with metal blade.)

2. Combine cucumbers, scallions, and broth in a 1½-quart saucepan. Bring to a boil, covered, over high heat. Turn heat to low and simmer, covered, stirring once or twice, for 30 minutes. Remove from heat and let cool to room temperature.

3. Ladle half of the soup into a blender or food processor fitted with metal blade. Run machine nonstop until you have a smooth purée. Transfer soup to a bowl and purée remaining soup. Stir in lemon juice and dill. Cover with plastic wrap and refrigerate for at least 4 hours or overnight.

4. One hour before serving, peel, halve lengthwise, seed, and finely dice reserved cucumber; set aside.

5. When ready to serve, stir yogurt into chilled soup with whisk or fork until completely blended. Season with salt and pepper. Place half of the diced cucumber in each soup bowl, ladle soup over, and serve immediately.

PER SERVING:	CAL. 82 (7% FROM FAT)	FAT .69 G	SOD. 227 MG
	PROT. 7 G	CARB. 12 G	CHOL. 2 MG

◆ COLD MELON SOUP

Brilliant orange color, a pleasure to look at, with a flavor that is totally refreshing. This light soup starts a warm-weather meal in the right direction.

YIELDS 2 CUPS
SERVES 2

¼ cup fresh orange juice, strained
1 tablespoon fresh lime juice, strained
¼ cup dry white wine
1 tablespoon honey, preferably orange blossom

⅛ teaspoon coarse salt
1½ cups extremely ripe diced cantaloupe, cut into 1-inch cubes
2 sprigs fresh mint leaves (optional garnish)

1. Place orange juice, lime juice, white wine, honey, and salt in a 1-cup glass measure. Stir with a fork until honey is dissolved and mixture is completely blended.

2. Put diced melon in food processor fitted with metal blade. Run machine until melon is finely chopped. With machine running, pour juice mixture through feed tube until mixture is a smooth purée, about 1 minute. Stop machine once and scrape down inside of work bowl with plastic spatula. Transfer soup to a 1½-pint jar. Chill in refrigerator for at least 3 hours, shaking jar once or twice to keep mixture blended.

3. When ready to serve, shake jar once again and pour cold soup into wine glasses, garnish with a sprig of mint, if desired, and serve.

VARIATION: You may substitute 1½ cups extremely ripe diced honeydew for the cantaloupe.

PER SERVING:	CAL. 110 (3% FROM FAT)	FAT .39 G	SOD. 13 MG
	PROT. 1 G	CARB. 23 G	CHOL. 0 MG

◆ LEFTOVER SOUP

This soup is made quite often in my household after a dinner party or at the end of the week when I have a collection of leftovers. I prefer a thick soup using a ratio of 1 cup broth to 1½ cups cooked vegetables. If you like a lighter soup, use 1 cup broth to 1 cup vegetables.

YIELDS 2½ CUPS

SERVES 2

1½ cups cooked vegetables such as carrots, peas, potatoes, green beans, broccoli, and the like
1 cup chicken or beef broth, preferably homemade (page 24 or page 22) or low-sodium canned
2 teaspoons minced Italian parsley leaves

1. Place vegetables and broth in a blender or food processor fitted with metal blade. Process until you have a smooth purée. Transfer soup to a 1½-quart saucepan.

2. Cook soup, covered, over low heat, stirring once or twice, for 20 minutes. Remove from heat and stir in parsley. Ladle into individual bowls and serve immediately.

PER SERVING:	CAL. 102 (2% FROM FAT)	FAT .19 G	SOD. 59 MG
	PROT. 6 G	CARB. 19 G	CHOL. OO MG

◆ LENTIL AND BROWN RICE SOUP

*A lusty one-dish meal! A great soup to serve family or friends for an infor-
mal Sunday-night supper. All that is needed as an accompaniment is a
lovely mixed green salad and some crisp rolls. If you have a food processor,
you can have this soup assembled in 5 minutes. Cut leek, parsnip, and carrots into 1-inch chunks before processing them, separately, with the metal
blade. Garlic can also be chopped in the food processor by turning the machine on first and dropping clove through the feed tube to mince.*

YIELDS 2 QUARTS
SERVES 6—MAIN COURSE

1 cup dried lentils
2 cups beef broth, preferably
  homemade (page 22) or low-
  sodium canned
2 cups water
½ cup brown rice, picked over
  to remove any dark brown
  grains
1 16-ounce can whole peeled
  tomatoes, coarsely chopped,
  juice included (can be chopped
  in food processor fitted with
  metal blade)
1 large leek (6 ounces), trimmed,

split in half, thoroughly washed,
  and finely chopped
1 teaspoon minced garlic
1 medium-sized parsnip (3 ounces),
  trimmed, peeled, and finely
  chopped
2 medium-sized carrots (5 ounces),
  peeled and finely chopped
1 tablespoon minced fresh basil or
  1 teaspoon crumbled dried basil
2 large bay leaves
¼ teaspoon coarse salt
½ teaspoon freshly milled black
  pepper

1. Spread lentils in a single layer on a flat plate and discard any bits of
foreign matter. Put lentils in a strainer and rinse with cold water.

2. In a 5-quart saucepan, combine broth and water. (If using frozen
beef broth, take directly from freezer, scrape off any solidified surface fat
with a small knife, and put the frozen block in the saucepan. Defrost
with the water over low heat.)

3. Add lentils, rice, tomatoes, leek, garlic, parsnip, carrots, basil, and
bay leaves to pan. Bring soup to a boil, uncovered, stirring once or twice,
over high heat. As soon as soup reaches a boil, turn heat to low, cover
pan, and simmer, stirring frequently, until lentils and rice are cooked
(test by tasting), about 45 to 55 minutes. Remove from heat and season
with salt and pepper. Let soup rest for 2 hours before serving so that all
the flavors meld together.

4. When ready to serve, remove bay leaves and reheat, covered, over
low heat. Ladle into individual bowls and serve immediately.

NOTE: Soup freezes very well and can be kept frozen up to 2 months. If soup is extremely thick after defrosting, add about ¼ cup water to each pint before reheating.

PER SERVING:	CAL. 217 (4% FROM FAT)	FAT 1 G	SOD. 263 MG
	PROT. 13 G	CARB. 41 G	CHOL. 0 MG

◆ MINESTRONE SOUP

Today, everyone seeks out hearty, robust soups, especially tasty with home-made bread in the winter months. Whenever it snows, friends and family usually call me because they always know bread is rising and this good old-fashioned soup is simmering away on my back burner. All of the vegetables can be prepared with the aid of a food processor. Cut onion, carrots, and celery into 1-inch chunks before processing, separately, with metal blade.

YIELDS 2 QUARTS
SERVES 6—MAIN COURSE

1 small head cabbage (8 ounces), preferably savoy
2 tablespoons olive oil
1 medium-sized yellow onion (6 ounces), finely chopped
1 28-ounce can whole peeled tomatoes, coarsely chopped, juice included (can be chopped in food processor fitted with metal blade)
1 teaspoon sugar
1 tablespoon minced fresh basil or 1 teaspoon crumbled dried basil
2 medium-sized carrots

(5 ounces), peeled and finely chopped
3 large celery ribs (6 ounces), strings removed, finely chopped
5½ cups water
¼ cup white rice, picked over to remove any dark grains
1 10½-ounce can red kidney beans, rinsed and well drained
¼ teaspoon coarse salt
½ teaspoon freshly milled black pepper
6 tablespoons freshly grated Parmesan cheese (1 tablespoon per serving)

1. Discard any bruised outer leaves from cabbage. Wash cabbage and blot dry with paper towel. Quarter cabbage and remove center core. Shred each quarter on the large holes of a grater or in food processor fitted with shredding disc. Set aside.

2. In a 5-quart saucepan, heat olive oil over medium-low heat. Add onion and sauté until soft but not brown, about 4 minutes. Add tomatoes, sugar, and basil. Cook sauce, partially covered, stirring frequently, until slightly thickened, about 10 minutes. Add cabbage, carrots, and celery. Cook, partially covered, stirring frequently, just until vegetables are slightly softened, about 8 minutes. Stir in water and bring to a boil, uncovered, over high heat. As soon as soup reaches a boil, turn heat to low, cover pot, and simmer, stirring frequently, until vegetables are cooked, about 45 minutes.

3. Stir in rice, cover pot, and cook undisturbed over low heat for 15 minutes. Stir in beans; cook, covered, for an additional 5 minutes. Remove pot from heat and season with salt and pepper. Let soup rest for 2 hours before serving so that all the flavors meld together.

4. When ready to serve, reheat over low heat. Ladle into individual bowls and sprinkle with freshly grated Parmesan cheese.

NOTE: Soup freezes very well and can be kept frozen up to 2 months. If soup is extremely thick after defrosting, add about ¼ cup water to each pint before reheating.

PER SERVING:	CAL. 182 (34% FROM FAT)	FAT 7 G	SOD. 436 G
	PROT. 8 G	CARB. 23 G	CHOL. 5 MG

◆ RAW MUSHROOM SOUP

The tender raw mushrooms in the heated beef broth add a refreshing, crisp touch to this excellent first course.

YIELDS 3 CUPS

SERVES 2

2 cups beef broth, preferably homemade (page 22) or low-sodium canned

4 medium-sized mushrooms (2 ounces), wiped, trimmed, and sliced paper-thin to make ¾ cup

1 tablespoon thinly sliced scallions

1 teaspoon minced Italian parsley leaves

⅛ teaspoon coarse salt

⅛ teaspoon freshly milled black pepper

1. In a 1½-quart saucepan, bring broth to a boil, covered, over high heat. Stir in mushrooms and cook, uncovered, until heated, about 30 seconds. Add scallions and parsley; remove from heat. Season with salt and pepper. Ladle into individual bowls and serve immediately.

PER SERVING:	CAL. 32 (4% FROM FAT)	FAT .16 G	SOD. 236 MG
	PROT. 4 G	CARB. 4 G	CHOL. 0 MG

◆ BUTTERNUT SQUASH AND APPLE SOUP

Easy to make for a delightful first course in late fall to reflect the season's golden hues.

YIELDS 2½ QUARTS

SERVES 6

1 tablespoon unsalted butter
1 medium-sized leek (4 ounces), white part and 4 inches of green, trimmed, split in half lengthwise, thoroughly washed, and thinly sliced to make 1½ cups
½ cup finely chopped celery, strings removed
1 cup peeled, finely chopped carrots
1 butternut squash (about 1½ pounds), ends trimmed, peeled, halved lengthwise, seeded, and cut into 1-inch cubes
3 medium-sized tart green apples (about 1 pound), peeled, halved, cored, and cut into 1-inch cubes
1½ quarts chicken broth, preferably homemade (page 24) or low-sodium canned
1 teaspoon freshly grated nutmeg
1 teaspoon coarse salt
½ teaspoon freshly milled black pepper

1. In a 5-quart saucepan, melt butter over low heat. Add leek, celery, and carrots; sauté, stirring frequently, until vegetables are slightly softened, about 4 minutes. (If vegetables start to stick to bottom of pan, loosen with 2 tablespoons of broth to prevent scorching.) Stir in butternut squash, apples, and broth. Turn heat to high and bring to a boil. As soon as soup reaches a boil, turn down to low and simmer, partially covered, until the squash is soft and can be crushed easily against the side of the pot with a fork, about 20 to 30 minutes. Remove from heat and let soup cool to almost room temperature.

2. Ladle about 3 cups of the soup into a blender or food processor fitted with metal blade. Run machine nonstop until you have a creamy purée. Transfer soup to clean pot and purée remaining soup. Add nutmeg and season with salt and pepper. (Soup can be made up to 4 hours before serving.)

NOTE: Soup freezes very well and can be kept frozen up to 2 months. If soup is extremely thick after defrosting, add 2 tablespoons water to each pint before reheating.

PER SERVING:	CAL. 114 (16% FROM FAT)	FAT 2 G	SOD. 187 MG
	PROT. 4 G	CARB. 21 G	CHOL. 5 MG

◆ GRATED POTATO SOUP

Select boiling potatoes for this textured soup. Baking potatoes (Idaho or russet) tend to be mealy and will break down more rapidly than the waxy boiling type. This recipe is an adaptation of one that was developed by my twin sister, Louisa, a fabulous soup-maker.

YIELDS 1 QUART
SERVES 4

2 cups beef broth, preferably homemade (page 22) or low-sodium canned
2 cups water
3 medium-sized white potatoes (1 pound), peeled and coarsely grated (can be grated in food processor fitted with shredding disk)
2 large celery ribs (4 ounces), strings removed, finely chopped

1 medium-sized yellow onion (6 ounces), peeled and finely chopped
1 large bay leaf
¼ teaspoon coarse salt
¼ teaspoon freshly milled white pepper
1 tablespoon minced Italian parsley leaves

1. In a 5-quart saucepan, combine broth and water; bring to a boil, covered, over high heat. Add potatoes, celery, onion, and bay leaf. Turn heat to low and simmer, covered, stirring frequently to prevent potatoes from sticking to bottom of pan, until potatoes are cooked, about 25 to 30 minutes. (Test by pressing a few shreds against the inside of saucepan

with a wooden spoon.) Season with salt and pepper. Remove from heat and let soup rest for 1 hour so that all the flavors meld together.

2. When ready to serve, remove bay leaf; reheat, covered, stirring frequently over low heat. Stir in parsley, ladle into individual bowls, and serve immediately.

PER SERVING:	CAL. 100 (2% FROM FAT)	FAT .23 G	SOD. 218 MG
	PROT. 4 G	CARB. 21 G	CHOL. 0 MG

◆ CHILLED TOMATO MINT SOUP

A refreshing starter for those hot summer days.

YIELDS 2 CUPS
SERVES 2

1½ cups low-fat yogurt
1½ cups tomato juice, preferably
    low-sodium
1 tablespoon fresh lime juice,
    strained
2 drops Tabasco sauce
1½ teaspoons minced fresh mint

or ½ teaspoon crumbled dried
mint
2 tablespoons minced fresh chives
1 teaspoon low-fat yogurt
    (garnish)
2 fresh mint leaves (garnish)

1. In a deep bowl, whip yogurt with a wire whisk until smooth. Add tomato juice, ½ cup at a time, and whisk until blended. Add remaining ingredients and stir with whisk to combine. Transfer to jar and refrigerate until well chilled, about 2 hours.

2. To serve, pour into bowls and garnish each serving with ½ teaspoon yogurt and 1 mint leaf in center. (For an unusual presentation, serve in stemmed goblets, omitting yogurt garnish.)

PER SERVING:	CAL. 143 (17% FROM FAT)	FAT 3 G	SOD. 140 G
	PROT. 11 G	CARB. 21 G	CHOL. 10 MG

◆ VEGETABLE BARLEY SOUP

Nothing is more satisfying than this flavorful soup to start a meal on crisp, chilly evenings. For a luncheon, try serving steaming bowls of it with Corn Muffins (page 207), fresh from the oven.

YIELDS 1 QUART
SERVES 4

1 quart beef broth, preferably homemade (page 22) or low-sodium canned
2½ tablespoons pearl barley
½ cup peeled, diced carrots (¼-inch cubes)
½ cup diced celery (¼-inch cubes), strings removed before dicing

4 ounces green beans, trimmed and cut into 1-inch lengths
1 8¾-ounce can whole-kernel corn, thoroughly rinsed and drained
¼ teaspoon coarse salt
⅓ teaspoon freshly milled black pepper

1. In a 5-quart saucepan, bring beef broth to a boil, covered, over medium-low heat. Turn heat to low, add barley, cover pan, and simmer until tender, about 45 minutes. Add carrots, celery, and green beans. Simmer, covered, until beans are cooked, about 20 minutes (test by tasting). Add corn and simmer, covered, for an additional 5 minutes. Season with salt and pepper. Remove from heat and let soup rest for 1 hour so that all the flavors meld together.

2. Reheat, covered, over low heat when ready to serve.

PER SERVING: CAL. 100 (5% FROM FAT)   FAT .61 G   SOD. 338 MG
PROT. 6 G   CARB. 20 G   CHOL. 0 MG

◆ JULIENNED VEGETABLE SOUP

The raw julienned vegetables add a touch of crispness, a splash of color, and delicate flavoring to this Japanese-style soup.

YIELDS 3 CUPS
SERVES 2

2 cups chicken broth, preferably homemade (page 24) or low-sodium canned
6 snow peas (1 ounce), washed, trimmed, strings removed, and sliced lengthwise into ¼-inch julienne strips
¼ cup peeled, grated carrots
3 small, tender romaine lettuce leaves (1 ounce), washed, drained, and sliced crosswise into ¼-inch julienne strips
1 teaspoon snipped fresh chives
1 teaspoon minced Italian parsley leaves
⅛ teaspoon coarse salt
⅛ teaspoon freshly milled black pepper

1. In a 1½-quart saucepan, bring broth to a boil, covered, over high heat. Add snow peas, carrots, and romaine and stir to combine. Cook, uncovered, until vegetables are heated, about 30 seconds. Add chives and parsley; remove from heat. Season with salt and pepper. Ladle into individual bowls and serve immediately.

PER SERVING:	CAL. 49 (1% FROM FAT)	FAT .07 G	SOD. 213 MG
	PROT. 7 G	CARB. 5 G	CHOL. 0 MG

PASTA AND SAUCES

TOMATO-BASED SAUCES

TOMATO BASIL SAUCE   45

SPAGHETTI WITH TOMATO BASIL SAUCE   46

LINGUINE WITH MARINARA SAUCE   47

FUSILLI WITH UNCOOKED TOMATO SAUCE AND
   RICOTTA   48

SPAGHETTINI WITH TOMATO AND CHICKEN SAUCE   49

VEGETABLE AND HERB SAUCES

SPAGHETTINI WITH CREAMY ARTICHOKE HEART
   SAUCE   50

VERMICELLI WITH ASPARAGUS   52

SMALL SHELLS WITH BEANS AND SAGE   53

LINGUINE WITH BROCCOLI   54

SPAGHETTINI WITH PARSLEY RICOTTA PESTO   55

   SPAGHETTINI WITH BASIL RICOTTA PESTO   55

   SPAGHETTINI WITH SPINACH RICOTTA PESTO   56

SHELLS WITH PEAS AND HERBS   56

LINGUINE WITH ZUCCHINI AND RICOTTA   57

PASTA SALADS

PASTA SALAD WITH CHICKEN AND BROCCOLI   58

PASTA SALAD WITH GREEN BEANS AND PIMIENTOS   59

SEAFOOD SAUCES

LINGUINE WITH SCALLOPS AND PARSLEY SAUCE   60

SPAGHETTINI WITH SHRIMP AND LEMON SAUCE   61

VERMICELLI WITH TOMATO TUNA SAUCE   62

So many dishes run their course—soar in popularity and then disappear. Not so with pasta. Americans have adopted this Italian staple, making it their own. It is easy to prepare and inexpensive. When it comes to creating a tasty topping for your favorite pasta, just about anything goes, from tomatoes, vegetables, and legumes to seafood. Pasta offers infinite possibilities of combinations for creating gastronomic delight.

I grew up in an Italian home where pasta was served at least three times a week, on Sunday, Tuesday, and Thursday evenings. I still remember trips to the local Italian grocer, where pasta was sold loose in bins lined with a dark blue tissuelike paper. The first packaged pasta I can recall seeing on the grocer's shelf was La Rosa. On the side of each box was a premium coupon. It was my job to cut off the coupons, which were saved until we accumulated enough to send for free gifts such as a colander or a large pasta pot. They even ran a baby contest, which my cousin Lorraine Mullen won. Although I haven't seen La Rosa pasta in years, I do see Lorraine regularly, and she is as beautiful now as she was when she won the contest.

Whenever possible, purchase the imported Italian varieties of pasta made from semolina flour. Semolina flour is made from hard durum wheat, which produces a pasta higher in fiber and contains the complex carbohydrates, protein, vitamins, and minerals essential to a well-balanced diet. Imported pasta also holds up better in cooking.

There isn't one sauce in the following pages that will take longer than 30 minutes to prepare. Many, in fact, will take much less time. Several can be readied while the pasta water comes to a boil. Many sauce and pasta combinations are hearty enough to constitute one-dish meals, especially when accompanied by crusty bread and a salad.

Note that I tend to favor the thinner types of pastas. Four ounces will serve two people. To measure 4 ounces, divide 1 pound of long pasta (such as spaghetti, vermicelli, or linguine) into 4 portions. If you cannot judge the correct amount, you can use a calibrated pasta measure, available in many department stores and gourmet shops.

PREPARING PERFECT PASTA

You'll need a large enough pot (at least 5 quarts) so that the pasta can swim freely; otherwise it will stick together.

For each 4 ounces of pasta, bring 3 quarts of water, covered, to a rolling boil. Add pasta and stir with a wooden fork. Cover pot briefly, just until the steam starts to escape around the rim of pot, bringing the water back to a rolling boil. (Watch carefully so that the water doesn't boil over the rim of pot.) Place a 12-inch wooden fork off to one side of the pot and place the lid tilted on top to partially cover pan while cooking pasta. (Tilting the lid at this angle allows the steam to escape while the pasta is boiling, and the fork is handy for frequent stirring.)

Stir the pasta frequently with the wooden fork to separate the pieces. (Don't leave the pot once the pasta has been added to the boiling water.) The cooking time will vary with the size and shape. Pasta will take anywhere from 5 to 20 minutes of boiling. The only way to tell whether it is done is to lift a piece from the water with a wooden fork and bite into it. The pasta should be cooked "al dente," which means it should be slightly resistant to the bite. Begin testing after 4 minutes of cooking time. Keep testing every few minutes until pasta is al dente. The moment the pasta is done, drain quickly in a large colander, shaking vigorously to remove excess liquid.

Transfer to a bowl and immediately toss the amount of sauce recommended in each recipe with the pasta. Since pasta cools very rapidly, the sauce should be ready to use the instant the pasta is drained. Sauce should be used sparingly. It should coat the pasta pieces evenly and thoroughly, but should never be so abundant that the pasta drowns or swims in it. The pasta should be drained, sauced, and served within moments of the time it leaves the pot.

TOMATO-BASED SAUCES

◆ TOMATO BASIL SAUCE

This savory sauce is alive with the flavor of basil, equally delectable mixed with cooked white or brown rice or spaghetti. You may want to double the recipe and freeze half. Sauce can be kept frozen up to three months. If doubling the recipe, increase cooking time to 40 minutes.

YIELDS 3 CUPS

2 tablespoons olive oil
½ cup minced red onion
⅓ cup peeled, minced carrot
1½ teaspoons minced garlic
1 28-ounce can Italian plum
  tomatoes with tomato purée,
  finely chopped, purée included
  (can be chopped in food
  processor fitted with metal blade)

½ teaspoon coarse salt
½ teaspoon freshly milled black
  pepper
1 teaspoon sugar
2 tablespoons minced fresh basil
  or 2 teaspoons crumbled dried
  basil

1. In a 12-inch nonstick skillet, heat olive oil over medium heat. Add onions and carrot; cook, stirring frequently, until soft but not brown, about 4 minutes. Add garlic and continue to cook for an additional minute. Stir in tomatoes, salt, pepper, sugar, and basil. Turn heat to high and bring to a boil. Reduce heat to medium-low and cook, stirring frequently, until slightly thickened, about 25 minutes. Remove from heat, cover pan, and let sauce rest for at least 1 hour before using.

PER ½ CUP:	CAL. 62 (43% FROM FAT)	FAT 3 G	SOD. 313 MG
	PROT. 2 G	CARB. 8 G	CHOL. 0 MG

◆ SPAGHETTI WITH TOMATO BASIL SAUCE

I like serving this tomato sauce with spaghetti, but it blends well with any type of thin pasta (spaghettini, linguine, or vermicelli). During the summer months, when fresh basil is available, sprinkle 2 teaspoons snipped fresh basil (instead of parsley) over pasta as a garnish.

SERVES 2

1½ cups Tomato Basil Sauce
   (page 45)
4 ounces spaghetti
2 teaspoons minced Italian parsley
   leaves (garnish)

2 tablespoons freshly grated
   Parmesan cheese (for serving)

1. Place tomato sauce in small saucepan and reheat over low heat while cooking pasta.

2. Cook pasta in 3 quarts lightly salted boiling water just until al dente. Drain pasta in colander and transfer to a bowl. Toss three-quarters of the sauce with pasta. Spoon remaining sauce on top and garnish with minced parsley. Serve with Parmesan cheese.

PER SERVING:	CAL. 331 (20% FROM FAT)	FAT 6 G	SOD. 782 M
	PROT. 12 G	CARB. 54 G	CHOL. 5 MG

◆ LINGUINE WITH MARINARA SAUCE

Anyone who adores garlic and hot pepper will just love this sauce. Adding the oregano after the sauce has finished cooking will give perfect flavoring and prevent a bitter aftertaste. Do not serve any cheese with this sauce; it would mask the flavors of garlic, tomato, and oregano.

SERVES 2

1 tablespoon extra virgin olive oil
2 teaspoons minced garlic
1 14½-ounce can diced peeled
   tomatoes
¼ teaspoon sugar
⅛ teaspoon coarse salt

⅛ teaspoon crushed red pepper
   flakes
1 tablespoon minced fresh
   oregano or 1 teaspoon
   crumbled dried oregano

1. In a 10-inch nonstick skillet, place olive oil and garlic. Turn heat to low and sauté garlic until very lightly golden. Add diced tomatoes to pan and crush with the back of a fork. Add sugar, salt, and pepper flakes. Bring sauce to a boil. Turn heat to low and cook, partially covered, stirring frequently, until sauce is slightly thickened, about 15 minutes. Stir in oregano and cook for an additional minute.

2. Cook pasta in 3 quarts lightly salted boiling water just until al dente. Drain pasta in colander and transfer to a bowl. Mix three-quarters of the sauce with pasta and spoon remaining sauce on top; serve immediately.

PER SERVING:	CAL. 321 (23% FROM FAT)	FAT 8 G	SOD. 680 MG
	PROT. 9 G	CARB. 53 G	CHOL. 0 MG

◆ FUSILLI WITH UNCOOKED TOMATO SAUCE AND RICOTTA

A refreshing dish to make during the summer months, when fresh basil and fully ripened tomatoes are available. This can be served hot or at room temperature. Green Bean and Zucchini Salad (page 185) would be a perfect choice to complete the meal.

SERVES 2

1 pound ripe tomatoes (6 large plum or 4 medium-sized round)
2 teaspoons extra virgin olive oil
1 large clove garlic, peeled and thinly sliced
1 tablespoon minced fresh basil or 1 teaspoon crumbled dried basil
1 tablespoon minced Italian parsley leaves

⅛ teaspoon coarse salt
⅛ teaspoon freshly milled black pepper
1½ cups fusilli
⅓ cup part-skim ricotta cheese or whipped part-skim ricotta cheese (page 9)
2 tablespoons freshly grated Parmesan cheese (for serving)

1. Plump fresh tomatoes in 3 quarts boiling water for 1 minute. Rinse under cold water, core tomatoes, and peel skins with a small paring knife. Cut in half crosswise. Gently squeeze each half and discard most of the seeds. Cut tomatoes into ½-inch cubes and place in strainer set over bowl; reserve juice.

2. In a 10-inch nonstick skillet, heat olive oil over low heat. Add garlic and sauté until lightly golden, pressing the garlic flat in pan with wooden spoon. With a slotted spoon, remove garlic and discard. (If you are a garlic lover, leave it in the pan.) Add cubed tomatoes to pan and immediately cover with a lid so that tomatoes will not splatter. Uncover pan, turn heat up to medium-high, and cook, stirring constantly, just until tomatoes are incorporated into the olive oil, about 30 seconds. Stir in basil and parsley. Season with salt and pepper; remove from heat.

3. Cook pasta spirals in 3 quarts lightly salted boiling water just until al dente.

4. While pasta is cooking, whisk ricotta in a small bowl with 2 tablespoons of the reserved tomato juice until smooth and creamy. (If using whipped ricotta, just stir in juice to blend.)

5. Drain cooked pasta in a colander and transfer to bowl. Spoon ricotta mixture and three-quarters of the tomato sauce over pasta and

toss well. Spoon remaining sauce on top and serve with Parmesan cheese.

NOTE: If serving at room temperature, reserve remaining quarter of sauce for topping. Cover dish with plastic wrap and leave at room temperature until needed, but no more than 2 hours. When ready to serve, toss pasta once again. If pasta seems a little dry, add 2 tablespoons of reserved juice and toss again. Spoon reserved sauce on top just before serving.

PER SERVING:	CAL. 405 (25% FROM FAT)	FAT 11 G	SOD. 382 MG
	PROT. 17 G	CARB. 60 G	CHOL. 17 MG

◆ SPAGHETTINI WITH TOMATO AND CHICKEN SAUCE

Tomatoes blended with succulent chicken breasts seasoned with the distinct flavor of sage makes this sauce truly elegant. All you need is a lovely mixed green salad to accompany this very satisfying entrée.

SERVES 2

2 teaspoons olive oil
2 boneless, skinless chicken breast halves (10 ounces total weight), well trimmed of fat
½ cup dry vermouth
¼ cup finely chopped yellow onion
¼ cup finely chopped carrots
1 14½-ounce can whole peeled tomatoes, coarsely chopped, juice included (can be chopped in food processor fitted with metal blade)

1½ teaspoons minced fresh sage or ½ teaspoon crumbled dried sage
⅛ teaspoon crushed red pepper flakes
⅛ teaspoon coarse salt
1½ teaspoons minced Italian parsley leaves
4 ounces spaghettini
2 tablespoons freshly grated Parmesan cheese (for serving)

1. In a 10-inch nonstick sauté pan, heat olive oil over medium-high heat. Add chicken and sear on both sides until lightly golden; transfer to

a small plate. (If chicken starts to stick to pan while searing, gently loosen with a wide metal spatula.) Add vermouth to pan, turn heat to high, and cook, stirring constantly, scraping bottom of pan to loosen any fragments that might be stuck. Continue cooking until vermouth is reduced by half, about 1 minute. Turn heat to low, stir in onion and carrots, and cook, stirring constantly, until soft but not brown, about 4 minutes. Add tomatoes, sage, and pepper flakes. Return chicken and any accumulated juices on plate to pan. Cook over low heat, partially covered, stirring and spooning sauce over chicken frequently to keep chicken moist, until sauce is slightly thickened, about 20 minutes. Season with salt; remove from heat. Cover pan and let sauce cool to room temperature so that all the flavors meld together.

2. Remove chicken from sauce. Slice halved breasts in half crosswise and then slice lengthwise into ¼-inch strips. Return chicken to sauce and mix well. When ready to serve, reheat sauce, covered, over low heat. Remove from heat and stir in minced parsley.

3. Cook pasta in 3 quarts lightly salted boiling water just until al dente. Drain pasta in a colander and transfer to bowl and quickly toss with three-quarters of the sauce. Spoon remaining sauce on top; serve with Parmesan cheese.

PER SERVING:	CAL. 500 (17% FROM FAT)	FAT 10 G	SOD. 896 MG
	PROT. 45 G	CARB. 57 G	CHOL. 87 MG

VEGETABLE AND HERB SAUCES

◆ SPAGHETTINI WITH CREAMY ARTICHOKE HEART SAUCE

The delectable flavor of artichoke hearts combined with whipped ricotta adds a smooth, creamy texture to this northern Italian pasta sauce.

SERVES 2

1 9-ounce package frozen
   artichoke hearts
2 teaspoons unsalted butter

¼ cup thinly sliced scallions
½ teaspoon minced garlic
¼ cup chicken broth,

preferably homemade
(page 24) or low-sodium
canned
¼ cup whipped part-skim ricotta
cheese (page 9)
⅛ teaspoon coarse salt
⅛ teaspoon freshly milled white
pepper

4 ounces spaghettini
2 teaspoons minced Italian parsley
leaves (garnish)
2 tablespoons freshly grated
Parmesan cheese (for serving)

1. Rinse frozen artichokes under warm water and very carefully separate. Cut each artichoke heart into ½-inch wedges and place in a strainer to drain (artichokes will be easier to slice if partially frozen). Set aside.

2. In a 10-inch nonstick skillet, melt butter over low heat. Add scallions and garlic. Cook, stirring constantly, until scallions are barely tender, about 1 minute. Add artichoke wedges and cook, partially covered, stirring once or twice, until tender when tested with a fork, about 4 minutes. Stir in chicken broth and cook, covered, for an additional minute. Stir in whipped ricotta and continue to cook, uncovered, on low heat, stirring constantly, until mixture is creamy, about 1 minute. Season with salt and pepper; remove from heat.

3. Cook pasta in 3 quarts lightly salted boiling water just until al dente. Drain pasta in colander and transfer to a bowl. Toss three-quarters of the sauce with pasta. Spoon remaining sauce on top and garnish with minced parsley. Serve with Parmesan cheese.

PER SERVING:	CAL. 373 (23% FROM FAT)	FAT 10 G	SOD. 420 MG
	PROT. 18 G	CARB. 56 G	CHOL. 25 MG

◆ VERMICELLI WITH ASPARAGUS

This pasta dish is made quite frequently in my household during early spring when asparagus is abundant at the market. To ensure even cooking, select asparagus of the same size.

SERVES 2

1 pound asparagus (about 16 medium-sized spears)
1 tablespoon olive oil
1 large clove garlic, peeled and thinly sliced
¼ cup chicken broth, preferably homemade (page 24) or low-sodium canned (see Note)

⅛ teaspoon coarse salt
⅛ teaspoon freshly milled black pepper
4 ounces vermicelli
2 tablespoons freshly grated Parmesan cheese (for serving)

1. Wash asparagus several times in cold water to get rid of sand. Using a sharp knife, cut off woody ends at base of spear. With a vegetable peeler, peel stalks from the base of the spear up, leaving tips intact. Slice stalks diagonally into 2-inch lengths; reserve tips.

2. In a 10-inch nonstick skillet, heat oil over medium heat. Add garlic, turn heat to low, and sauté until lightly golden, pressing the garlic flat in the pan with the back of a wooden spoon. With a slotted spoon, remove garlic and reserve. (If you are not a garlic lover, discard.) Place sliced asparagus stalks in pan and simmer, covered, stirring once or twice, until barely tender when tested with the tip of a knife, about 3 minutes. Add asparagus tips and continue cooking, covered, until barely tender when tested. Raise heat to high and continue cooking, uncovered, stirring constantly until asparagus are a light golden color. Stir in broth and season with salt and pepper; remove from heat.

3. Cook pasta in 3 quarts of lightly salted boiling water just until al dente. Drain pasta in a colander, transfer to bowl, and quickly toss with sautéed garlic and half of the asparagus mixture. Spoon remaining asparagus mixture on top and serve with Parmesan cheese.

NOTE: If you do not have chicken broth, remove ¼ cup of the pasta water before draining and substitute it for broth.

PER SERVING:	CAL. 345 (25% FROM FAT)	FAT 10 G	SOD. 323 MG
	PROT. 16 G	CARB. 50 G	CHOL. 5 MG

♦ SMALL SHELLS WITH BEANS AND SAGE

This is one of the Depression dishes that was served weekly during the winter months when I was a child. I, too, make this savory Tuscan dish quite often as a main course, accompanied with a Lettuce and Carrot Salad (page 187).

SERVES 2

1 tablespoon olive oil
½ cup finely chopped red onion
1 cup chicken broth,
    preferably homemade
    (page 24) or low-sodium
    canned
1½ teaspoons minced fresh sage or
    ½ teaspoon crumbled dried
    sage
1 10½-ounce can white

cannellini beans, rinsed and well
    drained
⅛ teaspoon coarse salt
⅛ teaspoon freshly milled black
    pepper
1 cup small pasta shells
2 teaspoons minced Italian parsley
    leaves
Freshly milled black pepper (for
    serving)

1. In a heavy 3½-quart saucepan, heat olive oil over low heat. Add onion and cook, covered, stirring once or twice, until soft but not brown, about 6 minutes. Add chicken broth and sage. Turn heat to high and bring to a boil. Add beans, turn heat to low, and cook, covered, for 2 minutes. Season with salt and pepper; remove from heat.

2. Cook pasta in 3 quarts lightly salted boiling water just until al dente. Drain in colander, transfer to saucepan containing bean mixture, and mix with a wooden spoon. Cover pan and let rest for 5 minutes before serving. (Allowing this dish to rest before serving enhances the flavor by letting the pasta absorb most of the broth.)

3. Stir in parsley, ladle into individual bowls, and serve with freshly milled black pepper.

PER SERVING:	CAL. 371 (21% FROM FAT)	FAT 8 G	SOD. 366 MG
	PROT. 17 G	CARB. 56 G	CHOL. 0 MG

◆ LINGUINE WITH BROCCOLI

This pasta dish for all of you broccoli lovers is alive with the pungent flavor of garlic and the tantalizing tinge of hot pepper.

SERVES 2

1 small bunch fresh broccoli
  (10 ounces)
1 tablespoon olive oil
½ cup thinly sliced red onion
⅛ teaspoon crushed red pepper
  flakes

⅛ teaspoon coarse salt
4 ounces linguine
2 tablespoons freshly grated
  Parmesan cheese (for serving)

1. Remove florets from broccoli, leaving about ½ inch of the stems. Cut or break florets into 1-inch pieces. Wash in cold water, drain, and set aside. Remove and discard the large coarse leaves from stems and cut off about ½ inch of tough lower part of stalk. Wash stalks thoroughly and peel with a vegetable peeler. Cut stalks in half lengthwise. (If stalks are more than 1 inch in diameter, cut into quarters.) Cut halved or quartered stalks into 1-inch pieces.

2. Bring 3 quarts of lightly salted water to a boil. Add broccoli stalks and cook until tender when tested with a fork, about 3 minutes. Add florets and continue cooking until tender when tested with fork, about 3 minutes. With a skimmer or slotted spoon, transfer broccoli to a colander and set aside to drain thoroughly. Reserve liquid for cooking pasta.

3. In a 10-inch nonstick skillet, heat olive oil over medium heat. Sauté onion until lightly golden. Stir in pepper flakes, add broccoli and cook, stirring constantly, until heated and well combined with onion mixture, about 1 minute. Season with salt and remove from heat.

4. Return water in which broccoli was cooked to a boil. Break pasta in half, add to pot, and cook just until al dente. (Breaking pasta in half before cooking will make it easier to toss with the broccoli mixture.) Before draining pasta, remove about ¼ cup pasta water and set aside. Drain pasta in colander and transfer to a bowl. Add three-quarters of the broccoli mixture and toss well. Add about 3 tablespoons of pasta water; toss quickly to loosen. Spoon remaining broccoli mixture on top and serve with Parmesan cheese.

PER SERVING:	CAL. 326 (27% FROM FAT)	FAT 10 G	SOD. 141 MG
	PROT. 13 G	CARB. 48 G	CHOL. 5 MG

◆ SPAGHETTINI WITH PARSLEY RICOTTA PESTO

This Ligurian favorite can be whipped up with the aid of a food processor in a matter of seconds while the pasta is cooking. See variations at bottom of recipe.

SERVES 2

¼ cup well-packed Italian parsley leaves

½ cup part-skim ricotta cheese or whipped part-skim ricotta cheese (page 9)

2 teaspoons extra virgin olive oil

⅛ teaspoon coarse salt

¼ teaspoon freshly milled black pepper

1 medium shallot (1 ounce), peeled and quartered

4 ounces spaghettini

2 tablespoons freshly grated Parmesan cheese (for serving)

1. Place parsley, ricotta, olive oil, salt, and pepper in food processor fitted with metal blade. Turn machine on and drop quartered shallot, one piece at a time, through the feed tube. Stop machine once or twice and scrape down inside work bowl with plastic spatula. Run machine until parsley and shallot are finely minced and mixture is a smooth, creamy consistency, about 1 minute.

2. Bring 3 quarts of lightly salted water to a boil. Break pasta in half, add to pot, and cook just until al dente. (Breaking pasta in half before cooking will make it easier to toss with the pesto sauce.) Before draining pasta, remove about ¼ cup pasta water and set aside. Drain pasta in colander, transfer to a bowl, and quickly toss with half of the pesto sauce and 2 tablespoons of pasta water; toss quickly to loosen. Add remaining pesto sauce and toss once again. Serve with Parmesan cheese.

PER SERVING:	CAL. 380 (29% FROM FAT)	FAT 12 G	SOD. 205 MG
	PROT. 18 G	CARB. 50 G	CHOL. 24 MG

VARIATIONS

BASIL RICOTTA PESTO

Follow procedure for Parsley Ricotta Pesto, substituting ¼ cup well-packed fresh basil leaves for the parsley and 1 small clove garlic, peeled and split in half, for the shallot. Use same food processor technique of dropping garlic through feed tube with machine running to mince.

PER SERVING:	CAL. 374 (30% FROM FAT)	FAT 12 G	SOD. 196 MG
	PROT. 18 G	CARB. 48 G	CHOL. 24 MG

SPINACH RICOTTA PESTO

Follow procedure for Parsley Ricotta Pesto, substituting 1 cup packed fresh spinach leaves (3 ounces), thoroughly washed and drained for the parsley and ¼ cup thinly sliced scallions for the shallot. Place scallions in food processor with pesto ingredients.

PER SERVING:	CAL. 377 (29% FROM FAT)	FAT 12. G	SOD. 230 MG
	PROT. 18 G	CARB. 48 G	CHOL. 24 MG

◆ SHELLS WITH PEAS AND HERBS

Allowing this dish to rest for 5 minutes before serving adds to the flavor by letting the pasta absorb most of the broth and providing time for the peas to search for shells to fill.

SERVES 2

2 teaspoons olive oil
⅓ cup finely chopped celery, strings removed
½ cup finely chopped yellow onion
1 cup frozen tiny peas, defrosted
1 cup chicken broth, preferably homemade (page 24) or low-sodium canned
1½ teaspoons minced fresh basil

or ½ teaspoon crumbled dried basil
1½ teaspoons minced fresh mint or ½ teaspoon crumbled dried mint
⅛ teaspoon coarse salt
⅛ teaspoon freshly milled black pepper
1¼ cups medium-sized pasta shells
2 teaspoons minced Italian parsley leaves

1. In a heavy 2½-quart saucepan, heat olive oil over low heat. Add celery and onion; cook, covered, stirring once or twice, until soft but not brown, about 8 minutes. Add peas and chicken broth. Cover pan and

simmer over low heat just until peas are tender, about 5 minutes. Stir in basil and mint. Season with salt and pepper; remove from heat.

2. Cook pasta in 3 quarts lightly salted boiling water just until al dente. Drain in a colander, transfer to saucepan containing pea mixture, and mix with wooden spoon. Cover pan and let rest for 5 minutes before serving. Stir in minced parsley, ladle into individual bowls, and serve immediately.

NOTE: Vegetable mixture can be prepared up to 3 hours before serving. Reheat, covered, over low heat while cooking pasta.

PER SERVING:	CAL. 349 (15% FROM FAT)	FAT 6 G	SOD. 139 MG
	PROT. 15 G	CARB. 59 G	CHOL. 0 MG

◆ LINGUINE WITH ZUCCHINI AND RICOTTA

For those days when you're just too busy to cook, here's a simple yet satisfying one-dish meal. All you need add is a salad of some sliced tomatoes drizzled with 2 teaspoons extra virgin olive oil, sprinkled with a pinch of salt and freshly milled black pepper, and topped off with a tablespoon of minced Italian parsley leaves—dinner is on the table in a matter of minutes.

SERVES 2

2 medium-sized zucchini (12 ounces)
1 tablespoon olive oil
½ cup thinly sliced red onion
1½ teaspoons minced fresh basil or ½ teaspoon crumbled dried basil
⅓ cup part-skim ricotta cheese

or whipped part-skim ricotta cheese (page 9)
⅛ teaspoon coarse salt
⅛ teaspoon freshly milled black pepper
4 ounces linguine
2 tablespoons freshly grated Parmesan cheese (for serving)

1. Scrub zucchini and blot dry with paper towel. Trim ends and cut zucchini into 2-inch lengths. Slice each piece in half lengthwise and slice into ¼-inch julienne strips.

2. In a 10-inch nonstick skillet, heat olive oil over medium heat. Add onion and cook, partially covered, stirring frequently with wooden spoon, until soft and very lightly golden, about 3 minutes. Add zucchini and cook, partially covered, stirring frequently, until tender, about 3 minutes. Stir in

basil and ricotta; cook, uncovered, stirring constantly, until mixture is creamy, about 30 seconds. Season with salt and pepper; remove from heat.

3. Cook pasta in 3 quarts lightly salted boiling water just until al dente. Before draining pasta, remove about ¼ cup pasta water and set aside. Drain pasta in colander and transfer to a bowl. Spoon half of the zucchini mixture over pasta and toss well. Add about 3 tablespoons of pasta water; toss quickly to loosen. Spoon remaining zucchini mixture on top; serve with Parmesan cheese.

PER SERVING:	CAL. 395 (29% FROM FAT)	FAT 13 G	SOD. 372 MG
	PROT. 17 G	CARB. 53 G	CHOL. 17 MG

PASTA SALADS

◆ PASTA SALAD WITH CHICKEN AND BROCCOLI

An inspiring entrée to make when you have leftover chicken. All that is needed to complete this meal is a lovely Red Onion and Tomato Salad (page 189).

SERVES 2

1½ cups broccoli florets, including ½ inch of stems, washed and broken or cut into ½-inch pieces
3 tablespoons low-fat yogurt
1½ tablespoons low-fat mayonnaise
1½ teaspoons snipped fresh dill or ½ teaspoon crumbled dried dillweed
¼ teaspoon Dijon mustard

½ teaspoon apple cider vinegar
¼ teaspoon sugar
⅛ teaspoon coarse salt
⅛ teaspoon freshly milled white pepper
1½ cups fusilli
1½ cups cooked chicken, skinned, boned, and cut into ½-inch cubes
2 tablespoons snipped fresh chives

1. Bring 3 quarts of lightly salted water to a boil. Add broccoli florets and cook until tender when tested with a fork, about 3 minutes. With a skimmer, transfer florets to a colander, refresh under cold water, drain

well, blot dry with paper towel, and set aside. Reserve liquid for cooking pasta.

2. Place yogurt, mayonnaise, dill, mustard, vinegar, sugar, salt, and pepper in a small bowl. Beat dressing with a fork or small whisk to combine.

3. Return water in which broccoli was cooked to a boil. Cook pasta spirals just until al dente. Drain pasta in colander and transfer to a bowl.

4. Toss hot pasta with dressing. Add chicken and chives and toss once again. Let pasta salad cool to room temperature, about 30 minutes. (Stir frequently to hasten cooling.)

5. Add broccoli, toss lightly once again, and serve. (Adding broccoli to cooled pasta will ensure a bright green color.)

NOTE: The entire salad may be made up to 2 hours before serving. Cover with plastic wrap and leave at room temperature. When ready to serve, lightly toss salad once again.

PER SERVING:	CAL. 499 (19% FROM FAT)	FAT 10 G	SOD. 465 MG
	PROT. 43 G	CARB. 57 G	CHOL. 95 MG

◆ PASTA SALAD WITH GREEN BEANS AND PIMIENTOS

A perfect do-ahead summer pasta salad, which can be prepared up to three hours before serving. This salad can also be a main course for lunch.

SERVES 2

4 ounces green beans, washed, trimmed, and sliced diagonally into 1-inch pieces to make about ¾ cup

2 teaspoons imported white wine vinegar

¼ teaspoon Dijon mustard

1½ teaspoons minced fresh basil or ½ teaspoon crumbled dried basil

¼ teaspoon sugar

⅛ teaspoon coarse salt

⅛ teaspoon freshly milled black pepper

1 tablespoon extra virgin olive oil

1½ cups fusilli

1 4-ounce jar whole pimientos, rinsed, blotted dry with paper towel, and sliced into 1-by-¼-inch strips

2 tablespoons thinly sliced scallions

1. Bring 3 quarts of lightly salted water to a boil. Add green beans and cook until tender when tested with a fork, about 5 minutes. With a skimmer, transfer beans to a colander, refresh under cold water, drain well, blot dry with paper towel, and set aside. Reserve liquid for cooking pasta.

2. Place vinegar, mustard, basil, sugar, salt, and pepper in a small bowl. Beat with a fork or small whisk to combine. Add oil, a little at a time, and beat dressing vigorously with a fork or whisk to incorporate; set aside.

3. Return water in which beans were cooked to a boil. Cook pasta spirals just until al dente. Drain pasta in colander and transfer to a bowl.

4. Whisk dressing once again and toss with hot pasta. Add pimientos and scallions; toss once again. Let pasta salad cool to room temperature, about 30 minutes. (Stir frequently to hasten cooling.)

5. Add green beans, toss once again, and serve. (Adding green beans to cooled pasta will ensure a bright green color.)

NOTE: Entire salad can be made up to 3 hours before serving. Cover with plastic wrap and leave at room temperature. When ready to serve, lightly toss salad once again.

PER SERVING:	CAL. 328 (22% FROM FAT)	FAT 8 G	SOD. 372 MG
	PROT. 10 G	CARB. 55 G	CHOL. 0 MG

SEAFOOD SAUCES

◆ LINGUINE WITH SCALLOPS AND PARSLEY SAUCE

Linguine paired with scallops and parsley is not only mouthwatering for seafood lovers but spectacular in presentation as well.

SERVES 2

8 ounces sea scallops
1 tablespoon unsalted butter
¼ cup minced Italian parsley leaves
1 tablespoon minced shallots
½ cup dry vermouth
⅛ teaspoon freshly grated nutmeg

⅛ teaspoon coarse salt
⅛ teaspoon freshly milled black pepper
4 ounces linguine
2 tablespoons freshly grated Parmesan cheese (for serving)

1. Wash scallops several times in cold water to remove sand. Place in a strainer and blot dry with paper towel. Cut scallops horizontally into ¼-inch slices.

2. In a 10-inch nonstick skillet, melt butter over medium heat. Add 2 tablespoons parsley and the shallots. Cook, stirring frequently, until shallots are soft but not brown, about 2 minutes. Turn heat to medium-high, add vermouth, and cook, stirring constantly, until reduced by one-third, about 30 seconds.

3. Turn heat down to medium, add scallops, and cook, stirring constantly, just until they turn opaque, about 2 minutes. Stir in remaining 2 tablespoons parsley, nutmeg, salt, and pepper; mix well and remove from heat.

4. Cook pasta in 3 quarts lightly salted boiling water just until al dente. Drain pasta in colander and transfer to a bowl. Toss three-quarters of the scallop mixture with pasta. Spoon remaining scallop mixture on top and serve with Parmesan cheese.

PER SERVING:	CAL. 379 (18% FROM FAT)	FAT 8 G	SOD. 343 MG
	PROT. 27 G	CARB. 49 G	CHOL. 53 MG

◆ SPAGHETTINI WITH SHRIMP AND LEMON SAUCE

This piquant sauce is ready in minutes, and guaranteed to please.

SERVES 2

8 ounces medium-sized shrimp (about 12)
1 tablespoon extra virgin olive oil
1 teaspoon minced garlic
2 tablespoons fresh lemon juice, strained
1 teaspoon finely grated lemon rind
1 tablespoon minced Italian parsley leaves
⅛ teaspoon coarse salt
⅛ teaspoon freshly milled black pepper
4 ounces spaghettini

1. Shell and devein shrimp (for directions, see page 148). Wash thoroughly in cold water, blot dry with paper towel, and set aside.

2. In a 10-inch nonstick skillet, heat olive oil over medium heat. Add garlic and sauté until very lightly golden. Add shrimp and cook, stirring constantly, just until shrimp turn pink, about 2 to 3 minutes. Add lemon juice and cook, stirring constantly until incorporated, about 15 seconds. Stir in lemon rind and parsley. Season with salt and pepper; remove from heat.

3. Cook pasta in 3 quarts lightly salted boiling water just until al dente. Drain pasta in colander and transfer to a bowl. Add three-quarters of the shrimp mixture and toss well. Spoon remaining shrimp mixture on top and serve immediately.

PER SERVING:	CAL. 377 (23% FROM FAT)	FAT 10 G	SOD. 337 MG
	PROT. 27 G	CARB. 45 G	CHOL. 141 MG

◆ VERMICELLI WITH TOMATO TUNA SAUCE

The addition of small nonpareil capers gives this pasta dish its intriguing flavoring. For this hearty entrée, all you need as an accompaniment is a lovely Cucumber and Radish Salad (page 183) or Lettuce and Carrot Salad (page 187).

SERVES 2

1 6½-ounce can water-packed solid white albacore tuna
2 teaspoons olive oil
½ cup finely chopped yellow onion
1 14½-ounce can whole peeled tomatoes, coarsely chopped
1½ teaspoons minced fresh basil

or ½ teaspoon crumbled dried basil
¼ teaspoon sugar
2 teaspoons nonpareil capers, thoroughly rinsed and drained
¼ teaspoon freshly milled black pepper
1 tablespoon minced parsley
4 ounces vermicelli

1. Place tuna in strainer and rinse thoroughly under cold water. Drain well and break into bite-sized pieces; set aside.

2. In a 10-inch nonstick skillet, heat olive oil over medium heat. Add onion, turn heat to low, and cook, covered, until onion is soft but not brown, about 5 minutes. Add chopped tomatoes, basil, and sugar. Bring sauce to a boil over high heat. Turn heat down to medium and cook sauce, covered, stirring once or twice, until thickened, about 10 minutes.

Add tuna and capers and cook, covered, stirring once or twice, for an additional 5 minutes. Season with pepper and remove from heat. Stir parsley into sauce just before tossing with pasta.

3. Cook pasta in 3 quarts lightly salted boiling water just until al dente. Drain pasta in colander, transfer to bowl, and quickly toss with three-quarters of the sauce. Spoon remaining sauce on top and serve immediately.

N O T E : Sauce may be prepared up to 3 hours before serving. Reheat, covered, over low heat while pasta is cooking.

PER SERVING:	CAL. 428 (17% FROM FAT)	FAT 8 G	SOD. 804 MG
	PROT. 33 G	CARB. 56 G	CHOL. 36 MG

RICE, BULGUR, AND BARLEY

When I go to the supermarket, it always amazes me to note the popularity of the many precooked and premixed varieties of grains, especially rice. To me these varieties are for those people who would rather eat fast than eat well. Almost all of the premixed varieties are too salty for my taste. My trial-testing experience has also proved that there is little if any time saved in their preparation compared with the recipes in this chapter.

Among all the grains, rice (white or brown) is arguably the most versatile of foods. Whether it is served plain, made into an elegant pilaf, or served cold as a salad, rice teams well with any poultry, meat, or seafood dish. Rice is by no means the only grain that offers a tempting range of presentations. For something just a little different as a side dish, you may want to try Bulgur Pilaf (page 79) or Barley and Mushroom Casserole (page 81). Both pair extremely well with many of the dishes with which you would team rice.

For all the recipes calling for white rice in this chapter, I have found Uncle Ben's converted rice to be the best. Parboiled or "converted" rice should not be confused with precooked rice. It is not an "instant rice." This type of rice is treated in a special steam-and-pressure process before milling. The grains remain firmer during cooking and are less likely to become sticky. When cooked, each grain is separate, with a smooth, clean appearance. Parboiled rice also gives a greater yield after cooking than regular milled rice.

For all the brown rice recipes, again I have found that Uncle Ben's parboiled brown rice cooks just perfectly. If you live near a health food store, you may want to try either the medium- or long-grain brown rice available there. The cooking time may vary just slightly from that of Uncle Ben's. Brown rice takes considerably longer to cook than white rice because when it is milled, the outer hull and only a small portion of the bran layer are removed, whereas white rice has the outer hull and all the bran layers removed. Because of the increased cooking time, brown rice requires more liquid. When cooked, brown rice has a nutlike taste and a pleasantly crunchy texture. Because of the bran layer, brown rice has a shorter shelf life than white rice, and should be stored in the refrigerator if kept for an extended period of time. This is my favorite type of rice. It is reasonable in price and excellent in taste.

Bulgur, or cracked wheat, is the staple grain of eastern Mediterranean countries and it is delicious! Bulgur is simply unbleached, cracked wheat berries with the nutty flavor of whole-grained bread. Look for it in the supermarket next to the rice and dried beans, or sometimes in the breakfast cereal section. It is also available in health food stores and specialty shops, where it is sold in bulk. Buy the unrefined brand, because the nutrients are mostly in the dark husk.

Pearl barley, sometimes called soup barley, is the whole kernel of barley groats, processed by a polishing method so that it is mild and tender when cooked. Pearl barley is ground in a revolving drum until the hull and germ are removed from the grains. In this process the grains are reduced to small balls called pearls. In addition to the two recipes in this chapter, you may want to try one of my favorite winter soups, Vegetable Barley Soup (page 38).

The recipes that follow have been designed to add variety to your menus and high fiber to your diet.

◆ WHITE RICE

This simple method of simmering long-grain white rice (such as Uncle Ben's converted) in a measured amount of water will produce moist, fluffy grains. Remember to keep the lid on the pot. After the rice is simmering, do not peek to see how it is doing. The heat must be low, but constant, so the simmer is even.

SERVES 2

1¼ cups cold water
⅛ teaspoon coarse salt
½ teaspoon olive oil

½ cup long-grain rice, picked over
to remove any dark grains

1. In a heavy 2-quart nonstick saucepan, bring water to a boil. Add salt, olive oil, and rice. Stir with a wooden spoon and bring to a boil. Cover pan with a tight-fitting lid; turn heat to low and simmer undisturbed for 20 minutes.

2. Remove pan from heat and let rice rest, covered, for at least 5 to 10 minutes before serving. (During the resting period, the grains will absorb any moisture left in pan.)

3. Remove cover and fluff rice with two forks before serving.

PER SERVING:	CAL. 169 (2% FROM FAT)	FAT .30 G	SOD. 2 MG
	PROT. 3 G	CARB. 37 G	CHOL. 0 MG

◆ HERB RICE

Adding the fresh herbs after the rice is cooked will guarantee a delicate flavor. I recommend you make this dish only if and when fresh herbs are available.

SERVES 2

2 teaspoons olive oil
¼ cup thinly sliced scallions
¼ cup finely chopped celery, strings removed
½ cup long-grain white rice, picked over to remove any dark grains
1⅓ cups chicken broth, preferably homemade (page 24) or low-sodium canned

1½ teaspoons minced fresh basil
1½ teaspoons minced fresh mint
1 tablespoon minced Italian parsley leaves
⅛ teaspoon coarse salt
⅛ teaspoon freshly milled white pepper

1. In a heavy 2½-quart nonstick saucepan, heat oil over low heat. Add scallions and celery and cook, covered, stirring frequently with a wooden spoon, until slightly softened but not brown, about 3 minutes. Add rice and stir until opaque and well coated with vegetable mixture. Add broth, turn heat to high, and bring to a boil, uncovered, stirring once or twice. Cover pan with a tight-fitting lid, turn heat to low, and simmer undisturbed for 25 minutes. At this point, the liquid should be completely absorbed into the cooked rice. If it isn't, cover pan and continue to cook for an additional minute or two.

2. Remove pan from heat and stir in basil, mint, and parsley. Season with salt and pepper. Cover pan and let rice rest for 5 minutes before serving so that all the flavors meld together. Transfer to bowl and serve immediately.

PER SERVING:	CAL. 242 (19% FROM FAT)	FAT 5 G	SOD. 59 MG
	PROT. 8 G	CARB. 41 G	CHOL. 0 MG

◆ LEMONY RICE

Lemony Rice is a good accompaniment to any of the main-dish fish or seafood recipes in this book.

SERVES 2

White Rice (page 69), prepared
   through Step 1
2 teaspoons unsalted butter,
   softened
½ teaspoon finely grated lemon
   rind

2 teaspoons fresh lemon juice,
   strained
⅛ teaspoon freshly milled white
   pepper
2 teaspoons snipped fresh chives

1. As soon as rice is cooked, stir in butter, lemon rind, lemon juice, and pepper. Cover pan and let rice mixture rest for 10 minutes so that all the flavors meld together.

2. Remove cover and fluff rice mixture with two forks. Stir in snipped chives, transfer to bowl, and serve immediately.

PER SERVING:	CAL. 205 (18% FROM FAT)	FAT 4 G	SOD. 3 MG
	PROT. 3 G	CARB. 38 G	CHOL. 10 MG

◆ RICE WITH PEAS

I love the flavor of rice, peas, and mint. See variation following this recipe using zucchini, which is equally good.

SERVES 2

White Rice (page 69), prepared
   through Step 1
2 teaspoons olive oil
1 tablespoon minced shallots
½ cup frozen tiny peas, defrosted
   and well drained

⅛ teaspoon freshly ground white
   pepper
1½ teaspoons minced fresh mint
   or ½ teaspoon crumbled dried
   mint

1. While rice is cooking, heat oil in a 1½-quart saucepan over medium heat. Sauté shallots, stirring constantly, until lightly golden, about 2 minutes. Stir in peas and cook, covered, stirring once or twice, until barely tender, about 2 minutes. Remove from heat and set aside.

2. As soon as rice is cooked, stir pea mixture into rice. Season with pepper and stir in mint. Cover pan and let rice mixture rest for 10 minutes so that all the flavors meld together.

3. Transfer to bowl and serve immediately.

PER SERVING:	CAL. 240 (19% FROM FAT)	FAT 5 G	SOD. 43 MG
	PROT. 5 G	CARB. 43 G	CHOL. 0 MG

VARIATION

RICE WITH ZUCCHINI

Substitute 1 medium-sized zucchini (6 ounces) for the peas. Scrub zucchini, trim ends, slice lengthwise and then crosswise into ½-inch lengths. Follow same procedure but cook zucchini 3 minutes.

PER SERVING:	CAL. 225 (20% FROM FAT)	FAT 5 G	SOD. 6 MG
	PROT. 4 G	CARB. 40 G	CHOL. 0 MG

◆ RICE WITH TOMATO SAUCE

A very simple dish to make when you have the Tomato Basil Sauce on hand. It is an excellent accompaniment to Turkey Cutlets with Mushrooms and Tarragon (page 134) or Oven-fried Fillet of Sole (page 153).

SERVES 2

White Rice (page 69), prepared
    through Step 1
⅓ cup Tomato Basil Sauce (page
    45), at room temperature
⅛ teaspoon freshly milled black
    pepper

2 tablespoons freshly grated
    Parmesan cheese
1 tablespoon minced Italian
    parsley leaves

1. As soon as rice is cooked, stir in sauce, pepper, Parmesan cheese, and parsley. Cover pan and let rice mixture rest for 10 minutes so that all the flavors meld together. Transfer to bowl and serve immediately.

PER SERVING:	CAL. 204 (10% FROM FAT)	FAT 2 G	SOD. 165 MG
	PROT. 5 G	CARB. 40 G	CHOL. 2 MG

◆ RICE SALAD

This salad is perfumed with the sweet, aromatic scent of basil and parsley. A good accompaniment to any of the main-dish fish recipes in this book.

SERVES 2

White Rice (page 69), prepared
    through Step 1
1 medium-sized zucchini
    (6 ounces)
1 tablespoon minced red
    onion
1½ teaspoons minced fresh basil
    or ½ teaspoon crumbled dried
    basil

1 tablespoon minced Italian
    parsley leaves
1½ teaspoons imported white
    wine vinegar
½ teaspoon freshly milled white
    pepper
1 tablespoon extra virgin
    olive oil

1. While rice is cooking, scrub zucchini under cold running water until the skin feels clean and smooth. Trim both ends. Cook zucchini, uncovered, in a 1-quart saucepan with 1½ cups boiling water until barely tender when tested with the tip of a knife, about 3 minutes. Transfer to a strainer and refresh under cold water. Blot dry with paper towel and cool to room temperature. Slice into 2-inch lengths. Slice each piece in half lengthwise and slice into ¼-inch julienne strips; set aside.

2. As soon as rice is cooked, transfer it to a strainer and refresh under cold water to hasten cooling. Place strainer over a bowl and thoroughly blot rice dry with paper towel.

3. Transfer rice to serving bowl and add zucchini, onion, basil, and parsley; thoroughly mix with two forks.

4. Place vinegar and pepper in a small bowl. Add olive oil a little at a time and stir with a fork or small whisk to combine. Pour dressing over salad and thoroughly mix with two forks. Cover bowl with plastic wrap

and refrigerate salad for at least 3 hours before serving. (Salad may be prepared up to 5 hours before serving.) Return to room temperature 30 minutes before serving.

5. Lightly toss salad once again and serve.

PER SERVING:	CAL. 246 (27% FROM FAT)	FAT 7 G	SOD. 6 MG
	PROT. 4 G	CARB. 41 G	CHOL. 0 MG

◆ BROWN RICE

Simmered, parboiled brown rice should be cooked in the size pan and with the exact amount of water recommended. If you follow this procedure, the rice will cook evenly and no liquid need be drained off after the rice has rested. Brown rice takes longer to cook than white but is well worth the time for its delightful, nutlike flavor and crunchy texture.

SERVES 2

1½ cups cold water
⅛ teaspoon coarse salt

½ teaspoon olive oil
½ cup long-grain brown rice

1. In a heavy 2½-quart nonstick saucepan, bring water to a boil. Add salt, olive oil, and rice. Stir with a wooden spoon and bring to a boil. Cover pan with a tight-fitting lid; turn heat to low and simmer undisturbed for 50 minutes.

2. Remove pan from heat and let rice rest, covered, for 2 minutes before serving. (As the rice rests, the grains will absorb any additional moisture left in pan.)

3. Remove cover and fluff rice with two forks before serving.

PER SERVING:	CAL. 171 (7% FROM FAT)	FAT 1 G	SOD. 3 MG
	PROT. 4 G	CARB. 36 G	CHOL. 0 MG

◆ BROWN RICE WITH CARROTS AND TARRAGON

Sweet-tasting carrots mixed with aromatic tarragon combine with the crunchy texture of simmered brown rice to create the intriguing flavor of this unusual side dish.

SERVES 2

Brown Rice (page 74), prepared through Step 1
2 medium-sized carrots (5 ounces), trimmed, peeled, and cut into ¼-inch cubes, to make ½ cup
2 teaspoons unsalted butter, softened

1½ teaspoons minced fresh tarragon or ½ teaspoon crumbled dried tarragon
⅛ teaspoon freshly milled black pepper
2 teaspoons minced Italian parsley leaves (garnish)

1. While rice is cooking, cook carrots in a 1½-quart saucepan with 2 cups boiling water until tender, about 4 minutes. Transfer to strainer and drain thoroughly. Set aside.

2. As soon as rice is cooked, stir butter, carrots, tarragon, and pepper into hot rice. Cover pan and let rice mixture rest, covered, for 10 minutes so that all the flavors meld together.

3. Transfer to serving bowl and garnish with minced parsley. Serve immediately.

PER SERVING:	CAL. 223 (21% FROM FAT)	FAT 5 G	SOD. 18 MG
	PROT. 4 G	CARB. 40 G	CHOL. 10 MG

◆ BROWN RICE PILAF

The tasty combination of onion, celery, and beef broth brings out the full fla-vor of this rice pilaf.

SERVES 2

2 teaspoons extra virgin olive oil
¼ cup finely chopped yellow
   onion
¼ cup finely chopped celery,
   strings removed
½ cup brown rice, picked over to
   remove any dark brown grains
1 cup beef broth,
preferably homemade
   (page 22) or low-sodium canned
⅔ cup water
⅛ teaspoon coarse salt
⅛ teaspoon freshly milled black
   pepper
1 tablespoon minced Italian
   parsley leaves (garnish)

1. In a heavy 2½-quart nonstick saucepan, heat olive oil over low heat. Add onion and celery; cook, covered, stirring frequently, until slightly softened but not brown, about 4 minutes. Add rice and stir until opaque and well coated with the vegetable mixture. Add broth and wa-ter, turn heat to high, and bring to a boil, uncovered, stirring once or twice. Cover pan with a tight-fitting lid, turn heat to low, and simmer undisturbed for 50 minutes. At this point the rice should be tender and all the liquid completely absorbed. Test by tasting a few grains. If rice is still chewy, cover pan and continue cooking over low heat for an addi-tional 2 to 3 minutes. Season with salt and pepper; remove from heat. Cover pan and let rice rest for 10 minutes before serving so that all the flavors meld together.

2. Transfer rice to serving bowl, garnish with parsley, and serve immediately.

PER SERVING:	CAL. 234 (23% FROM FAT)	FAT 6 G	SOD. 61 MG
	PROT. 6 G	CARB. 39 G	CHOL. 0 MG

◆ BROWN RICE WITH RED KIDNEY BEANS

A good, hearty winter side dish and a delicious partner to Oven-fried Beef and Spinach Patties (page 86) or Turkey Cutlets with Mushrooms and Tarragon (page 134).

SERVES 2

Brown Rice (page 74), prepared through Step 1
2 teaspoons extra virgin olive oil
¼ cup finely chopped red onion
½ cup canned red kidney beans, rinsed and thoroughly drained

1½ teaspoons minced fresh savory or ½ teaspoon crumbled dried savory
⅛ teaspoon freshly milled black pepper

1. While rice is cooking, heat olive oil in a 1½-quart saucepan over medium heat. Sauté red onion, stirring constantly, until lightly golden, about 3 minutes. Add beans and savory, turn heat to low, and cook, stirring once or twice, just until beans are heated, about 1 minute. Remove from heat, cover pan, and set aside.

2. As soon as rice is cooked, stir bean mixture into rice. Season with pepper. Cover pan and let rice mixture rest for 10 minutes so that all the flavors meld together.

3. Transfer rice to bowl and serve immediately.

PER SERVING: CAL. 270 (21% FROM FAT)	FAT 6 G	SOD. 92 MG
PROT. 8 G	CARB. 46 G	CHOL. 0 MG

◆ FRUITY BROWN RICE SALAD

Easy on the budget, easy to make, and an excellent accompaniment to Yummy Pork Chops (page 101).

SERVES 2

Brown Rice (page 74), prepared through Step 1
2 tablespoons dark seedless raisins
1 small Golden Delicious apple (4 ounces), peeled, halved, cored, and cut into ¼-inch cubes to make ¾ cup
¼ cup low-fat yogurt

1 tablespoon honey, preferably orange blossom
⅛ teaspoon freshly ground nutmeg
2 teaspoons fresh lemon juice, strained
2 large lettuce leaves (garnish)

1. As soon as rice is cooked, stir raisins into hot rice. Cover pan and let rice rest, covered, until raisins are plumped, about 10 minutes. Transfer mixture to strainer set over a bowl and cool to room temperature. (Stir frequently with fork to hasten cooling.) Thoroughly squeeze out any excess moisture with your hands.

2. Place rice mixture in a bowl, add apple, and stir to combine.

3. Place yogurt, honey, nutmeg, and lemon juice in a small bowl. Stir dressing with a fork or small whisk to combine. Add dressing to salad and mix thoroughly with a fork. Cover bowl with plastic wrap and refrigerate salad for at least 2 hours before serving. (Salad may be prepared up to 4 hours before serving.)

4. When ready to serve, arrange lettuce leaves on two salad plates. Lightly toss salad with fork once again, spoon onto lettuce leaves, and serve immediately.

PER SERVING:	CAL. 280 (6% FROM FAT)	FAT 2 G	SOD. 26 MG
	PROT. 6 G	CARB. 61 G	CHOL. 2 MG

◆ BULGUR PILAF

I was introduced to bulgur pilaf by a friend who lived in Lebanon. When cooked, the bulgur has the chewy consistency and nutlike flavor of good whole-grained bread. I like serving it with grilled lamb chops and frequently use it as a substitute for rice.

SERVES 2

2 teaspoons extra virgin olive oil
1½ tablespoons minced shallots
2 tablespoons minced celery,
   strings removed
½ cup bulgur
1½ cups chicken broth,
   preferably homemade

(page 24) or low-sodium
   canned
⅛ teaspoon coarse salt
⅛ teaspoon freshly milled black
   pepper
1 tablespoon minced Italian
   parsley leaves

1. In a heavy 2½-quart nonstick saucepan, heat olive oil over low heat. Add shallots and celery. Cook, covered, stirring frequently with a wooden spoon, until slightly softened but not brown, about 2 minutes. Add bulgur and stir until the grains are well coated with the vegetable mixture. Add broth, turn heat to high, and bring to a boil, uncovered, stirring once or twice. Cover pan with a tight-fitting lid, turn heat to low, and simmer undisturbed until the broth is completely absorbed into the grain, about 20 minutes. Season with salt and pepper. Remove from heat and let pilaf rest for 5 minutes before serving.

2. Stir in parsley, transfer to bowl, and serve immediately.

PER SERVING:	CAL. 192 (22% FROM FAT)	FAT 5 G	SOD. 59 MG
	PROT. 9 G	CARB. 30 G	CHOL. 0 MG

◆ TABBOULEH

This unusual Lebanese salad is a distinctive, delicious combination of bulgur, red onion, mint, and lots of parsley in a tangy, lemony dressing. The texture is pleasantly chewy because the grains are soaked in hot water rather than cooked. I make this salad quite often in the summer months, when fresh mint is available. It is an excellent accompaniment to any of the grilled meat dishes or broiled fish dishes in this book.

SERVES 2

½ cup bulgur
2 cups boiling water
2 tablespoons finely chopped red
   onion
¼ cup minced Italian parsley leaves
1 tablespoon minced fresh mint
1 tablespoon fresh lemon juice,
   strained
⅛ teaspoon coarse salt

⅛ teaspoon freshly milled black
   pepper
1 tablespoon extra virgin olive oil
1 medium tomato (4 ounces),
   halved, cored, seeded, and cut
   into ¼-inch cubes
4 small romaine lettuce leaves
   (garnish)

1. Place bulgur in a deep ovenproof bowl. Pour boiling water over and let bulgur soak for 1 hour. Transfer to a fine mesh strainer and drain thoroughly. Place strainer over a bowl and thoroughly squeeze out excess moisture with your hands.

2. Transfer bulgur to a bowl. Add red onion, parsley, and mint. Mix thoroughly with fork to combine.

3. Place lemon juice, salt, and pepper in a small bowl. Stir with a fork or small whisk to combine. Add olive oil, a little at a time, and beat with fork or whisk to combine. Spoon dressing over salad and mix thoroughly with fork. Cover with plastic wrap and refrigerate for at least 3 hours before serving. (Salad may be prepared up to 5 hours before serving.) Remove from refrigerator 30 minutes before serving.

4. Lightly toss salad with two forks. Add tomatoes and toss once again. (Adding the tomatoes just before serving will prevent the salad from getting soggy.)

5. Arrange two romaine leaves on each salad plate. Spoon salad onto romaine and serve.

PER SERVING:	CAL. 204 (32% FROM FAT)	FAT 8 G	SOD. 17 MG
	PROT. 5 G	CARB. 32 G	CHOL. 0 MG

◆ BARLEY AND MUSHROOM CASSEROLE

If you are a lover of barley mushroom soup, you will like this casserole just as well. I often serve this dish as an accompaniment to Broiled Rock Cornish Hen (page 131) or Chicken Breast with Piquant Vinegar Sauce (page 121).

SERVES 2

1 tablespoon unsalted butter
2 tablespoons minced shallots
4 ounces medium-sized
   mushrooms, wiped, trimmed,
   and thinly sliced
⅓ cup pearl barley
⅛ teaspoon coarse salt

⅛ teaspoon freshly milled black
   pepper
1¼ cups beef broth, preferably
   homemade (page 22) or low-
   sodium canned, heated
2 teaspoons minced Italian parsley
   leaves (garnish)

1. Adjust rack to center of oven and preheat to 350 degrees. Lightly grease bottom and sides of a shallow 1-quart ovenproof casserole; set aside.

2. In a 10-inch nonstick skillet, heat butter over medium heat. Add shallots and sauté, stirring frequently with a wooden spoon, until lightly golden, about 2 minutes. Add mushrooms and sauté, stirring constantly, just until they begin to exude their juices, about 1 minute. Add barley and stir until opaque and well coated with mushroom mixture, about 30 seconds. Season with salt and pepper. Spoon barley mixture into greased casserole and spread evenly with the back of spoon. Pour heated broth over barley mixture.

3. Cover casserole and cook in preheated oven until barley is tender and all the liquid is completely absorbed, about 45 to 50 minutes. Garnish with minced parsley and serve immediately.

PER SERVING:	CAL. 187 (21% FROM FAT)	FAT 4 G	SOD. 208 MG
	PROT. 7 G	CARB. 32 G	CHOL. 10 MG

◆ BARLEY PILAF WITH RAISINS

A spicy way to prepare barley and a wonderful side dish with Pork Tender-loin with Apples and Prunes (page 102) or Poached Chicken with Apricot Sauce (page 125).

SERVES 2

2 teaspoons extra virgin olive oil
¼ cup finely chopped yellow
   onion
⅓ cup pearl barley
1 small bay leaf
⅛ teaspoon ground cinnamon

1⅓ cups water
⅛ teaspoon coarse salt
⅛ teaspoon freshly milled black
   pepper
2 tablespoons dark seedless raisins

1. In a heavy 2½-quart nonstick saucepan, heat olive oil over medium heat. Add onion and sauté, stirring frequently with a wooden spoon, until lightly golden, about 5 minutes. Add barley and stir until opaque and well coated with onion mixture. Add bay leaf, cinnamon, and water. Turn heat to high and bring to a boil, stirring once or twice with wooden spoon. Cover pan, turn heat to low, and simmer undisturbed for 35 minutes. At this point barley should be tender and all the liquid completely absorbed. Test by tasting a few grains. If barley is still chewy, cover pan and continue cooking over low heat until tender, about 3 to 5 minutes more.

2. Remove pan from heat and season with salt and pepper. With a fork, stir in raisins. Cover pan and let pilaf rest until raisins are plumped, about 5 minutes. Remove bay leaf, transfer to serving bowl, and serve immediately.

PER SERVING:	CAL. 193 (22% FROM FAT)	FAT 5 G	SOD. 5 MG
	PROT. 4 G	CARB. 35 G	CHOL. 0 MG

MEATS

BEEF

OVEN-FRIED BEEF AND SPINACH PATTIES 86

STIR-FRIED BEEF WITH BROCCOLI AND SESAME SEEDS 87

GRILLED SKIRT STEAK WITH PARSLEY CAPER SAUCE 88

GRILLED FILET MIGNON 89

BRAISED CUBE STEAKS WITH SHALLOTS AND
    ORANGE SAUCE 90

VEAL

GRILLED VEAL CHOPS 91

VEAL CHOPS WITH CARROTS AND ONION 92

VEAL SCALLOPS WITH MUSHROOMS 93

VEAL PICCATA 94

VEAL CUTLETS WITH PARMESAN TOPPING 95

SWEET AND SOUR VEAL CHOPS 96

VEAL STEW 97

PORK

OVEN-FRIED PORK CHOPS 98

GRILLED PORK CHOPS WITH ROSEMARY 99

STUFFED PORK CHOPS 100

YUMMY PORK CHOPS 101

PORK TENDERLOIN WITH APPLES AND PRUNES 102

PORK SCALOPPINE 103

PORK LOIN WITH HERBED VEGETABLE SAUCE 104

LAMB

The following sections offer step-by-step instructions for the different methods of cooking beef, veal, pork, and lamb: broiling, grilling, braising, roasting, sautéing, and stir-frying.

Since nutritionists recommend that we all reduce our intake of meats, especially red meats, it is increasingly important to become more conscientious consumers. The cuts recommended for these recipes are the choicest, leanest cuts of meat. Judgment and guidance are often needed to make the best selections.

Most butchers will give you friendly advice at no extra charge. If you can deal with a butcher personally, either in his own shop or in the specialty section of a supermarket, he will assist you by carefully choosing, cutting, and trimming the meat. If, however, you must shop at a supermarket where a butcher is unavailable for consultation, here are a few pointers:

- Check expiration dates on all packaged meats. Packaged meat should look silky, not wet.
- Where there are bones, they should be sawn smoothly, not chopped jaggedly.
- Select meat that is neatly trimmed, particularly chops and steaks, with most of the excess fat removed.
- Always unwrap meat as soon as you get home and store in the coldest part of the refrigerator loosely wrapped in foil so that a little air can circulate around.
- Always use fresh meat within one to two days of purchase.
- If freezing meat, remove all excess fat before wrapping for the freezer. For freezing, wrap meat in plastic wrap first and then in heavy-duty foil or extra-thick moisture- and vapor-proof freezer bags. If using freezer bags, make sure that all of the air is expelled before sealing them so that the meat will not develop freezer burn. Always defrost frozen meat in the refrigerator.

BEEF

◆ OVEN-FRIED BEEF AND SPINACH PATTIES

These meat patties have great flavor and are a cinch to make with the aid of a food processor.

SERVES 2

½ cup tightly packed spinach leaves (2 ounces), thoroughly washed, blotted dry with paper towel, and snipped into 1-inch pieces
¼ cup wheat germ
1 tablespoon freshly grated Parmesan cheese
1½ teaspoons snipped fresh basil leaves or ½ teaspoon crumbled dried basil
⅛ teaspoon coarse salt
⅛ teaspoon freshly milled black pepper

1 medium-sized shallot (1 ounce), peeled and quartered
½ large egg (beat 1 large egg lightly and use half, about 2 tablespoons)
8 ounces very lean ground round or sirloin steak
¼ cup Tomato Basil Sauce (page 45)
1 teaspoon minced Italian parsley leaves (optional garnish)

1. Adjust oven rack to top shelf of oven and preheat to 400 degrees. Lightly grease a shallow baking pan; set aside.

2. Place spinach leaves, wheat germ, Parmesan cheese, basil, salt, and pepper in food processor fitted with metal blade. Turn machine on and drop quartered shallot, one piece at a time, through the feed tube. Stop machine once and scrape down inside work bowl with plastic spatula. Run machine until spinach and shallot are finely minced, about 30 seconds. Add egg and run machine for 5 seconds to combine. Transfer mixture to a bowl. Add meat and mix well with your hands. In same bowl, divide meat mixture into 4 portions. Roll them with the palms of your hands and shape into 4 patties, each about 2½ inches in diameter and 1 inch thick.

3. Place patties in prepared pan and cook in preheated oven until underside is lightly golden, about 10 to 12 minutes. Turn patties with a broad metal spatula and continue cooking until second side is golden, about 7 to 9 minutes.

4. Transfer patties to serving platter. Heat sauce over low heat and

spoon 1 tablespoon over each patty. Garnish with minced parsley, if desired, and serve immediately.

PER SERVING:	CAL. 383 (56% FROM FAT)	FAT 24 G	SOD. 250 MG
	PROT. 30 G	CARB. 12 G	CHOL. 134 MG

◆ STIR-FRIED BEEF WITH BROCCOLI AND SESAME SEEDS

The garlic and hot pepper flakes add zestful flavoring to this one-dish meal, which should be accompanied with cooked white rice. If you do not have any beef broth on hand for the sauce, you can substitute water.

SERVES 2

FOR THE MARINADE

1 teaspoon sugar
1½ teaspoons reduced-sodium soy sauce
1 tablespoon dry sherry

8 ounces boneless sirloin, cut across the grain into ¼-inch slices

FOR THE SAUCE

2 teaspoons cornstarch
2 teaspoons reduced-sodium soy sauce
½ cup beef broth, preferably homemade (page 22) or low-sodium canned

1 teaspoon Oriental sesame oil
½ teaspoon imported white wine vinegar
½ teaspoon sugar

FOR STIR-FRY

4 teaspoons vegetable oil
1 teaspoon minced garlic
⅛ teaspoon crushed red pepper flakes
2 cups broccoli florets, including

¼ inch of stems, washed and broken into bite-sized pieces
1 tablespoon unhulled sesame seeds

1. Prepare the beef: In a small bowl, stir together sugar, soy sauce, and dry sherry. Add beef strips, toss well to coat each piece, and marinate at room temperature for 20 minutes.

2. Make the sauce while the beef is marinating. In a small bowl, dissolve cornstarch in soy sauce, then stir in broth, sesame oil, vinegar, and sugar.

3. Heat wok or large, heavy skillet over high heat until hot, add 2 teaspoons vegetable oil, and heat until it just begins to smoke. Stir-fry beef, patted dry, in oil for 1 minute, or until it is no longer pink, and transfer with slotted spoon to a plate. Add remaining 2 teaspoons oil and swirl pan to coat. Turn heat to medium-high, add garlic and pepper flakes, and stir-fry for 30 seconds. Add broccoli and stir-fry for 1 minute. Stir sauce, add to wok with beef and any juices that have accumulated on the plate, and cook mixture, stirring, for 2 minutes, or until sauce is thickened and beef is heated through. Sprinkle sesame seeds in pan and toss to combine. Transfer mixture to a heated platter and serve.

PER SERVING:	CAL. 286 (50% FROM FAT)	FAT 16 G	SOD. 310 MG
	PROT. 22 G	CARB. 13 G	CHOL. 43 MG

◆ GRILLED SKIRT STEAK WITH PARSLEY CAPER SAUCE

This steak can also be cooked on a lightly greased, ridged grill pan.

SERVES 2

2 tablespoons minced Italian parsley leaves
1 small clove garlic, minced and mashed to a paste with ¼ teaspoon coarse salt
1 teaspoon Worcestershire sauce
2 teaspoons fresh lemon juice
¼ teaspoon freshly milled black pepper
Olive oil cooking spray
12 ounces skirt steak, well trimmed of fat, halved crosswise
2 tablespoons nonpareil capers, thoroughly rinsed and drained

1. In a small bowl, stir together parsley, garlic paste, Worcestershire sauce, lemon juice, and pepper until well combined.

2. Lightly grease grill rack with olive oil cooking spray. Preheat char-

coal grill until coals have turned a gray ashy color. Preheat gas or electric grill according to manufacturer's suggested time.

3. Place steak on grill about 4 inches from heat source. Grill steak for 4 minutes on each side for medium-rare meat. Transfer steak to a cutting board, let it stand for 5 minutes, and cut it across the grain into thin slices. Divide steak between 2 plates.

4. Stir sauce once again to combine, and spoon over each steak. Sprinkle 1 tablespoon capers over each portion and serve.

PER SERVING:	CAL. 266 (45% FROM FAT)	FAT 14 G	SOD. 292 MG
	PROT. 21 G	CARB. 16 G	CHOL. 43 MG

◆ GRILLED FILET MIGNON

This section of the whole tenderloin is also called tournedos of beef. After trimming all the fat, make sure you remove the thin blue-gray membrane around the steak's outside edge before cooking. Always give the raw meat time to reach room temperature so that it will cook evenly. These steaks are best when served medium rare or medium.

SERVES 2

2 slices filet mignon, each 1 inch thick (12 ounces total weight), well trimmed of fat and any attached membrane
1 large clove garlic, peeled and split in half

1 teaspoon olive oil (approximately)
¼ teaspoon freshly milled black pepper
8 sprigs curly parsley (optional garnish)

1. Preheat charcoal grill until coals have turned a gray ashy color. Preheat gas or electric grill according to manufacturer's suggested time.

2. Using a piece of paper towel, thoroughly blot dry both surfaces of steaks. Place steaks on a flat plate and rub each steak with garlic on both sides. Sprinkle a few drops of oil on the surface of meat and thoroughly spread across surface with your fingertips. Turn steaks over and repeat on other surface. (Rubbing a little oil into both surfaces will prevent steaks from sticking when placed on heated grill, and will help brown the meat as well.)

3. Place steaks on grill about 4 inches from the heat source. Sear the

steaks 1 minute on each side, turning meat with long-handled tongs. Approximate cooking time after searing is 2 minutes on each side for medium rare, or 3 minutes on each side for medium. Red droplets appearing on the steak's seared upper surface while the second side is still cooking indicate the meat is medium rare. Pink juices mean the steak is medium.

4. Transfer to platter and sprinkle both surfaces of steak with freshly milled black pepper. Garnish with parsley sprigs, if desired, and serve immediately.

PER SERVING:	CAL. 293 (48% FROM FAT)	FAT 15 G	SOD. 81 MG
	PROT. 36 G	CARB. 1 G	CHOL. 107 MG

◆ BRAISED CUBE STEAKS WITH SHALLOTS AND ORANGE SAUCE

An excellent dish served with a border of brown rice and Parsleyed Baby Carrots (page 164). There will be ample sauce for spooning over rice as well.

SERVES 2

2 cube steaks (about 12 ounces total weight)
¼ teaspoon coarse salt
¼ teaspoon freshly milled black pepper
2 teaspoons canola oil
⅓ cup thinly sliced shallots
⅓ cup beef broth, preferably

homemade (page 22) or low-sodium canned
1½ teaspoons finely grated orange rind
⅓ cup fresh orange juice
1½ teaspoons reduced-sodium soy sauce

1. Pat steaks dry between paper towels and season with salt and pepper.
2. In a 10-inch nonstick skillet, heat oil over moderately high heat until hot but not smoking, and brown steaks on both sides. Transfer steaks with tongs to a plate.
3. Turn heat down to medium and cook shallots, stirring frequently, until softened, about 5 minutes. Stir in broth, orange rind, juice, and soy sauce and cook, stirring constantly, for 1 minute. Return steaks to pan and

simmer, uncovered, until steaks are tender, about 7 to 8 minutes. Transfer to individual plates, spoon sauce over each, and serve immediately.

PER SERVING:	CAL. 293 (42% FROM FAT)	FAT 15 G	SOD. 265 MG
	PROT. 45 G	CARB. 4 G	CHOL. 100 MG

VEAL

◆ GRILLED VEAL CHOPS

Rubbing a little garlic on the chops before grilling adds just the right taste to this dish, which is dressed with a little pepper and lime juice as soon as the meat is taken off the grill.

SERVES 2

2 veal rib chops, each ½ inch thick (1 pound total weight), well trimmed of fat
1 large clove garlic, peeled and split in half
1 teaspoon olive oil
¼ teaspoon freshly milled black pepper
2 tablespoons fresh lime juice

1. Place veal chops on a flat plate. Rub split garlic over both surfaces of chops. With your fingers, rub ½ teaspoon oil onto both surfaces of each chop. (Rubbing a little oil on surface of chops will prevent them from sticking when placed on heated grill.)

2. Preheat charcoal grill until coals have turned a gray ashy color. Preheat gas or electric grill according to manufacturer's suggested time.

3. Place chops on grill 4 inches from heat source. Sear the chops 1 minute on each side, turning meat with long-handled tongs. Continue cooking chops 2 more minutes on each side. To test for doneness, insert the tip of a small knife into the thickest part near the bone. If the juices run clear, with no traces of pink, the chops are done. If not, continue cooking for an additional 2 minutes. Test for doneness once again.

4. Transfer to platter and sprinkle both sides of chops with pepper. Spoon lime juice over chops and serve immediately.

PER SERVING:	CAL. 217 (43% FROM FAT)	FAT 10 G	SOD. 104 MG
	PROT. 28 G	CARB. 2 G	CHOL. 123 MG

◆ VEAL CHOPS WITH CARROTS AND ONION

Cooking the chops smothered with carrots and onion will keep them extremely moist and juicy.

SERVES 2

2 tablespoons Wondra flour
¼ teaspoon freshly milled black
  pepper
2 veal rib chops, each ½ inch thick
  (1 pound total weight), well
  trimmed of fat
2 teaspoons olive oil
½ cup finely diced carrots
½ cup minced yellow onion

1 teaspoon grated lemon rind
1½ tablespoons fresh lemon juice
1½ teaspoons minced fresh thyme
  or ½ teaspoon crumbled dried
  thyme
2 to 4 tablespoons water
2 teaspoons minced Italian parsley
  leaves (garnish)

1. In a wide, shallow bowl, combine flour and pepper. Dredge chops in seasoned flour and shake off excess. (Dredge just before sautéing or flour coating will become gummy.)

2. In a 10-inch nonstick skillet, heat oil over medium-high heat. Sauté the chops, turning once, until lightly golden on both sides, about 1½ minutes on each side. Transfer to plate.

3. Turn heat down to medium, add carrots and onion, and sauté, stirring constantly, scraping any fragments that cling to bottom of pan with a wooden spoon. Cook until carrots are barely tender, about 2 minutes. Stir in lemon rind, juice, and thyme. Return chops to pan and spoon all of the vegetable mixture on top. Spoon 2 tablespoons water around chops. Cover pan, turn heat to low, and cook until chops are tender when tested with the tip of a knife, about 8 minutes. Check liquid in pan after 4 minutes of cooking. If liquid has evaporated, spoon remaining 2 tablespoons water around chops.

4. Transfer chops to serving plate, spoon vegetable mixture over top, garnish with minced parsley, and serve immediately.

PER SERVING:	CAL. 261 (35% FROM FAT)	FAT 10 G	SOD. 141 MG
	PROT. 29 G	CARB. 13 G	CHOL. 113 G

◆ VEAL SCALLOPS WITH MUSHROOMS

Rice with Peas (page 71) would be a delicious accompaniment to this succulent entrée.

SERVES 2

2 tablespoons Wondra flour
¼ teaspoon freshly milled black
   pepper
4 veal scallops, each ¼ inch thick
   (8 ounces total weight)
1 tablespoon olive oil
1 tablespoon minced shallots

½ cup dry white wine
4 ounces medium-sized
   mushrooms, trimmed, wiped,
   and thinly sliced
2 teaspoons minced Italian parsley
   leaves
⅛ teaspoon coarse salt

1. In a shallow bowl, combine flour and pepper. Lightly dredge each piece of veal in seasoned flour and shake off excess. (Dredge just before sautéing or the flour coating will become gummy.)

2. In a 10-inch nonstick skillet, heat oil over medium-high heat. Sauté veal, turning once, until lightly golden on both sides, about 1½ minutes on each side. Remove veal and set aside.

3. Add shallots to pan and sauté over medium heat until lightly golden, scraping any fragments that cling to bottom of pan with a wooden spoon, about 30 seconds. Add wine and turn heat to high. Cook, stirring constantly, until wine is reduced to half, about 1 minute.

4. Add mushrooms, turn heat down to medium-high, and cook, stirring constantly, until barely tender when tested with a fork, about 20 seconds. Return veal to pan and cook, spooning pan juices and mushrooms over veal, for an additional 30 seconds. Stir in parsley and season with salt; remove from heat.

5. Transfer veal to platter, spoon mushroom mixture over veal, and serve immediately.

PER SERVING:	CAL. 227 (35% FROM FAT)	FAT 9 G	SOD. 79 MG
	PROT. 26 G	CARB. 10 G	CHOL. 88 MG

◆ VEAL PICCATA

This specialty is fast and simple to prepare. Vermouth and lemon juice provide its piquant flavoring.

SERVES 2

2 tablespoons Wondra flour
¼ teaspoon freshly milled black
  pepper
4 veal scallops, each ¼ inch thick
  (8 ounces total weight)
1 tablespoon olive oil
1 large clove garlic, thinly sliced

¼ cup dry vermouth
2 tablespoons fresh lemon juice
1 teaspoon grated lemon rind
1 tablespoon minced Italian
  parsley leaves
⅛ teaspoon coarse salt

1. In a shallow bowl, combine flour and pepper. Lightly dredge each piece of veal in seasoned flour and shake off excess. (Dredge just before sautéing or the flour coating will become gummy.)

2. In a 10-inch nonstick skillet, heat oil over medium-high heat. Add garlic and sauté until lightly golden. Using a slotted spoon, remove garlic and discard.

3. Sauté veal, turning once, until lightly golden on both sides, about 1½ minutes on each side. Remove veal and set aside.

4. Add vermouth, turn heat to high, and cook, scraping any fragments that cling to bottom of pan with wooden spoon, until vermouth is reduced by half, about 30 seconds. Stir in lemon juice. Return veal to pan and cook, spooning pan juices over veal, for an additional 30 seconds.

5. Remove pan from heat; stir in lemon rind and parsley. Season with salt. Transfer veal to platter, spoon pan juices over veal, and serve immediately.

NOTE: You may substitute one whole boneless, skinless chicken breast (10 ounces) for the veal. Slice breast in half lengthwise and lightly pound between pieces of waxed paper. Slice each halved breast lengthwise into 3 even pieces.

PER SERVING:	CAL. 220 (36% FROM FAT)	FAT 9 G	SOD. 77 MG
	PROT. 25 G	CARB. 9 G	CHOL. 88 MG

◆ VEAL CUTLETS WITH PARMESAN TOPPING

Sprinkling the cutlets with Parmesan cheese after they are cooked adds a flavor bonus to the crusty coating.

SERVES 2

2 tablespoons Wondra flour
⅛ teaspoon freshly milled black
  pepper
1 large egg
1½ teaspoons cold water
½ cup fine dry bread crumbs
2 teaspoons minced Italian parsley
  leaves

2 veal cutlets, each ¼ inch thick
  (about 8 ounces total weight)
1 tablespoon olive oil
4 teaspoons freshly grated
  Parmesan cheese
½ lemon, sliced into 4 wedges
  (garnish)

1. In a shallow bowl, combine flour and pepper. In another bowl, beat egg and cold water with a fork. On a flat plate, combine bread crumbs and parsley. Dredge cutlets in seasoned flour, dip in beaten egg, and then thoroughly coat with bread crumb mixture. Refrigerate cutlets in a single layer on plate lined with waxed paper for at least 1 hour (chilling prevents coating from coming off during sautéing).

2. In a 10-inch nonstick skillet, heat oil over medium-high heat. Sauté the cutlets until lightly golden on both sides, about 1½ minutes on each side. As soon as second side is golden, sprinkle 2 teaspoons Parmesan cheese over each cutlet. Partially cover pan and cook until cheese melts, about 20 seconds.

3. Transfer to platter and serve with lemon wedges.

PER SERVING:	CAL. 435 (31% FROM FAT)	FAT 15 G	SOD. 450 MG
	PROT. 45 G	CARB. 29 G	CHOL. 242 MG

◆ SWEET AND SOUR VEAL CHOPS

The sweet taste of yellow or red bell pepper complements the vinegar, adding a piquant touch to the veal.

SERVES 2

2 tablespoons Wondra flour
⅛ teaspoon freshly milled black
  pepper
2 veal loin chops, ½ inch thick
  (1 pound total weight), well
  trimmed of fat
1 tablespoon olive oil
1 large yellow or red bell pepper
  (8 ounces), halved, cored,

seeded, and sliced lengthwise
  into ¼-inch strips
½ cup thinly sliced red onion
2 tablespoons imported white
  wine vinegar
2 teaspoons water
½ teaspoon sugar
⅛ teaspoon coarse salt

1. In a shallow bowl, combine flour and pepper. Dredge chops in seasoned flour and shake off excess. (Dredge just before sautéing or flour coating will become gummy.)

2. In a 10-inch nonstick skillet, heat oil over medium-high heat. Sauté the chops, turning once, until lightly golden on both sides, about 1½ minutes on each side. Transfer to plate.

3. Turn heat down to medium; add bell pepper and onion slices. Sauté, stirring constantly with wooden spoon, scraping any fragments that cling to bottom of pan. Cook until peppers are crisp tender when tested with fork, about 3 minutes. Remove pan from heat. Return chops to pan and arrange vegetables over top.

4. In a small bowl, combine vinegar, water, and sugar. Stir mixture together until the sugar is completely dissolved (this is best done with your index finger so that you can feel when sugar is dissolved). Spoon vinegar mixture over top of vegetables.

5. Cover pan and return it to low heat. Simmer, basting frequently with pan juices, until chops are extremely tender when tested with the tip of a knife, about 10 minutes. Season with salt, and additional pepper if needed.

6. Arrange chops on platter with a border of vegetables; serve immediately.

PER SERVING:	CAL. 142 (44% FROM FAT)	FAT 7 G	SOD. 14 MG
	PROT. 4 G	CARB. 17 G	CHOL. 7 MG

◆ VEAL STEW

This stew can be prepared up to three hours before serving and reheated over very low heat. Serve cooked white or brown rice or boiled potatoes to round out this hearty one-dish meal.

SERVES 2

1 tablespoon olive oil
8 ounces boned shoulder of veal, well trimmed of fat and cut into 1½-inch cubes
½ cup thinly sliced yellow onion
1 large carrot (4 ounces), trimmed, peeled, and sliced diagonally into 1-inch pieces
½ cup coarsely chopped canned tomatoes, juice included
1½ teaspoons minced fresh sage or

½ teaspoon crumbled dried sage
1 large bay leaf
¼ pound green beans, washed, trimmed, and sliced diagonally into 1-inch lengths
1 teaspoon grated lemon rind
⅛ teaspoon coarse salt
⅛ teaspoon freshly milled black pepper

1. In a 3-quart dutch oven, heat oil over medium heat. Add veal and sauté, stirring frequently, until lightly golden. Remove with a slotted spoon. Add onion and carrot; sauté, stirring constantly, scraping any fragments that cling to bottom of pan with wooden spoon.

2. Add tomatoes, sage, and bay leaf. Return meat to pan and bring to a boil, uncovered, over high heat, stirring constantly. Turn heat to low and cook, partially covered, stirring frequently, until meat is extremely tender when pierced with the tip of a knife, about 45 minutes. (Watch cooking liquid; if it starts to evaporate, add about 2 tablespoons hot water.) Add green beans and cook, covered, stirring frequently, until barely tender, about 15 minutes. Discard bay leaf, stir in lemon rind; season with salt and pepper.

3. When ready to serve, transfer stew to platter, and serve immediately.

PER SERVING:	CAL. 260 (36% FROM FAT)	FAT 11 G	SOD. 229 MG
	PROT. 25 G	CARB. 17 G	CHOL. 98 MG

PORK

◆ OVEN-FRIED PORK CHOPS

The savory bread crumb coating seals the chops so that they are juicy and tender when served.

SERVES 2

1½ teaspoons olive oil
   (approximately)
½ cup fine dry bread crumbs
1 tablespoon minced Italian
   parsley leaves
1 teaspoon crushed fennel seeds
   (see Note)

4 boneless center cut pork chops,
   each about ¼ inch thick
   (12 ounces total weight), well
   trimmed of fat

1. Place olive oil in a shallow bowl. On a flat plate, combine bread crumbs, parsley, and crushed fennel seeds. Hold one end of each pork chop with your fingertips over bowl of olive oil and lightly brush both surfaces with oil. Firmly dredge pork chop in bread crumb mixture to coat both sides thoroughly; repeat with remaining pork chops. Refrigerate chops in a single layer on a platter lined with waxed paper for at least 1 hour (chilling prevents coating from coming off during cooking).

2. Adjust rack to top shelf of oven and preheat to 375 degrees. Lightly grease bottom of a shallow 9-by-13-by-2-inch baking pan.

3. Place pork chops in prepared pan and cook in preheated oven until underside is lightly golden and slightly crispy, about 15 minutes (check by lifting with a broad metal spatula). Carefully turn chops with metal spatula and continue cooking until second side is slightly golden and crispy, about 15 minutes. Transfer to platter and serve immediately.

NOTE: Crush fennel seeds in an electric minichopper, or place them in a mound on a cutting board, give them a good thump with the broad side of a chef's knife to partially crush, and then finely chop with a knife.

PER SERVING:	CAL. 378 (33% FROM FAT)	FAT 14 G	SOD. 347 MG
	PROV. 41 G	CARB. 20 G	CHOL. 107 MG

◆ GRILLED PORK CHOPS WITH ROSEMARY

Use only fresh rosemary for this grilled pork recipe. If rosemary is unavailable, you may substitute 8 whole sage leaves or 1 tablespoon minced fresh thyme. The strong taste of the rosemary mellows as it cooks, delicately flavoring the meat. The chops can also be broiled in a preheated oven 4 inches from the heat source.

SERVES 2

4 pork loin chops, each ½ inch
   thick (1 pound total weight),
   well trimmed of fat
2 teaspoons extra virgin olive oil
1 tablespoon minced fresh
   rosemary

⅛ teaspoon freshly milled black
   pepper
8 sprigs curly parsley (optional
   garnish)

1. Place pork chops on a flat plate. With your fingers, rub ½ teaspoon olive oil on both surfaces of each chop. (Rubbing a little oil on surface of chops will prevent them from sticking when placed on heated grill.) With fingertips, press minced rosemary into both surfaces of chops. Let the chops stand at room temperature for 1 hour to allow the rosemary flavor to penetrate each chop.

2. Preheat charcoal grill until coals have turned a gray ashy color. Preheat gas or electric grill according to manufacturer's suggested time.

3. Place chops on grill about 4 inches from heat source. Sear the chops 1 minute on each side, turning meat with long-handled tongs. Cook chops for an additional 3 minutes on each side. To test for doneness, insert the tip of a small knife into the thickest part near the bone. If the juices run clear, with no traces of pink, the chops are done. If not, continue cooking for an additional 2 minutes. Test for doneness once again.

4. Transfer to platter, season with pepper, garnish with parsley, and serve immediately.

PER SERVING:	CAL. 289 (51% FROM FAT)	FAT 16 G	SOD. 76 MG
	PROT. 34 G	CARB. 25 G	CHOL. 93 MG

◆ STUFFED PORK CHOPS

The savory blending of fruit, sage, and white wine gives this dish its full-bodied flavor. This recipe is an adaptation of one developed by my daughter Joanne—a gifted artist and mother of my two grandsons, John Paul and Colin Edward.

SERVES 2

2 pork rib chops, each 1 inch thick (1 pound total weight)
1 tablespoon minced shallots
2 tablespoons dark seedless raisins, plumped in hot water, thoroughly drained, and finely chopped
2 tablespoons applesauce
1½ teaspoons minced fresh sage or ½ teaspoon crumbled dried sage

⅛ teaspoon freshly ground nutmeg
¼ cup fresh bread crumbs
⅛ teaspoon coarse salt
⅛ teaspoon freshly milled black pepper
2 teaspoons olive oil
½ cup dry white wine

1. With a small paring knife, trim excess fat from chops. To make pockets in pork for stuffing, cut a lateral slit down the center and the full length of each chop right to the bone (or have this done by the butcher). Place chops on a flat surface and open the pockets.

2. In a small bowl, combine shallots, raisins, applesauce, sage, nutmeg, bread crumbs, salt, and pepper. Divide stuffing in half.

3. Stuff each chop, bringing flaps together to enclose stuffing. Fasten the edges with 2 toothpicks.

4. In a 10-inch nonstick skillet, heat oil over medium heat. Add pork chops and brown lightly on both sides. Remove chops to a plate and pour off all the drippings. Add ¼ cup wine and turn heat to high, scraping any fragments that cling to pan with wooden spoon; remove pan from heat.

5. Return chops to pan and add remaining wine. Cover pan and cook chops over low heat, basting every 10 minutes with pan juices, until chops are tender when pierced with the tip of a knife, about 35 minutes. If pan juices seem to be evaporating during cooking, add 2 teaspoons water.

6. Transfer chops to serving platter, remove toothpicks, and pour pan juices over each chop. Serve immediately.

NOTE: The pork chops may be cooked up to 2 hours before serving; keep covered after cooking and baste frequently with pan juices. When ready to serve, reheat over low heat for 10 minutes; check pan juices and add a little more white wine if needed.

PER SERVING:	CAL. 305 (44% FROM FAT)	FAT 15 G	SOD. 91 MG
	PROT. 29 G	CARB. 13 G	CHOL. 71 MG

◆ YUMMY PORK CHOPS

The onion, lemon, brown sugar, and ketchup form a mahogany glaze for these succulent chops. This happens to be one of my husband John's favorite pork dishes, especially when served with either Applesauce Raisin Loaf (page 199), or Cranberry Nut Bread (page 202).

SERVES 2

2 teaspoons olive oil
4 pork rib chops, each ½ inch thick (1 pound total weight), well trimmed of fat
1 small yellow onion (5 ounces), peeled and sliced into paper-thin rounds

1 lemon (4 ounces), ends removed, sliced into 8 thin rounds
2 teaspoons ketchup
4 teaspoons dark brown sugar
2 to 3 tablespoons water

1. In a 10-inch nonstick skillet, heat oil over medium-high heat. Lightly brown chops on both sides, about 1 minute on each side; transfer to a platter. Remove skillet from heat, discard any pan drippings, and wipe pan out with paper towel.

2. In same skillet, arrange pork chops in a single layer. Arrange onion slices over chops in an overlapping pattern. Place 2 slices of lemon on top of each chop, spoon ½ teaspoon of ketchup over each chop, and sprinkle 1 teaspoon dark brown sugar over each. Add 2 tablespoons water to bottom of pan.

3. Cover pan and cook chops over low heat until cooking liquid forms a glaze, about 15 minutes. Continue cooking, covered, basting frequently, until chops are extremely tender when pierced with the tip of a knife, about 15 minutes. If glaze gets extremely thick while basting, stir in another tablespoon of water.

4. Transfer chops to a platter with a spatula, and spoon glaze from bottom of pan over each. Serve immediately.

PER SERVING:	CAL. 320 (40% FROM FAT)	FAT 14 G	SOD. 124 MG
	PROT. 29 G	CARB. 20 G	CHOL. 71 MG

◆ PORK TENDERLOIN WITH APPLES AND PRUNES

Although this is a hearty winter dish, I strongly suggest that you try it in late summer, when fresh Italian purple prune plums are in season. Substitute 4 plums (4 ounces), halved, pitted, and quartered, for the prunes. Bulgur Pilaf (page 79) would be an excellent accompaniment.

SERVES 2

2 tablespoons Wondra flour
¼ teaspoon freshly milled black
 pepper
1 8-ounce pork tenderloin, well
 trimmed of fat and any
 connecting membrane
2 teaspoons olive oil
¼ to ⅓ cup dry vermouth
1 large shallot (2 ounces), peeled
 and thinly sliced to make ¼ cup
1 medium-sized tart apple

(6 ounces), such as Granny
 Smith or greening, peeled,
 halved, cored, seeded, and cut
 into ½-inch slices
4 large prunes, pitted and sliced
 into ½-inch strips to make
 ⅓ cup
1 scant teaspoon minced fresh
 rosemary or ¼ teaspoon
 chopped dried rosemary
⅛ teaspoon coarse salt

1. On a piece of waxed paper, combine flour and pepper. Lightly dredge pork in seasoned flour and shake off excess. (Dredge just before browning or flour coating will become gummy.)

2. In a 10-inch nonstick skillet, heat olive oil over medium-high heat. Lightly brown meat on all sides; transfer to platter.

3. Add ¼ cup vermouth to skillet; turn heat to high, scraping any fragments that cling to bottom of pan. Cook, stirring constantly with wooden spoon, until vermouth is reduced to about 1 tablespoon, about 1 minute. Add shallot and cook, stirring constantly, until barely tender, about 30 seconds. Remove pan from heat.

4. Arrange apple slices in bottom of skillet; arrange prunes over apples. Place tenderloin on top of fruit mixture. Sprinkle rosemary and salt

over pork. Cover pan and simmer over medium heat just until apple slices start to exude their juices, about 5 minutes. Spoon some of the fruit mixture over pork and continue cooking, covered, basting pork with fruit frequently, for 25 minutes. If pan juices evaporate during cooking, add an additional tablespoon or more of vermouth.

5. Transfer pork to cutting board, cover loosely with foil, and let rest for 10 minutes before slicing.

6. To serve, slice tenderloin into ½-inch slices; arrange in a single row down center of platter in a slightly overlapping pattern. Spoon fruit mixture around pork; serve immediately.

PER SERVING:	CAL. 324 (24% FROM FAT)	FAT 9 G	SOD. 64 MG
	PROT. 26 G	CARB. 37 G	CHOL. 74 MG

◆ PORK SCALOPPINE

The tomato mushroom sauce enhances the flavorful essence of these tender medallions.

SERVES 2

2 tablespoons Wondra flour
¼ teaspoon freshly milled black
  pepper
1 8-ounce pork tenderloin, well
  trimmed of fat and any
  connecting membrane
2 teaspoons olive oil
¼ cup dry vermouth
½ cup thinly sliced shallots
½ cup finely diced

canned tomatoes, well
  drained
¼ pound crimini or button
  mushrooms, wiped, stems
  discarded and sliced ¼ inch
  thick
1½ teaspoons minced fresh
  rosemary or ½ teaspoon
  chopped dried rosemary
⅛ teaspoon coarse salt

1. On a piece of waxed paper, combine flour and pepper. Lightly dredge pork tenderloin in seasoned flour and shake off excess. (Dredge just before sautéing or the flour coating will become gummy.)

2. In a 10-inch nonstick skillet, heat oil over medium-high heat. Sauté pork, turning several times, until lightly golden on all sides; transfer to platter. Remove pan from heat and stir in vermouth. Turn heat to medium-high and scrape any fragments that cling to bottom of pan with

a wooden spoon. Cook until vermouth is reduced by half, about 30 seconds. Add shallots and cook, stirring constantly, until slightly golden, about 2 minutes. Stir in tomatoes and cook, stirring constantly, until there are no tomato juices left in bottom of pan, about 1 minute. Add mushrooms and continue cooking, stirring constantly, for an additional minute.

3. Turn heat down to medium and return pork to pan. Cook, partially covered, stirring and spooning vegetable mixture over meat, for an additional 5 minutes. Stir in rosemary; season with salt and cook for an additional minute.

4. Transfer pork to platter and slice into ½-inch rounds. Spoon vegetable mixture and sauce over top; serve immediately.

PER SERVING:	CAL. 251 (32% FROM FAT)	FAT 9 G	SOD. 75 MG
	PROT. 27 G	CARB. 16 G	CHOL. 74 MG

◆ PORK LOIN WITH HERBED VEGETABLE SAUCE

It is best if you have the butcher butterfly the pork loin. You can also substitute an 8-ounce butterflied pork tenderloin for the small roast.

SERVES 2

⅓ cup chopped celery with leaves

1 medium clove garlic, split in half

¼ cup coarsely chopped shallots

½ large red bell pepper, cored, seeded, and cut into 1-inch pieces

2 teaspoons fresh thyme leaves or ½ teaspoon

crumbled dried thyme

2 sprigs Italian parsley leaves

⅛ teaspoon cayenne pepper

⅛ teaspoon coarse salt

8 ounces whole boneless pork loin, butterflied and halved crosswise

½ cup water

1. In a food processor or blender fitted with metal blade, purée celery, garlic, shallots, bell pepper, thyme, and parsley. Transfer purée to a small bowl and stir in cayenne pepper and salt.

2. Wrap a double layer of aluminum foil around handle of a 10-inch

skillet to prevent it from burning under broiler. Adjust oven rack to up-per third of oven (about 5 to 6 inches from heat source) and preheat broiler for 10 minutes.

3. Broil pork halves in skillet for 10 minutes. Turn pork halves and spread them with two-thirds of vegetable purée, spooning remaining purée around them. Broil pork for 8 to 10 minutes more, or until meat thermometer registers 150 degrees. Transfer meat to platter and tent with foil to keep warm while making sauce.

4. Add water to skillet and bring to a boil over high heat, scraping up any brown bits, and reduce liquid to about ⅓ cup. Strain sauce into a small bowl, pressing hard on the solids. Spoon sauce around and over pork and serve.

PER SERVING:	CAL. 409 (36% FROM FAT)	FAT 16 G	SOD. 71 MG
	PROT. 42 G	CARB. 24 G	CHOL. 101 MG

LAMB

◆ BROILED LAMB STEAKS WITH THYME

Broiling either in the oven or on an outdoor grill produces the most succu-lent lamb steaks. To avoid spattering and smoking when cooking, the meat should be well trimmed of fat. See bottom of recipe for grilling method.

SERVES 2

2 center cut lamb steaks cut from leg, each ½ inch thick (1¼ pounds total weight), well trimmed of fat
2 teaspoons olive oil
1 tablespoon minced fresh thyme

or 1½ teaspoons crumbled dried thyme
⅛ teaspoon freshly milled black pepper
1 tablespoon fresh lemon juice, strained

1. Place lamb steaks on a flat plate. With your fingers, rub 1 teaspoon olive oil on both surfaces of each steak. (Rubbing a little oil on surface of steaks will prevent them from sticking to the rack when broiled or when placed on heated grill.) With your fingertips, press thyme into both surfaces of steaks. Let the steaks rest at room temperature for 1 hour to allow the flavor of the thyme to penetrate the meat.

2. Remove broiler rack and pan from oven and preheat broiler for 15 minutes.

3. Place steaks on rack over broiler pan. Position broiler pan 4 inches from heat source. Broil until surface of meat is seared and lightly browned, about 3 minutes. Turn steaks and continue broiling on second side, 2 minutes for medium rare, 3 minutes for medium, 5 minutes for well done.

4. Remove steaks from broiler pan (or grill) and place on a cutting board. With a sharp knife, carve around the leg bone (small, round bone); discard bone. Slice the boned steak down center. Repeat with remaining steak. Season both sides of halved steaks with pepper.

5. Place steaks on platter, spoon lemon juice over steaks, and serve immediately.

NOTE: To grill lamb steaks, preheat charcoal grill until coals have turned a gray ashy color. Preheat gas or electric grill according to manufacturer's suggested time. Place steaks on grill 4 inches from heat source. Sear steaks on both sides, about 1 minute on each side, turning meat with long-handled tongs. Approximate cooking time after searing is 2 minutes on each side for medium rare, 3 minutes on each side for medium, or 4 minutes on each side for well done.

PER SERVING:	CAL. 276 (43% FROM FAT)	FAT 13 G	SOD. 113 MG
	PROT. 37 G	CARB. 1 G	CHOL. 116 MG

◆ LAMB SHOULDER CHOPS WITH MUSTARD AND DILL

This tangy combination keeps the chops juicy and moist when broiling, and adds a special zip to the lamb.

SERVES 2

2 lamb shoulder chops, each ½ inch thick (1¼ pounds total weight), well trimmed of fat

2 teaspoons Dijon mustard

1 tablespoon minced fresh dill or

1 teaspoon crumbled dried dillweed

⅛ teaspoon freshly milled black pepper

Several short sprigs fresh dill (optional garnish)

1. Place chops on a flat plate. Spread mustard over both surfaces of each chop. With fingertips, press dill into both surfaces of chops. Let chops stand at room temperature for 1 hour to allow the mustard and dill flavors to penetrate the meat.

2. Remove broiler rack and pan from oven and preheat broiler for 15 minutes. Lightly grease broiler rack.

3. Place chops on prepared rack over broiler pan. Position broiler pan 4 inches from heat source. Broil until surface of meat is seared and lightly browned, about 3 minutes. Turn chops and continue broiling on second side, 2 minutes for medium rare, 3 minutes for medium, or 5 minutes for well done.

4. Transfer to platter and season with pepper; garnish with fresh dill, if desired, and serve immediately.

PER SERVING:	CAL. 272 (46% FROM FAT)	FAT 13 G	SOD. 226 MG
	PROT. 34 G	CARB. 1 G	CHOL. 118 MG

◆ PIQUANT GRILLED LAMB CHOPS

These tasty chops may also be broiled on top of the stove in a ridged grill pan. If raspberry vinegar is unavailable, you can substitute white wine vinegar.

SERVES 2

3 tablespoons raspberry vinegar
1 teaspoon minced garlic
1½ teaspoons minced fresh
　marjoram or ½ teaspoon
　crumbled dried marjoram
4 lamb loin chops, each 1 inch

thick (1¼ pounds total weight),
　well trimmed of fat
⅛ teaspoon freshly milled black
　pepper
Several sprigs curly parsley
　(optional garnish)

1. Place vinegar, garlic, and marjoram in a small bowl; stir with fork to combine.

2. Place chops in a single layer in shallow dish. Spoon marinade over chops, turning once to coat completely; marinate at room temperature for 30 minutes.

3. Preheat charcoal grill until coals have turned a gray ashy color. Preheat gas or electric grill according to manufacturer's suggested time.

4. Remove chops from marinade and gently blot dry with paper towel; discard marinade.

5. Lightly brush the grill rack with a little vegetable or olive oil to prevent chops from sticking while grilling.

6. Place chops on grill about 4 inches from heat source. Sear meat on both sides, about 1 minute on each side, turning meat with long-handled tongs. Approximate cooking time after searing is 2 minutes on each side for medium rare, 3 minutes on each side for medium, or 4 minutes on each side for well done.

7. Place chops on platter, season with pepper, garnish with parsley sprigs, if desired, and serve immediately.

PER SERVING:	CAL. 242 (41% FROM FAT)	FAT 11 G	SOD. 92 MG
	PROT. 33 G	CARB. 1 G	CHOL. 103 MG

◆ RACK OF LAMB

The crusty bread crumb and parsley coating seals in natural juices while it provides a handsome presentation.

SERVES 2

1 6-rib rack of lamb (about 1¼ pounds total weight)
1 teaspoon Dijon mustard
1 teaspoon olive oil
1 teaspoon minced garlic (mince to a paste)
1½ teaspoons minced fresh thyme or ½ teaspoon crumbled dried thyme
1½ teaspoons minced fresh rosemary or ½ teaspoon chopped dried rosemary

¼ teaspoon freshly milled black pepper
½ cup fresh bread crumbs, preferably made from whole wheat bread
1 tablespoon minced Italian parsley leaves
½ bunch watercress, tough ends trimmed (garnish)
1 small lemon, cut into wedges (garnish)

1. Ask your butcher to make ½-inch cuts between the ribs so that carving will be easier. Have him also trim about 2 inches of fat and meat from between ribs to dress up the rack. Trim all the fat from the top of the meat.

2. Combine mustard, olive oil, garlic, thyme, rosemary, and pepper in a small bowl. Rub marinade all over meat; place rack in a shallow bowl and cover with plastic wrap. Refrigerate for at least 3 hours or overnight.

3. When ready to roast, adjust oven rack to center of oven and preheat to 375 degrees.

4. Wrap each exposed bone end of the chops with foil to prevent burning while roasting.

5. Place lamb meat side down on a rack in roasting pan. Roast until meat thermometer registers 140 degrees for medium rare, about 35 minutes, or 145 degrees for medium, about 45 minutes.

6. While lamb is roasting, combine bread crumbs and parsley in a small bowl; set aside.

7. Remove lamb from oven and turn it over (meat side up). Firmly press crumb mixture over top of lamb. Return to oven and bake until crumb mixture is lightly browned and crusty, about 10 minutes. Remove foil from bone ends and let lamb rest for 10 minutes before serving (this will make carving easier).

8. Place rack of lamb on an oval platter and garnish with a border of watercress and lemon wedges. Carve between ribs to serve.

PER SERVING:	CAL. 303 (47% FROM FAT)	FAT 16 G	SOD. 227 MG
	PROT. 29 G	CARB. 12 G	CHOL. 88 MG

◆ BRAISED LAMB SHANKS

The savory blending of herbs, wine, lemon, and broth gives this hearty winter dish its full-bodied flavor. It happens to be one of my husband John's favorites. Plain cooked rice (either white or brown) would be an excellent accompaniment to the lamb shanks because there will be ample sauce from the shanks to spoon over the rice as well.

SERVES 2

2 tablespoons Wondra flour
¼ teaspoon freshly milled black pepper
2 lamb shanks (about 1½ pounds total weight), well trimmed of fat and any attached membrane
2 teaspoons olive oil
⅓ cup minced yellow onion
⅓ cup peeled, minced carrots
⅓ cup minced celery, strings removed
½ cup dry white wine

1 teaspoon minced garlic
1½ teaspoons grated lemon rind
½ cup chicken broth, preferably homemade (page 24) or low-sodium canned
1 tablespoon minced fresh thyme or 1 teaspoon crumbled dried thyme
2 small bay leaves
1 tablespoon minced Italian parsley leaves (garnish)

1. Adjust rack to center of oven and preheat to 350 degrees.
2. Combine flour and pepper in a shallow bowl. Dredge lamb shanks in seasoned flour. (Dredge just before searing or flour coating will become gummy.)
3. In a 10-inch nonstick ovenproof sauté pan, heat oil over high heat. Sear lamb shanks on all sides until lightly golden. Transfer to a plate.
4. Turn heat down to medium and add onion, carrots, and celery. Sauté, stirring constantly, until soft but not brown, scraping any fragments that cling to bottom of pan, about 3 minutes. (If vegetables start to stick to bottom of pan while sautéing, add about 2 tablespoons of the wine to loosen.) Add garlic and lemon rind; mix well. Add wine, turn heat to high, and cook, stirring constantly, until slightly reduced, about 2 minutes. Add broth, thyme, and bay leaves to pan; cook until broth comes to a boil. Remove pan from heat and place shanks on top of vegetable mixture.
5. Cover pan and bake for 30 minutes. Remove pan from oven and spoon half of the vegetable mixture over shanks. Continue to bake, cov-

ered, basting frequently with pan juices until meat is very tender when pierced with fork, about 35 minutes. The meat is finished cooking when it almost falls from the bone.

6. Transfer lamb shanks to platter; discard bay leaves from sauce. Spoon sauce over lamb shanks and garnish with minced parsley; serve immediately.

NOTE: The lamb shanks may be cooked up to 3 hours before serving; keep covered after cooking and baste frequently with pan juices. When ready to serve, reheat in 300-degree oven for 20 minutes.

PER SERVING:	CAL. 400 (33% FROM FAT)	FAT 15 G	SOD. 188 MG
	PROT. 52 G	CARB. 13 G	CHOL. 151 MG

◆ LAMB STEW

These lamb shoulder chops deliver good flavor when made into a stew and make for a speedy braise for weeknight dinners.

SERVES 2

3 teaspoons olive oil
2 lamb shoulder chops, each ¾ inch thick (1½ pounds total weight), well trimmed of fat
½ cup chopped yellow onion
1 teaspoon minced garlic
½ cup coarsely chopped canned tomatoes, juice included
1 bay leaf
1½ teaspoons minced fresh thyme or 1 teaspoon crumbled dried thyme
1 large carrot (4 ounces), peeled

and sliced diagonally into ½-inch pieces
2 medium-sized white potatoes (10 ounces), peeled and cut into 1½-inch cubes
1 cup frozen tiny peas, defrosted and well drained
⅛ teaspoon coarse salt
¼ teaspoon freshly milled black pepper
2 teaspoons minced Italian parsley leaves

1. In a 12-inch nonstick skillet, heat 1½ teaspoons olive oil over medium heat. Add chops and sauté until golden on both sides, about 3 minutes on each side. Transfer chops to plate and pour off any fat from pan.

2. Return skillet to medium heat and add remaining 1½ teaspoons olive oil. Add onion and garlic and sauté, stirring constantly, until onion is barely tender, about 1 minute. Add tomatoes, bay leaf, and thyme. Return chops to pan and spoon tomato mixture over top. Turn heat to low and simmer, covered, until chops are cooked through but tender, about 20 to 25 minutes. Add carrot and potatoes and continue simmering, covered, over low heat until vegetables are done, about 10 minutes. Add peas and cook an additional 2 minutes. Discard bay leaf, season with salt and pepper, and stir in minced parsley. Transfer chops to each plate and spoon vegetables and sauce over each.

NOTE: Stews can be prepared up to 4 hours before serving and reheated over low heat when ready to serve. Add parsley just before serving.

PER SERVING:	CAL. 415 (30% FROM FAT)	FAT 16 G	SOD. 314 MG
	PROT. 45 G	CARB. 36 G	CHOL. 116 MG

POULTRY

CHICKEN

ROAST CHICKEN WITH ROSEMARY 117

ROAST CHICKEN BREAST WITH POTATOES AND RED
   PEPPER 119

CURRIED BRAISED CHICKEN WITH TOMATO,
   GREEN PEPPER, AND RAISINS 120

CHICKEN BREAST WITH PIQUANT VINEGAR SAUCE 121

CHICKEN BREAST WITH ARTICHOKE HEARTS 122

CHICKEN BREAST WITH LEMON CAPER TARRAGON
   SAUCE 123

SPICY BROILED CHICKEN STRIPS 124

POACHED CHICKEN WITH APRICOT SAUCE 125

STIR-FRIED CHICKEN STRIPS WITH CARROTS AND
   ZUCCHINI 126

CHICKEN SALAD WITH YOGURT MINT DRESSING 128

OVEN-BARBECUED CHICKEN THIGHS 129

PEACHY DRUMSTICKS WITH ORANGE SAUCE 130

ROCK CORNISH HEN

BROILED ROCK CORNISH HEN 131

GLAZED ROCK CORNISH HEN 132

TURKEY

TURKEY CUTLETS WITH MUSHROOMS AND TARRAGON 134

TURKEY CUTLETS WITH TOMATO SAUCE 135

I can still remember my childhood days, when poultry was served every Sunday, most often chicken. Each Saturday morning I would walk to the market, holding my father's hand with my left hand and pulling my little wagon with my right. After my father made his choice of chickens, either broilers or fryers, the farmer would tie the legs and wings in place with twine and place the bound chickens in my wagon for the walk home. I distinctly remember two different occasions when the chickens broke loose and I had to go running down the street to catch them. After the chickens were killed and plunged in boiling water, my job was to pluck and singe the feathers. How I dreaded that job. But the taste of those free-range birds was my reward. No matter how they were prepared—broiled, roasted, grilled, or sautéed—that taste was memorable.

Very few people today, however, are fortunate enough to get barnyard-reared (free-range), freshly killed poultry. Instead, poultry must be bought in butcher shops or supermarkets.

Most of the recipes in this chapter call for boneless, skinless poultry, but here are a few suggestions on selecting and preparing the poultry before cooking it.

- When buying packaged poultry, either whole, parts, or boneless, skinless breasts, always check the expiration date. Make sure the outer wrapping on the package is completely sealed.
- The skin of whole birds or cut-up parts should look smooth and there should be no discoloration.
- Some birds have a few small feathers still attached, especially around the vent and wings. These feathers can easily be removed by hand or with tweezers. If there are any hairs on the flesh, carefully pass the birds over a low flame (either a gas burner or a candle) to singe them off.
- Poultry is extremely perishable and should be used within two days of purchase.
- Wash poultry as soon as you get it home, or soak it in cold water with a little lemon juice. Rinse whole birds, parts, or boneless, skinless breasts thoroughly and blot dry with paper towel.

- If you are not going to use it the same day, rub a cut lemon all over the poultry. The acid in the lemon will keep it fresh-smelling. Place in a nonaluminum bowl, cover with plastic wrap, and refrigerate overnight.
- Before cooking poultry, either whole or parts, be sure to remove any traces of fat. Although this book includes just a few recipes in which poultry is cooked with the skin on, I suggest that you remove the skin before eating.
- Many of the recipes for chicken (whole, parts, and boneless, skinless breasts), Rock Cornish hens, and turkey cutlets are interchangeable. There are many in this chapter for you to choose from, so use your imagination in the preparation of poultry for your table.

URRIED BRAISED CHICKEN WITH TOMATO,
REEN PEPPER, AND RAISINS

*inter fare just bursts with the flavor of curry. Cooked white or brown
ould be an excellent accompaniment, since there will be ample sauce
n over.*

s 2

spoons Wondra flour	halved, cored, seeded,
oon freshly milled black	and cut into ¼-inch pieces to
er	make ¾ cup
ess, skinless chicken breast	1 teaspoon minced garlic
s (10 ounces total weight),	½ teaspoon curry powder
rimmed of fat	1 cup coarsely chopped canned
oon olive oil	tomatoes, juice included
ry white wine	2 tablespoons dark seedless
inced red onion	raisins
m-sized green bell	⅛ teaspoon coarse salt
r (5 ounces),	

a shallow bowl, combine flour and pepper. Lightly dredge
ieces in seasoned flour. (Dredge just before sautéing or flour
ill become gummy.)
10-inch nonstick skillet, heat oil over medium-high heat. Place
pan and sauté until lightly golden on both sides, about 2 min-
ach side. Transfer chicken to platter. Discard any oil or pan

¼ cup wine to pan and turn heat to high, scraping any frag-
cling to bottom of pan with wooden spoon. Turn heat to me-
stir in onion and bell pepper. Cook vegetables, stirring
until they are soft, about 5 minutes. Stir in garlic and cook,
nstantly, until soft, about 1 minute. Stir in remaining ¼ cup
, tomatoes, and raisins. Bring sauce to a boil, uncovered, stir-
r twice.
n chicken to pan and spoon sauce over. Simmer, partially cov-
ow heat, stirring and spooning sauce over chicken frequently,
n is tender, about 15 to 20 minutes. Season with salt and reheat. (Chicken can be cooked up to 2 hours before serving,
d and reheated over low heat.)
ve, arrange on a platter and spoon some sauce over chicken;

CHICKEN

◆ ROAST CHICKEN WITH ROSEMARY

*Placing the herbed mixture under the skin will help retain natural moisture
and add distinctive flavoring to the chicken, a flavor that is not lost when the
skin is later removed. See bottom of recipe for suggestions for leftovers.*

SERVES 4

1 whole frying chicken (about 3 pounds)	½ teaspoon dry mustard
1 teaspoon minced garlic	2 teaspoons unsalted butter, softened
1½ teaspoons minced fresh rosemary or ½ teaspoon chopped dried rosemary	1 lemon (4 ounces), cut in half crosswise
¼ teaspoon freshly milled black pepper	½ cup water
	1 small bunch curly parsley (optional garnish)

1. Adjust rack to center of oven and preheat to 350 degrees.
2. Remove fat from rear cavity of the chicken. Cut off wing tips at the first joint and discard. Rinse chicken under cold water and blot dry inside and out with paper towel. Place chicken on work surface with breast side up. Using your index finger, gently loosen skin from flesh of chicken breast, thighs, and upper portion of leg. Be careful not to puncture skin; set chicken aside.
3. In a small bowl, combine garlic, rosemary, pepper, mustard, and softened butter. Mix with spoon until herb mixture is a smooth paste.
4. With one hand, gently pull back the skin at one side of the neck to expose half of the breast flesh. With your other hand, rub half of the herbed mixture over breast and leg area; repeat same process on the other half of chicken. Pat the skin back in place. Rub outside of bird with half of lemon. Squeeze the other half inside chicken and leave in cavity. Truss chicken with kitchen twine or simply tie legs and wings in place with twine.
5. Place chicken on rack in roasting pan, breast side up. Roast until skin is nicely browned and crisp, about 1 hour. To test for doneness, remove chicken from roasting rack with two forks and tip it up on its tail over a white plate. If the juices that run out are a pale yellow color, the chicken is done. If the juices are a pale pink color, cover chicken with a loose tent of foil, return to oven, and roast for an additional 10 to 15 minutes. Test for doneness once again.

6. Transfer chicken to platter and let rest for 10 minutes before carving.

7. Skim off any surface fat from roasting pan. Add ½ cup water to pan and place over medium-high heat. Cook pan juices, scraping any fragments that cling to bottom of pan. Strain pan juices through a strainer set over a small pan; keep warm over low heat.

8. Remove twine from chicken and discard lemon from rear cavity.

9. Quarter chicken and place on serving platter. Garnish with parsley, if desired, and serve with pan juices.

TRUSSING CHICKEN WITH TWINE

1. Place chicken on its back on work surface. Cut a piece of kitchen twine approximately 45 to 50 inches in length (using a generous length of twine will simplify the job when it comes to pulling tightly, and excess will be cut off after knotting). Place center of twine underneath its tail.

2. Cross the twine ends over tail and loop each end over and around the opposite drumstick.

3. Pull both ends of the twine away from the bird to draw the drumstick and tail tightly over the vent.

4. Pull twine under legs and up along sides of thigh and over wings. Make sure that wings are secure under twine as you pull.

5. Knot at top of neck and cut off excess twine.

NOTE: Leftover chicken makes a delicious meal when added to pasta for a salad. See Pasta Salad with Chicken and Broccoli (page 58). For another variation, you may want to try Chicken Soup with Herbs (page 28).

PER SERVING:	CAL. 252 (41% FROM FAT)	FAT 11 G	SOD. 105 MG
	PROT. 35 G	CARB. 1 G	CHOL. 113 MG

◆ ROAST CHICKEN BREAST WI___ POTATOES AND RED PEPPER

Simplicity is the keynote to this tasty one-dish mea___
doubled if entertaining.

SERVES 2

1 medium-sized red onion
  (6 ounces), peeled and
  quartered
2 teaspoons minced garlic
1 tablespoon olive oil
1 large red bell pepper (8 ounces),
  halved, cored, seeded, and cut
  into 1-inch pieces
4 small red-skinned potatoes
  (12 ounces), halved
1 tablespoon minced fresh thyme
  or 1½ teaspoons crumbled
  dried thyme

⅛ teaspo___
¼ teaspo___
  pepp___
1 whole___
  skin___
½ cup___
  hon___
  sod___
4 spri___
  gar___

1. Adjust rack to upper third of oven a___

2. In a 12-inch ovenproof skillet, com___ olive oil, bell pepper, potatoes, thyme, ___ chicken breast halves with remaining te___ them, skin sides up, on top of the veget___

3. Roast chicken for 20 minutes, re___ grees, and continue roasting until chi___ cooked through, and the potatoes are t___

4. Transfer chicken and vegetables ___ and tent with foil to keep warm while ___

5. Stir broth into skillet, scraping ___ pan with wooden spoon. Boil mixtu___ through a sieve over the chicken, ga___ and serve immediately.

PER SERVING:	CAL. 438 (20% FROM FA___
	PROT. 51 G

serve remaining sauce separately. Or you can present both chicken and sauce on a bed of cooked rice.

| PER SERVING: | CAL. 377 (23% FROM FAT) | FAT 10 G | SOD. 325 MG |
| | PROT. 46 G | CARB. 27 G | CHOL. 107 MG |

◆ CHICKEN BREAST WITH PIQUANT VINEGAR SAUCE

Deglazing the pan with white wine vinegar adds flavor and body to the sauce.

SERVES 2

1 tablespoon olive oil
2 boneless, skinless chicken breast halves (10 ounces total weight), well trimmed of fat
2 tablespoons minced shallots
3 tablespoons imported white wine vinegar
¾ cup chicken broth, preferably homemade (page 24) or low-sodium canned
2 teaspoons minced Italian parsley leaves
⅛ teaspoon coarse salt
⅛ teaspoon freshly milled black pepper

1. Adjust oven rack to middle of oven and preheat to 200 degrees.
2. In a 10-inch nonstick skillet, heat oil over medium heat. Sauté breast pieces, turning once with metal spatula, until lightly golden, about 2 minutes on each side. (If chicken starts to stick to bottom of pan, loosen gently with metal spatula.) Remove pan from heat and transfer chicken to ovenproof platter; cover loosely with a tent of foil. Place in oven while making sauce.
3. Add shallots to pan and sauté over medium heat until lightly golden, scraping any fragments that cling to bottom of pan with wooden spoon, about 30 seconds. Add vinegar and turn heat to high. Cook, stirring constantly, until vinegar is reduced to 1 teaspoon and shallots are lightly glazed, about 1 minute. Stir in broth and continue cooking, stirring once or twice, until broth is reduced to about ¼ cup and sauce is slightly thickened, about 2 to 3 minutes. Stir in parsley. Season with salt

and pepper; remove from heat. Stir in any juices that have accumulated on platter. Spoon sauce over chicken breasts; serve immediately.

PER SERVING:	CAL. 239 (33% FROM FAT)	FAT 9 G	SOD. 116 MG
	PROT. 35 G	CARB. 3 G	CHOL. 82 MG

♦ CHICKEN BREAST WITH ARTICHOKE HEARTS

A savory and nutritious accompaniment to this chicken dish would be Brown Rice Pilaf (page 76).

SERVES 2

2 boneless, skinless chicken breast halves (10 ounces total weight), well trimmed of fat
2 tablespoons Wondra flour
¼ teaspoon freshly milled black pepper
1 tablespoon olive oil
½ cup thinly sliced red onion

¼ cup Madeira wine
1 9-ounce package frozen artichoke hearts, defrosted and well drained
1½ teaspoons minced fresh lemon thyme or ½ teaspoon crumbled dried lemon thyme
⅛ teaspoon coarse salt

1. Holding knife at a slight angle, slice breast halves crosswise into 2-inch pieces. (You will be slicing on a bias and cutting against the grain.)

2. In a shallow bowl, combine flour and pepper. Lightly dredge chicken pieces in seasoned flour and shake off excess. (Dredge just before sautéing or flour coating will become gummy.)

3. In a 10-inch nonstick skillet, heat oil over medium-high heat. Add chicken and sauté, turning once, until lightly golden on both sides, about 2 minutes on each side. Using tongs, transfer chicken to plate.

4. Turn heat down to medium, add onion, and cook, stirring constantly and scraping any fragments that cling to bottom of pan. Add wine, turn heat to high, and cook, stirring constantly, until wine has reduced to half, about 1 minute. Stir in artichoke hearts, turn heat down to medium, and cook, partially covered, stirring frequently, until they are barely tender when tested with the tip of a knife, about 3 minutes. Stir in lemon thyme. Return chicken to pan and spoon artichoke mixture on

top. Continue cooking over low heat, partially covered, for an additional 2 minutes. Season with salt and remove from heat.

5. Transfer chicken to platter and spoon artichoke mixture around chicken; serve immediately.

PER SERVING:	CAL. 352 (25% FROM FAT)	FAT 9 G	SOD. 160 MG
	PROT. 38 G	CARB. 23 G	CHOL. 82 MG

◆ CHICKEN BREAST WITH LEMON CAPER TARRAGON SAUCE

The delicate taste of sautéed chicken breast is enhanced with a hint of sharpness from the lemon caper tarragon sauce, adding vigor to this dish.

SERVES 2

2 boneless, skinless chicken breast halves (10 ounces total weight), well trimmed of fat
1 tablespoon olive oil
1 tablespoon fresh lemon juice
½ cup chicken broth, preferably homemade (page 24) or low-sodium canned
2 teaspoons nonpareil capers, thoroughly rinsed and drained

1½ teaspoons minced fresh tarragon or ½ teaspoon crumbled dried tarragon
1 teaspoon cornstarch
1 tablespoon water
⅛ teaspoon coarse salt
⅛ teaspoon freshly milled black pepper

1. Adjust rack to middle of oven and preheat to 200 degrees.
2. Place breast halves between waxed paper and lightly pound until each piece is about ¼ inch thick.
3. In a 10-inch nonstick skillet, heat oil over medium heat. Sauté chicken, turning once with metal spatula, until lightly golden, about 1½ minutes on each side. (If chicken starts to stick to bottom of pan, loosen gently with metal spatula.) Remove pan from heat and transfer chicken to an ovenproof serving platter. Cover loosely with a tent of foil and place in oven while making sauce.
4. Discard any oil remaining in the skillet. Add lemon juice and broth to pan; bring to a boil over high heat, scraping any fragments that cling

to bottom of pan with a wooden spoon. Turn heat to low, stir in capers and tarragon, and cook, stirring constantly, for 30 seconds.

5. In a small bowl, dissolve cornstarch in water. Stir into sauce and continue cooking over low heat until slightly thickened, about 30 seconds. Season with salt and pepper; remove from heat. Stir in any juices that have accumulated on serving dish. Spoon sauce over chicken and serve immediately.

PER SERVING:	CAL. 234 (33% FROM FAT)	FAT 9 G	SOD. 234 MG
	PROT. 34 G	CARB. 3 G	CHOL. 82 MG

◆ SPICY BROILED CHICKEN STRIPS

For an attractive presentation, arrange Shredded Zucchini with Garlic (page 177) in an outer border on platter; fill center with these spicy morsels of chicken.

SERVES 2

2 boneless, skinless chicken breast halves (10 ounces total weight), well trimmed of fat
2 small tomatoes (6 ounces), halved, cored, seeded, but not peeled, cut into 1-inch cubes
2 teaspoons olive oil

1 tablespoon apple cider vinegar
¼ teaspoon crushed fennel seeds
¼ teaspoon ground cinnamon
½ teaspoon Tabasco sauce
1 teaspoon Worcestershire sauce
1 small clove garlic, peeled and halved

1. Cut each breast half lengthwise into strips about ½ inch wide. Place chicken strips in low, shallow bowl.

2. In food processor fitted with metal blade, place tomato, oil, vinegar, crushed fennel seeds, cinnamon, Tabasco, and Worcestershire. Turn machine on and drop garlic, one piece at a time, through the feed tube. Stop machine once or twice and scrape down inside work bowl with plastic spatula. Run machine until tomato and garlic are finely minced and marinade is a smooth, creamy consistency, about 1 minute.

3. Pour marinade over chicken and stir to coat thoroughly. Cover with plastic wrap and marinate in refrigerator for at least 3 hours. Remove from refrigerator ½ hour before broiling.

4. Adjust broiler pan 6 inches from heat source and preheat oven on broil setting for 15 minutes.

5. In a shallow baking pan, place chicken strips in a single layer, about ½ inch apart. Spoon any remaining marinade over chicken. Broil chicken until meat turns white and strips feel firm to the touch, about 4 to 6 minutes.

6. Transfer chicken to a platter. Spoon pan juices over chicken; serve immediately. (If some of the pan juices stick to bottom of pan, add 1 tablespoon hot water and stir with a spoon to loosen.)

PER SERVING:	CAL. 213 (28% FROM FAT)	FAT 6 G	SOD. 132 MG
	PROT. 33 G	CARB. 4 G	CHOL. 82 MG

◆ POACHED CHICKEN WITH APRICOT SAUCE

The apricot sauce lightly coats the chicken, while the grapes add a stylish touch to this flavorful entrée.

SERVES 2

2 boneless, skinless chicken breast halves (10 ounces total weight), well trimmed of fat
¼ cup water
1 5½-ounce can apricot nectar
2 teaspoons fresh lemon juice
⅛ teaspoon freshly grated nutmeg
1½ teaspoons minced fresh mint or ½ teaspoon crumbled dried mint

1½ teaspoons cornstarch
1 tablespoon water
⅛ teaspoon coarse salt
⅛ teaspoon freshly milled white pepper
½ cup small seedless green grapes, sliced in half lengthwise

1. Adjust rack to center of oven and preheat to 200 degrees.
2. Place chicken in a 10-inch nonstick skillet.
3. In a bowl, combine ¼ cup water and apricot nectar and pour over chicken. Cover pan and bring to a boil over medium heat. As soon as diluted nectar reaches a boil, reduce heat to low. Poach chicken, covered, spooning nectar over chicken frequently, until chicken is cooked and feels springy to the touch, about 15 to 20 minutes. Using a pair of tongs,

transfer chicken to an ovenproof serving platter. Cover loosely with a tent of foil. Place in oven while making sauce.

4. Add lemon juice to pan and bring to a boil over high heat. Cook, stirring constantly, until sauce is reduced to about half, about 3 minutes. Stir in nutmeg and mint.

5. In a small bowl, mix cornstarch with 1 tablespoon water and stir until dissolved. Add to sauce and cook over low heat, stirring constantly, until slightly thickened, about 30 seconds. Season with salt and pepper. Stir in grapes and remove from heat. Spoon sauce and grapes over and around chicken; serve immediately.

PER SERVING:	CAL. 243 (8% FROM FAT)	FAT 2 G	SOD. 96 MG
	PROT. 33 G	CARB. 22 G	CHOL. 82 MG

◆ STIR-FRIED CHICKEN STRIPS WITH CARROTS AND ZUCCHINI

Traditionally, this dish is served with 2 cups cooked white rice, but I prefer brown rice as an accompaniment. The nutty flavor of the brown rice truly complements the stir-fried chicken and vegetables. Cook brown rice 1 hour before you start to stir-fry.

SERVES 2

FOR THE MARINADE

2 teaspoons cornstarch
1 teaspoon sugar
2 teaspoons reduced-sodium soy
   sauce
½ teaspoon peeled, minced fresh
   gingerroot
2 teaspoons dry sherry

1 tablespoon water
2 boneless, skinless chicken breast
   halves (10 ounces total weight),
   well trimmed of fat, cut
   lengthwise into ⅛-inch thick
   strips

FOR STIR-FRYING

1 tablespoon vegetable oil
½ cup thinly sliced scallions
⅛ teaspoon crushed red pepper
    flakes
2 medium-sized carrots (5 ounces),
    trimmed, peeled, and thinly
    sliced diagonally to make ½ cup
2 small zucchini (8 ounces),
    trimmed, halved lengthwise,
and sliced diagonally into
    ½-inch pieces
½ cup chicken broth, preferably
    homemade (page 24) or low-
    sodium canned
1 teaspoon cornstarch
1 tablespoon water

1. Prepare the marinade: In a small bowl, stir together cornstarch, sugar, soy sauce, gingerroot, sherry, and water. Add chicken strips, toss well to coat each piece, and marinate at room temperature for 15 minutes.

2. Heat wok or large, heavy skillet over high heat until hot, add 2 teaspoons vegetable oil, and heat until it just begins to smoke. Stir-fry chicken strips, patted dry, in oil until meat turns white, about 1 to 1½ minutes. Transfer chicken to plate with slotted spoon. Add remaining teaspoon oil and swirl pan to coat. Turn heat to medium-high, add scallions and pepper flakes, and stir-fry for 5 seconds. Add carrots and zucchini and continue to stir-fry for 30 seconds. Stir in broth, turn heat to high, and continue to stir-fry just until carrots and zucchini pieces are barely tender, about 1 minute.

3. In a small bowl, combine cornstarch with water and stir until cornstarch is dissolved.

4. Return chicken to pan and stir to combine over high heat. Pour cornstarch mixture into pan and continue to stir-fry until glaze coats chicken and vegetables, about 30 seconds. Transfer to platter and serve immediately.

PER SERVING:	CAL. 234 (32% FROM FAT)	FAT 9 G	SOD. 294 MG
	PROT. 12 G	CARB. 15 G	CHOL. 49 MG

◆ CHICKEN SALAD WITH YOGURT MINT DRESSING

Chicken tossed with grapes and pineapple and enveloped in this silky dressing makes a most refreshing salad to serve during hot weather. Warm Corn Muffins (page 207) would be an excellent accompaniment.

SERVES 2

1 whole boneless, skinless chicken
    breast (10 ounces), well
    trimmed of fat

FOR THE DRESSING

1½ tablespoons low-fat
    mayonnaise
3 tablespoons low-fat yogurt
3 teaspoons fresh lemon juice,
    strained
½ teaspoon honey, preferably
    orange blossom

⅛ teaspoon coarse salt
⅛ teaspoon freshly milled white
    pepper
1½ teaspoons minced fresh mint
    or ½ teaspoon crumbled dried
    mint

FOR THE SALAD

¼ cup thinly sliced celery, strings
    removed
½ cup seedless green grapes, sliced
    in half lengthwise
½ cup unsweetened pineapple
    tidbits, thoroughly drained

1 small bunch watercress
    (5 ounces), coarse stems
    discarded
1 tablespoon toasted slivered
    almonds (optional garnish)

1. Place chicken in a 3½-quart saucepan, cover with water by 1 inch, and remove chicken. Lightly salt the water, bring to a boil, and add chicken. Poach chicken, uncovered, at a bare simmer for 15 minutes. Remove pan from heat and cool chicken in liquid 30 minutes. Drain chicken and let stand until cool enough to handle. (Chicken may be poached 1 day ahead and chilled, covered.) Cut breasts into 1-inch cubes and set aside.

2. Make the dressing: In a small bowl, place mayonnaise, yogurt, lemon juice, honey, salt, pepper, and mint. Whisk to combine.

3. In a deep bowl, place chicken, sliced celery, grapes, and pineapple. Pour dressing over salad and lightly toss to combine. Cover with plastic wrap and refrigerate for 2 hours. (Salad can be made up to 4 hours before serving.)

4. When ready to serve, arrange watercress in an outer border on platter. Lightly toss salad once again, spoon in center, garnish with toasted almonds, if desired, and serve.

PER SERVING:	CAL. 353 (17% FROM FAT)	FAT 7 G	SOD. 341 MG
	PROT. 44 G	CARB. 28 G	CHOL. 116 MG

◆ OVEN-BARBECUED CHICKEN THIGHS

To many, barbecuing means cooking outdoors on a grill. This indoor version bakes in the oven with an authentic, zippy hot sauce.

SERVES 2

⅓ cup minced yellow onion
2 tablespoons ketchup
2½ tablespoons light brown sugar
¼ teaspoon dry mustard
¼ teaspoon crushed red pepper flakes
2 tablespoons apple cider vinegar
½ cup apple juice

⅛ teaspoon coarse salt
¼ teaspoon freshly milled black pepper
4 large boneless, skinless chicken thighs (1 pound total weight), well trimmed of fat
Several sprigs curly parsley (optional garnish)

1. In a 1½-quart saucepan, combine onion, ketchup, brown sugar, mustard, pepper flakes, vinegar, and apple juice. Bring mixture to a boil over high heat. Turn heat to medium and cook, uncovered, stirring frequently, until barbecue sauce is slightly thickened, about 6 minutes. Remove from heat and let cool to room temperature.

2. Lightly salt and pepper chicken thighs. Place thighs on a plate and spoon 1 tablespoon barbecue sauce over each; reserve remaining sauce for basting. Cover chicken with plastic wrap and marinate in refrigerator for at least 2 hours, turning chicken twice. Place chicken, meaty side down, in a 1½-quart ovenproof casserole. Discard any remaining marinade left on plate.

3. Adjust oven rack to center of oven and preheat to 350 degrees.

4. Cook chicken, covered, in preheated oven for 25 minutes. Remove chicken from oven and turn temperature up to 375 degrees. Turn thighs meaty side up and spoon reserved barbecue sauce over chicken. Return to oven and continue cooking, uncovered, basting frequently, until thighs are golden and glazed, about 25 minutes. Transfer to platter and spoon sauce over chicken. (If some of the sauce sticks to bottom of pan, add 2 teaspoons hot water and stir to loosen with a wooden spoon.) Garnish with parsley sprigs, if desired, and serve immediately.

PER SERVING:	CAL. 262 (23% FROM FAT)	FAT 7 G	SOD. 277 MG
	PROT. 32 G	CARB. 17 G	CHOL. 134 MG

◆ PEACHY DRUMSTICKS WITH ORANGE SAUCE

The slight hint of ginger adds zest to the orange sauce. A spicy accompaniment to this dish is Barley Pilaf with Raisins (page 82).

SERVES 2

4 large skinless chicken legs
   (1¼ pounds total weight)
1 8¾-ounce can (Del Monte)
   sliced yellow cling peaches in
   heavy syrup
½ cup fresh orange juice, strained

2 teaspoons reduced-sodium soy
   sauce
2 teaspoons cornstarch
1 teaspoon freshly grated
   gingerroot or ½ teaspoon
   ground ginger

1. Adjust rack to center of oven and preheat to 350 degrees.
2. Place chicken legs in a single layer in a 1½-quart ovenproof casserole.
3. Drain peaches in a strainer set over a bowl. Reserve ¼ cup of the syrup; discard remaining syrup.
4. In a small saucepan, place ¼ cup peach syrup, orange juice, soy sauce, cornstarch, and ginger. Stir with whisk until cornstarch is completely dissolved. Cook, uncovered, over medium heat, whisking constantly, until sauce is slightly thickened, about 1 to 2 minutes.
5. Spoon orange sauce over chicken. Cook, covered, in preheated oven for 20 minutes. Remove chicken from oven and turn temperature up to 375 degrees.
6. Return chicken to oven and continue cooking, uncovered, basting

and turning legs every 5 minutes until lightly golden and glazed, about 20 minutes longer. Add peaches to casserole and spoon some of the sauce over them. Continue cooking, uncovered, just until peaches are heated, about 2 minutes. Transfer to a platter and serve immediately.

PER SERVING:	CAL. 323 (18% FROM FAT)	FAT 6 G	SOD. 347 MG
	PROT. 34 G	CARB. 33 G	CHOL. 129 MG

ROCK CORNISH HEN

◆ BROILED ROCK CORNISH HEN

To ensure that bird will turn crisp, brown without burning, and cook through evenly, broil 6 inches from the heat source. Always remove the wing tips so that protruding wings will not char during the time it takes the breast to cook.

SERVES 2

2 tablespoons fresh lemon juice, strained
½ teaspoon minced garlic
½ teaspoon Dijon mustard
1½ teaspoons minced fresh savory or ½ teaspoon crumbled dried savory

¼ teaspoon freshly milled black pepper
2 teaspoons olive oil
1 Rock Cornish hen (about 1½ pounds) halved lengthwise
Several sprigs curly parsley (garnish)

1. Place lemon juice, garlic, mustard, savory, and pepper in a small bowl. Using a fork or small whisk, beat to combine. Add oil a little at a time and whisk to thoroughly combine marinade.

2. Place split hen in a shallow bowl. Using your hands, rub marinade into both surfaces of hen. Cover with plastic wrap and marinate in refrigerator for at least 3 hours, turning twice in marinade. Remove from refrigerator ½ hour before broiling.

3. Remove broiler rack and pan from oven and preheat broiler for 15 minutes. Lightly grease broiler rack.

4. Using a narrow metal spatula or the back of a knife, scrape marinade off both surfaces of split hen into bowl; reserve marinade. Blot hen dry with paper towel.

5. Place hen halves, skin sides down, on prepared rack over broiler pan and position hen 6 inches from heat source. Broil until lightly golden, about 15 minutes. Remove from oven and brush half of the reserved marinade over surface. Return to oven and continue broiling until golden brown, about 15 minutes longer. Remove from oven and, using long-handled tongs, carefully turn the hen halves skin side up. (Using tongs will prevent piercing the flesh and letting the juices run out.) Return to oven and broil until skin is a light golden color, about 15 minutes more. Remove from oven and baste with remaining marinade. Return to oven and broil until the skin has turned a deep golden brown, about 15 minutes longer.

6. To test for doneness, place split hen on a white plate with skin sides down. Using a small knife, make a slit about ½ inch deep into the thickest part of the thigh. If the juices that run out are pale yellow, the bird is done. If the juices are pink, turn oven temperature down to 375 degrees, cover pan with a loose tent of foil, and place in oven. Cook for an additional 10 minutes. Test for doneness once again.

7. Place split hen on a platter, garnish with parsley, if desired, and serve immediately.

PER SERVING:	CAL. 420 (66% FROM FAT)	FAT 31 G	SOD. 122 MG
	PROT. 32 G	CARB. 2 G	CHOL. 187 MG

◆ GLAZED ROCK CORNISH HEN

The delicate taste of this glazed Cornish hen is enhanced by the light honey orange sauce made with the pan juices.

SERVES 2

1 Rock Cornish hen (about
  1½ pounds)
1 large clove garlic, split in half
¼ cup fresh orange juice, strained
2 teaspoons reduced-sodium soy
  sauce
2 teaspoons honey, preferably
  orange blossom

1 teaspoon freshly grated
  gingerroot or ½ teaspoon
  ground ginger
1 teaspoon apple cider vinegar
¼ cup water
Several sprigs curly parsley
  (optional garnish)

1. Adjust rack to center of oven and preheat to 350 degrees.

2. Rinse hen under cold water and blot dry inside and out with paper towel. Thoroughly rub surface of hen with split garlic, then place garlic in rear cavity. Truss hen with kitchen twine or simply tie legs and wings in place with twine.

3. Place orange juice, soy sauce, honey, ginger, and vinegar in a small bowl. Beat with a fork or small whisk to combine; set aside.

4. Place hen on rack in roasting pan, breast side up. Roast until skin is a very light golden color, about 50 minutes. To test for doneness, remove hen from roasting rack with two forks and tip it up on its tail over a white plate. If the juices that run out are a pale yellow, the hen is done. If the juices are pale pink, cover hen with a loose tent of foil, return to oven, and roast for an additional 10 minutes. Test for doneness once again.

5. Remove pan from oven and pour off any drippings in bottom of pan. If using foil, discard.

6. Whisk glaze once again. Turn hen breast side down on rack. Brush with half of the glaze and bake until bottom surface is glazed, about 5 minutes. Remove from oven and turn hen breast side up. Brush with remaining glaze and bake until top surface of hen is glazed, about 5 to 7 minutes.

7. Transfer hen to platter and let rest for 10 minutes before serving.

8. Add ¼ cup water to pan and place over medium-high heat. Cook pan juices, scraping any fragments that cling to bottom of pan with wooden spoon. Pour sauce through a strainer set over a small pan; keep warm over low heat.

9. Remove twine from hen and discard garlic from rear cavity. Place hen on a serving platter and garnish with parsley, if desired. Serve sauce separately.

PER SERVING:	CAL. 415 (58% FROM FAT)	FAT 26 G	SOD. 293 MG
	PROT. 33 G	CARB. 11 G	CHOL. 187 MG

TURKEY

♦ TURKEY CUTLETS WITH MUSHROOMS AND TARRAGON

Deglazing the pan with dry vermouth enriches the sauce of this mushroom-and-tarragon-garnished entrée.

SERVES 2

2 turkey cutlets, each ¼ inch thick (8 ounces total weight)

2 teaspoons Wondra flour

¼ teaspoon freshly milled black pepper

1 tablespoon olive oil

¼ cup dry vermouth

1 large shallot (2 ounces), peeled and thinly sliced to make ¼ cup

4 ounces medium-sized mushrooms, wiped, trimmed, and sliced in half

1½ teaspoons minced fresh tarragon or ½ teaspoon crumbled dried tarragon

⅛ teaspoon coarse salt

2 teaspoons minced Italian parsley leaves (garnish)

1. Holding knife at a slight angle, slice each cutlet crosswise into 2 pieces. (You will be slicing on a bias and cutting against the grain.)

2. In a shallow bowl, combine flour and pepper. Lightly dredge each piece of turkey in seasoned flour and shake off excess. (Dredge just before sautéing or the flour coating will become gummy.)

3. In a 10-inch nonstick skillet, heat oil over medium-high heat. Sauté turkey pieces, turning once, until lightly golden on both sides, about 1½ minutes on each side. Transfer turkey to a plate.

4. Add vermouth and turn heat to high, scraping any fragments that cling to bottom of pan with wooden spoon. Cook until vermouth is reduced by half, about 1 minute. Stir in shallots and sauté until crisp tender, about 1 minute. Stir in mushrooms and sauté just until they start to exude their juices, about 2 minutes. Stir in tarragon and mix well to combine. Return turkey to pan and cook, spooning mushrooms and pan juices over turkey for an additional 30 seconds. Season with salt; remove from heat.

5. Transfer to platter, garnish with minced parsley, and serve immediately.

PER SERVING:	CAL. 261 (31% FROM FAT)	FAT 8 G	SOD. 64 MG
	PROT. 30 G	CARB. 10 G	CHOL. 71 MG

◆ TURKEY CUTLETS WITH TOMATO SAUCE

The slight hint of lemon rind in the bread crumb coating adds a distinctive taste to these cutlets.

SERVES 2

2 tablespoons Wondra flour
⅛ teaspoon freshly milled black
  pepper
1 large egg
1½ teaspoons cold water
½ cup fine dry bread crumbs
1 teaspoon minced Italian parsley
  leaves
1 teaspoon finely grated lemon
  rind

2 turkey cutlets, each ¼ inch thick
  (8 ounces total weight)
1 tablespoon olive oil
¼ cup Tomato Basil Sauce
  (page 45)
1 teaspoon minced Italian parsley
  leaves (garnish)

1. In a shallow bowl, combine flour and pepper. In another shallow bowl, beat egg and cold water with a fork. On a flat plate, combine bread crumbs, parsley, and lemon rind. Dredge cutlets in seasoned flour, dip in beaten egg, and then thoroughly coat with bread crumb mixture. Refrigerate cutlets in a single layer on a plate lined with waxed paper for at least 1 hour (chilling prevents coating from coming off during sautéeing).

2. In a 12-inch nonstick skillet, heat oil over medium-high heat. Sauté the cutlets on one side until lightly golden, about 2 minutes. Turn the cutlets, partially cover the skillet, and sauté on second side until cutlets feel firm but springy to the touch, about 2 minutes more. Transfer cutlets to serving platter.

3. While cutlets are sautéing on second side, heat Tomato Basil Sauce over low heat.

4. Spoon 2 tablespoons of the sauce over each cutlet and garnish each with a little minced parsley; serve immediately.

PER SERVING:	CAL. 371 (30% FROM FAT)	FAT 12 G	SOD. 399 MG
	PROT. 36 G	CARB. 28 G	CHOL. 176 MG

FISH AND SEAFOOD

A fish-eating society has been evolving during the past twenty years. I attribute this to people being more aware of healthy eating habits and to the improved marketing and distribution of fresh fish and seafood.

When you add fresh fish to your diet, you are adding taste, variety, and valuable nutrients. Fresh fish has little waste and loses little of its food value when cooked properly. It is high in protein, low in calories, and a source of important vitamins and minerals. Because of its nutritional value, fish is often referred to as nature's most nearly perfect food, ideal for people of all ages, from young toddlers to senior citizens.

With today's efficient cross-country transportation in refrigerated trucks and planes, it is possible to purchase fresh fish and seafood of the highest quality at local supermarkets or fish markets.

All over the country, people are developing a new appreciation for fish, are learning how to handle it more comfortably and cook it with imagination and style. Whether it be broiled, grilled, baked, poached, or oven-fried, whether served hot or cold, fish and shellfish are indispensable to today's cook, especially to those who are in a hurry or do not want to spend hours in the kitchen. Many cuts of meat, notably beef and pork, require longer periods of cooking to become tender, but all fish and seafood are by contrast naturally tender and require relatively brief cooking times.

Most of my childhood summer vacations were spent with my family at the New Jersey shore. As we sat on the beach, we could see the fishing boats come into the inlet of the Manasquan River. It was always fun to go down to the fishing pier and watch the sea captains and crew unload the catch of the day. Like any curious child, I enjoyed looking at the fish with their clear, protruding eyes and black pupils, bright red gills, and shiny, tightly adhering scales. Naturally, my inquisitive instinct always prompted me to touch the fish and feel the firm, elastic flesh spring back when pressed with my finger. I can still remember the faintly sweet, appetizing aroma of the sea as the fish were sorted, cleaned, and packed in ice to be shipped to restaurants or local markets. Little did I know then that I was being taught my first lesson in using my eyes and nose to sharpen my sea sense in selecting fresh fish.

The following pointers are offered to help sharpen *your* sea sense:

- Remember, freshness is the key to quality. When a recipe requires a particular fish that is not available fresh, substitute another appropriate fresh fish, if possible, or choose a different recipe.
- Watch closely when your fish seller picks up the fish. The flesh of the fillet should be white or almost translucent and should appear firm and resilient. If the fillets have a yellow tinge along the cut surface, the fish is spoiling.
- Do not purchase fish that is prewrapped. In selecting fresh fish, the first thing to do is smell the fish. There should be no smell at all or a mild, fresh aroma like seawater or seaweed. Reject any fish that has a fishy odor—this is an early sign of decomposition.
- Always make the fish store or fish department in the supermarket your last stop when shopping so that your purchase is unrefrigerated for the shortest possible time. When you get home, unwrap fish immediately, thoroughly wash in cold water, and pat dry with paper towel.
- Fresh fish should be eaten the same day of purchase. If the fish must be stored, cover it loosely with plastic wrap and keep it in the coldest part of your refrigerator, but no longer than two days.

The recipes in this chapter offer flavorful opportunities to create dishes that should be just right to introduce you to a culinary pleasure you may have been missing.

◆ COD STEW

This stew has a tantalizing mild and subtle flavor. The careful layering of ingredients adds to its delicate appeal. Broccoli with Garlic and Lemon (page 163) would be an excellent accompaniment to this hearty one-dish meal.

SERVES 2

1 skinless fillet of cod about 1 inch thick (12 ounces)
1 tablespoon olive oil
1 medium-sized yellow onion (6 ounces), peeled, halved, and cut into ½-inch slices
2 large celery ribs (4 ounces), strings removed, cut into 2-inch lengths
1 large Idaho potato (8 ounces),

peeled and sliced into ½-inch rounds
⅛ teaspoon coarse salt
¼ teaspoon freshly milled black pepper, divided
2 medium bay leaves, broken in half
½ cup coarsely chopped canned tomatoes, juice included
2 tablespoons water

1. Rinse fillet with cold water and blot dry with paper towel. Cut fillet crosswise into 4 even pieces; set aside.

2. Drizzle 1 teaspoon olive oil in bottom of a 3-quart saucepan. Place onion in a single layer in pan. Arrange celery in a single layer on top of onion. Place sliced potatoes on top of celery in a single layer and sprinkle with salt and ⅛ teaspoon pepper. Place cut cod fillet in a single layer on top of potatoes. Place ½ bay leaf on top of each piece of fillet. Spoon chopped tomatoes on top of fish and season with remaining ⅛ teaspoon pepper. Drizzle remaining 2 teaspoons olive oil over tomatoes and add water to bottom of pan.

3. Cover pan and cook over medium-low heat, basting frequently with cooking liquid, until potatoes are cooked when tested with the tip of a fork, about 30 to 40 minutes. Check cooking liquid frequently; if the saucepan is not a heavy one, you may have to add a few more teaspoons of water to keep mixture moist. Remove from heat and discard bay leaves.

4. Use two large serving spoons to carefully lift portions into individual bowls. Spoon a little of the pan juices on top and serve immediately.

PER SERVING:	CAL. 315 (23% FROM FAT)	FAT 8 G	SOD. 246 MG
	PROT. 34 G	CARB. 26 G	CHOL. 73 MG

◆ POACHED FISH ROLLS IN TOMATO WINE SAUCE

Turbot is a delicate, sweet-tasting fish that is a member of the flatfish or flounder family. If turbot is unavailable, you may substitute fillets of lemon sole.

SERVES 2

2 skinless fillets of turbot, each
¼ inch thick (about 8 ounces
total weight)
2 teaspoons olive oil
½ teaspoon minced garlic
½ cup finely chopped canned
tomatoes, juice included
⅓ cup dry white wine

¼ teaspoon dry mustard
1 small bay leaf
1 scant teaspoon minced fresh
thyme or ¼ teaspoon crumbled
dried thyme
⅛ teaspoon coarse salt
⅛ teaspoon freshly milled black
pepper

1. Wash fillets under cold water and blot dry with paper towel. Place fillets on a work surface. Cut each fillet in half lengthwise. With skinned side down, and starting from broad end, roll each piece jelly-roll fashion into a cylinder.

2. Adjust rack to center of oven and preheat to 200 degrees.

3. In a 10-inch nonstick skillet, heat oil over medium-low heat. Add garlic and sauté until very lightly golden, about 1 minute. Add tomatoes, wine, mustard, and bay leaf. Bring sauce to a boil and cook for 1 minute, stirring constantly with a wooden spoon. Turn heat down to low. Arrange fish rolls seam side down in single layer in pan. Cover pan and poach rolls, basting frequently, until easily flaked when tested with a toothpick, about 6 to 7 minutes. Remove from heat.

4. Using two forks, carefully transfer rolls to an ovenproof serving platter. Place in oven to keep warm while finishing sauce.

5. Turn heat to high and cook sauce, stirring constantly, until slightly thickened, about 1½ to 2 minutes. Stir in thyme. Season with salt and pepper and remove from heat. Remove bay leaf from sauce. Spoon sauce over fish rolls and serve immediately.

PER SERVING:	CAL. 293 (69% FROM FAT)	FAT 20 G	SOD. 101 MG
	PROT. 17 G	CARB. 4 G	CHOL. 52 MG

◆ BROILED FLOUNDER WITH THYME

Nothing is better than a piece of simply broiled fish. The bread crumb coating on the surface of the fillet will keep fish moist during broiling.

SERVES 2

1 skinless fillet of flounder, ½ inch thick (about 12 ounces)
1 tablespoon dry bread crumbs
⅛ teaspoon coarse salt
⅛ teaspoon paprika
1 scant teaspoon minced fresh

thyme or ¼ teaspoon crumbled dried thyme
2 teaspoons olive oil
1 tablespoon fresh lemon juice, strained

1. Remove broiler rack and pan from oven and preheat broiler for 15 minutes. Lightly grease broiler rack.

2. Wash fillet in cold water and thoroughly blot dry with paper towel. Slice fillet in half crosswise and place pieces about 2 inches apart on prepared rack.

3. In a small bowl, combine bread crumbs, salt, paprika, and thyme. Using a small pastry brush, evenly spread 1 teaspoon oil over entire surface of each half of the fillet. Sprinkle bread crumb mixture on top of fish.

4. Position broiler pan so that the fish will be 5 inches from heat source. Broil until surface of fish is lightly golden and barely flakes when tested with a fork, about 7 to 8 minutes. (The fish does not have to be turned.)

5. Remove from oven and transfer to platter. Spoon lemon juice over each portion and serve immediately.

PER SERVING:	CAL. 210 (29% FROM FAT)	FAT 7 G	SOD. 167 MG
	PROT. 33 G	CARB. 3 G	CHOL. 82 MG

◆ BROILED HALIBUT STEAKS WITH HERBS

Marinating the halibut before cooking adds subtle flavor and will keep steaks juicy and moist while broiling. Swordfish or salmon steaks may be substituted for the halibut.

SERVES 2

2 halibut steaks, each about 1 inch thick (12 ounces total weight)
¼ cup fresh lemon juice, strained
1 teaspoon minced garlic
1 scant teaspoon minced fresh

oregano or ¼ teaspoon crumbled dried oregano
1½ teaspoons snipped fresh dill or ½ teaspoon crumbled dried dillweed

1. Rinse steaks under cold water and blot dry with paper towel. Place steaks in a single layer in a shallow dish.

2. Place lemon juice, garlic, oregano, and dill in a small bowl. Beat with fork or small whisk to combine marinade. Spoon marinade over fish and turn the steaks once to coat thoroughly. Marinate at room temperature for 30 minutes.

3. Remove broiler rack and pan from oven and preheat broiler for 15 minutes. Lightly grease broiler rack.

4. Using a pair of tongs, lift steaks out of marinade. Scrape marinade off steaks with the back of a knife; reserve marinade for basting.

5. Place steaks about 2 inches apart on prepared rack. Position broiler pan so that the fish will be 5 inches from heat source. Broil steaks, basting once with half of the reserved marinade, until surface is golden, about 5 minutes. Remove broiler pan and carefully turn steaks with a wide metal spatula. Spoon remaining marinade over steaks and broil until second side is golden, about 5 minutes. To test for doneness, slip a small knife between the bone and the flesh; if the fish is sufficiently cooked, the flesh will separate easily from the bone. Transfer to platter and serve immediately.

PER SERVING:	CAL. 162 (18% FROM FAT)	FAT 3 G	SOD. 75 MG
	PROT. 29 G	CARB. 3 G	CHOL. 44 MG

◆ BROILED MONKFISH WITH MUSTARD AND CHIVES

This fish was once called the "poor man's lobster" because of its sweet flavor. This recipe is equally as good with tilefish, grouper, or sea bass fillets.

SERVES 2

1 skinless monkfish fillet, 1 inch thick (12 ounces)
¼ teaspoon freshly milled white pepper

2 teaspoons Dijon mustard
1 tablespoon olive oil
1 tablespoon minced chives

1. Preheat oven on broil setting for 15 minutes. Lightly grease a shallow ovenproof baking dish large enough to hold the monkfish; set aside.

2. Wash fillet in cold water and thoroughly blot dry with paper towel.

3. Rub pepper into both surfaces of fish. Place fillet in prepared pan. Using a small pastry brush, brush surface of fish with 1 teaspoon mustard. Spoon 1½ teaspoons olive oil over fish.

4. Position baking dish so that the fish will be 5 inches from the heat source. Broil fillet until very lightly golden, about 3 to 4 minutes. Remove from oven and carefully turn fish with a wide metal spatula. Brush surface with remaining mustard and spoon remaining olive oil over top. Return to oven and broil until second side of fish is lightly golden and barely flakes when tested with a fork, about 4 to 5 minutes.

5. Remove from oven and sprinkle chives over surface; serve immediately.

PER SERVING:	CAL. 176 (39% FROM FAT)	FAT 7 G	SOD. 151 MG
	PROT. 25 G	CARB. .24 G	CHOL. 43 MG

◆ POACHED SALMON WITH DILL SAUCE

Poaching the salmon steaks in this court bouillon will keep them very moist.
The court bouillon will be transformed into a delicate dill sauce to grace-
fully dress these steaks. The Grapefruit Salad with Watercress Dressing
(page 183) would be an excellent accompaniment to this entrée.

SERVES 2

2 salmon steaks, each about
   1 inch thick (12 ounces total
   weight)
2 teaspoons olive oil
⅓ cup minced shallots
¼ cup peeled, minced carrots
¼ cup minced celery, strings
   removed
½ teaspoon coarse salt
⅛ teaspoon freshly milled black
   pepper

1 cup dry white wine, preferably
   sauvignon blanc
1½ teaspoons cornstarch
2½ tablespoons cold water
1½ teaspoons minced fresh dill or
   ½ teaspoon crumbled dried dillweed
2 teaspoons minced Italian parsley
   leaves

1. Rinse steaks under cold water and blot dry with paper towel.

2. In a 10-inch nonstick skillet, heat olive oil over medium heat. Add
shallots, carrots, and celery; cover pan and cook, stirring once, until
vegetables are soft but not brown, about 5 minutes. Remove pan from
heat. Place steaks on top of vegetable mixture and season with salt and
pepper. Add wine to pan (wine should barely cover top of steaks; add more
if necessary). Bring the court bouillon to a simmer and poach the steaks,
covered, at a bare simmer until they barely flake, about 6 to 8 minutes.

3. Adjust oven rack to center of oven and preheat to 200 degrees.

4. Transfer steaks with a slotted spoon to an ovenproof platter and
spoon 2 tablespoons of the court bouillon on top of steaks to keep moist
while making sauce. Pour court bouillon through strainer set over a
bowl; reserve solids in strainer. Transfer ½ cup strained liquid and reserved solids to food processor or blender fitted with metal blade; discard remaining liquid. Run machine nonstop until vegetables are finely
puréed; transfer to a 1½-quart saucepan.

5. In a small bowl, dissolve cornstarch in cold water and whisk into
pureed mixture. Cook over medium-high heat, stirring constantly, until
slightly thickened, about 1 minute. Stir in dill and parsley and remove
from heat.

6. Spoon 2 tablespoons of heated sauce on individual plates. Place steaks in center of plates and spoon an additional 2 tablespoons of sauce on top of each and serve.

PER SERVING:	CAL. 383 (55% FROM FAT)	FAT 23 G	SOD. 126 MG
	PROT. 35 G	CARB. 7 G	CHOL. 100 MG

◆ SAUTÉED SCALLOPS WITH MUSHROOM HERB SAUCE

The sauce adds tantalizing flavor to the tender sautéed scallops. A good addition to this entrée would be Rice with Zucchini (page 72).

SERVES 2

8 ounces sea scallops
2 tablespoons Wondra flour
¼ teaspoon freshly milled black
    pepper
1 tablespoon olive oil
½ cup thinly sliced scallions
8 medium-sized mushrooms
    (4 ounces), trimmed, wiped,
    and thinly sliced to make 1 cup
¼ cup dry vermouth
1 cup diced canned tomatoes, well
    drained

1 scant teaspoon minced fresh
    thyme or ¼ teaspoon crumbled
    dried thyme
1½ teaspoons minced fresh basil
    or ½ teaspoon crumbled dried
    basil
⅛ teaspoon coarse salt
1 tablespoon fresh lemon juice,
    strained
1 tablespoon minced Italian
    parsley leaves

1. Wash scallops in cold water and thoroughly blot dry with paper towel. If scallops are more than 1 inch in diameter, slice in half crosswise.

2. In a shallow bowl, combine flour and pepper. Lightly dredge scallops in seasoned flour and shake off excess. (Dredge just before sautéing or the flour coating will become gummy.)

3. In a 10-inch nonstick skillet, heat oil over medium-high heat. Sauté scallops, turning once, just until they are lightly golden and feel slightly firm to the touch, about 1½ minutes on each side. Using a slotted spoon, transfer scallops to a plate.

4. Turn heat down to medium, add scallions, and cook until crisp tender, about 1 minute, scraping any fragments that cling to bottom of

pan with wooden spoon. Turn heat to high, add mushrooms, and sauté, stirring constantly, just until they begin to exude their juices, about 30 seconds. Add vermouth, stirring constantly until liquid in pan is reduced by half, about 30 seconds. Stir in diced tomatoes, thyme, and basil. Continue cooking over high heat, stirring constantly, until very little liquid is left in bottom of pan and sauce is slightly thickened, about 1 minute.

5. Return scallops and any accumulated juices on plate to pan. Cook mixture, stirring constantly, over medium-high heat, until scallops are heated through, about 30 seconds. Season with salt; stir in lemon juice and parsley. Remove from heat. Transfer to platter and serve immediately.

PER SERVING:	CAL. 230 (31% FROM FAT)	FAT 8 G	SOD. 199 MG
	PROT. 22 G	CARB. 18 G	CHOL. 37 MG

CLEANING SHRIMP

Using a sharp pair of kitchen shears, cut shell down back of shrimp to tail (you will be exposing the black intestinal vein as you cut). Peel off shell to tail. With your thumb and index finger, pinch tail and pull off remaining tail shell (this will leave tail meat intact). Under cold running water lift out intestinal vein with fingers and discard. Wash shrimp in cold water and thoroughly blot dry with paper towel.

On underside of shrimp, cut 3 slits ¼ inch deep and ½ inch apart; this will minimize curling when cooking.

◆ SPEEDY SHRIMP SCAMPI

This delectable scampi recipe is simple to prepare and can be on the table in a matter of minutes.

SERVES 2

1 tablespoon olive oil
½ teaspoon minced garlic
8 ounces medium-sized shrimp
  (about 12), shelled and
  deveined (see directions for
  cleaning, above)

1 tablespoon lemon juice, strained
2 tablespoons dry white wine
1 tablespoon dry bread crumbs
⅛ teaspoon coarse salt
⅛ teaspoon freshly milled black
  pepper

2 teaspoons minced Italian parsley leaves   2 lemon wedges (optional garnish)

1. In a 10-inch nonstick skillet, heat oil over low heat. Add garlic and sauté, stirring constantly with a wooden spoon, until very lightly golden, about 1 minute. Add shrimp, turn heat to medium-high, and sauté, stirring constantly, until they turn pink, about 1½ minutes. Turn heat to high; stir in lemon juice and wine. Cook, stirring constantly, just until blended, about 20 seconds. Stir in bread crumbs and cook, stirring constantly, until crumbs absorb most of the pan juices. Season with salt and pepper; stir in minced parsley and remove from heat.

2. Transfer to individual serving plates and garnish each plate with a lemon wedge, if desired; serve immediately.

PER SERVING:	CAL. 185 (44% FROM FAT)	FAT 8 G	SOD. 169 MG
	PROT. 19 G	CARB. 4 G	CHOL. 141 MG

◆ SHRIMP AND SNOW PEA SALAD

An eye-catching, delicious salad that can be served as a main course for lunch or supper. An excellent first course for this entrée would be a cup of Chilled Cucumber Soup (page 29).

SERVES 2

5 teaspoons fresh lemon juice, strained
8 ounces medium-sized shrimp (about 12), shelled and deveined (see directions for cleaning, page 148)
1 tablespoon minced scallions, white part only (reserve 2 tablespoons thinly sliced scallion greens for garnish)

¼ teaspoon Dijon mustard
⅛ teaspoon coarse salt
¼ teaspoon sugar
⅛ teaspoon freshly milled white pepper
1 tablespoon extra virgin olive oil
16 snow peas (about 3 ounces), trimmed and strings discarded

1. In a 12-inch nonstick skillet, bring 2 cups lightly salted water to a boil with 3 teaspoons lemon juice. Cook shrimp just until they turn pink,

about 2 minutes. Drain in strainer, cool to room temperature, and blot dry. Transfer to bowl.

2. In a small bowl, place remaining 2 teaspoons lemon juice, minced scallions, Dijon mustard, salt, sugar, and pepper. Add oil and whisk dressing to combine. Pour dressing over shrimp and toss lightly. Cover with plastic wrap and refrigerate for 2 hours (do not marinate any longer or shrimp will become soggy).

3. Blanch snow peas in 1 quart boiling water just until they start to puff up, about 1 minute. Transfer to strainer, refresh under cold water, and blot dry. Place on small plate lined with paper towel and refrigerate until needed.

4. When ready to serve, arrange 8 snow peas in an outer border on each salad plate. Toss shrimp in dressing once again and spoon into center of each plate; garnish with scallion greens and serve.

PER SERVING:	CAL. 183 (43% FROM FAT)	FAT 9 G	SOD. 155 MG
	PROT. 20 G	CARB. 6 G	CHOL. 141 MG

◆ POACHED RED SNAPPER WITH TOMATO DILL SAUCE

The assertive flavoring of this sauce enhances the poached snapper. It is equally delicious with fillet of sole sliced to a thickness of ½ inch so that poaching time will be the same. This recipe is an adaptation of one developed by my daughter Amy for a popular Manhattan restaurant.

SERVES 2

2 unskinned boneless red snapper fillets, each about ½ inch thick (12 ounces total weight)
2 teaspoons olive oil
½ teaspoon minced garlic
½ cup finely chopped canned tomatoes, well drained
⅛ teaspoon sugar

1 scant teaspoon minced fresh dill or ¼ teaspoon crumbled dried dillweed
⅛ teaspoon coarse salt
⅛ teaspoon freshly milled black pepper
2 medium-sized limes (6 ounces), ends trimmed and each sliced into 6 thin rounds

½ cup dry white wine, preferably
   sauvignon blanc
½ to ¾ cup water

1 tablespoon minced Italian
   parsley leaves (garnish)

1. Rinse fillets under cold water and blot dry with paper towel; set aside.

2. In a small saucepan, heat oil over medium heat. Add garlic and sauté, stirring constantly with wooden spoon, until very lightly golden, about 30 seconds. Add tomatoes and sugar. Turn heat to high and bring sauce to a boil, stirring constantly. As soon as sauce reaches a boil, turn heat down to low. Cook, partially covered, stirring frequently, until sauce is slightly thickened, about 5 to 7 minutes. Stir in dill; season with salt and pepper. Cover pan and remove from heat. (Sauce may be made up to 2 hours before poaching fish. Reheat, covered, over low heat just before serving.)

3. Line bottom of a 10-inch nonstick skillet with lime slices. Place fillets on top of lime slices, skin sides down. Add wine and enough water to pan to barely cover top of fillets. Cover pan and bring liquid to a low boil over medium-low heat. As soon as liquid comes to a low boil, turn heat to low. Poach fillets, covered, just until they are firm and opaque and barely begin to flake when tested with a toothpick, about 5 minutes.

4. Using a slotted spatula or two forks, transfer fillets to individual dinner plates with skin side down. Spoon heated sauce over fillets, garnish with minced parsley, and serve immediately.

PER SERVING:	CAL. 268 (25% FROM FAT)	FAT 7 G	SOD. 211 MG
	PROT. 36 G	CARB. 12 G	CHOL. 63 MG

◆ TUNA AND ORANGE SALAD

This salad is alive with the flavor of mint. It is an excellent one-dish meal for lunch, especially when served with homemade Corn Muffins (page 207).

SERVES 2

1 large navel orange (10 ounces)
1 6½-ounce can water-packed
   solid white albacore tuna
1 tablespoon snipped fresh chives
   or thinly sliced scallions (green
   part only)
1½ teaspoons minced fresh mint
   or ½ teaspoon crumbled dried
   mint

2 teaspoons minced Italian parsley
   leaves
⅛ teaspoon coarse salt
⅛ teaspoon freshly milled black
   pepper
1 tablespoon extra virgin olive oil
4 medium-sized lettuce leaves
   (garnish)

1. With sharp knife, cut a small slice from top and bottom of orange. With tip of knife, divide orange skin into 8 sections. Peel each section, removing most of the white membrane as you peel. With a vegetable peeler, remove all the white membrane from orange. Cut out each orange segment, removing its protective membrane as you cut. Cut each segment in half and place in a strainer set over a bowl for at least 15 minutes to drain off excess juice; reserve 1 tablespoon juice for dressing.

2. Place tuna in another strainer and thoroughly rinse under cold water. Drain well and break into bite-sized pieces.

3. Place orange segments, tuna, chives or scallions, mint, and parsley in a bowl. Lightly toss with two forks to combine.

4. Place reserved tablespoon of orange juice, salt, and pepper in a small bowl. Beat with a fork or small whisk to combine. Add oil a little at a time and whisk thoroughly to incorporate. Pour dressing over salad and toss lightly with two forks to combine.

5. Arrange lettuce on salad plates. Spoon salad on top and serve.

PER SERVING:	CAL. 226 (36% FROM FAT)	FAT 10 G	SOD. 340 MG
	PROT. 24 G	CARB. 12 G	CHOL. 36 MG

◆ OVEN-FRIED FILLET OF SOLE

Baking in the upper portion of the oven will help keep the sole moist without losing its crunchy coating.

SERVES 2

2 skinless fillets of lemon or gray sole (12 ounces total weight)
¼ cup low-fat or skim milk
½ cup dry bread crumbs
1 teaspoon grated lemon rind
½ teaspoon minced garlic
1 tablespoon minced Italian parsley leaves

1½ teaspoons minced fresh oregano or ½ teaspoon crumbled dried oregano
¼ teaspoon freshly milled black pepper
2 teaspoons olive oil
2 lemon wedges (garnish)

1. Adjust rack to top shelf of oven and preheat to 450 degrees. Lightly grease bottom of a shallow 9-by-13-by-2-inch baking pan; set aside.

2. Wash fillets in cold water and thoroughly blot dry with paper towel.

3. Place milk in a shallow bowl. On a flat plate, combine bread crumbs, lemon rind, garlic, parsley, oregano, and pepper. Dip fillets in milk and then dredge in bread crumb mixture. Place fillets in prepared pan and drizzle 1 teaspoon oil over each fillet.

4. Bake in preheated oven until surface of fish is lightly golden and barely flakes when tested with a fork, about 5 to 7 minutes, depending on thickness of fish. The fish does not have to be turned.

5. Using a wide metal spatula, transfer fillets to platter, garnish with lemon wedges, and serve immediately.

PER SERVING:	CAL. 318 (24% FROM FAT)	FAT 8 G	SOD. 387 MG
	PROT. 37 G	CARB. 22 G	CHOL. 83 MG

◆ SAUTÉED SWORDFISH WITH KALAMATA OLIVES AND CAPER VINAIGRETTE

In this dish the olives and caper vinaigrette complements the succulent sautéed swordfish.

SERVES 2

2 swordfish steaks, each 1 inch thick (about 14 ounces total weight)

4 teaspoons extra virgin olive oil

6 Kalamata olives, pitted and finely chopped

1 tablespoon capers, thoroughly rinsed and drained, and finely chopped

2 tablespoons minced shallots

1 tablespoon minced Italian parsley leaves

½ tablespoon white balsamic vinegar

⅛ teaspoon coarse salt

⅛ teaspoon freshly milled black pepper

1. Rinse steaks under cold water and blot dry with paper towel.

2. In a 10-inch nonstick skillet, heat 2 teaspoons olive oil over moderately high heat until hot but not smoking. Sauté swordfish steaks on each side until they barely flake when tested with the tip of a knife, about 4 to 5 minutes on each side.

3. While the fish is cooking, stir together olives, capers, shallots, parsley, vinegar, remaining 2 teaspoons olive oil, salt, and pepper in a small bowl.

4. Transfer swordfish to two plates, spoon the sauce over, and serve.

PER SERVING:	CAL. 261 (28% FROM FAT)	FAT 8 G	SOD. 242 MG
	PROT. 36 G	CARB. 10 G	CHOL. 69 MG

◆ BROILED SWORDFISH STEAKS

Purchase steaks that are at least ¾ inch thick so that they will remain juicy while cooking. Leaving the outer skin on the steak will protect the flesh from breaking while broiling.

SERVES 2

2 swordfish steaks, each about
 ¾ inch thick (12 ounces total
 weight)
1 teaspoon finely grated orange
 rind
¼ cup fresh orange juice, strained
2 teaspoons reduced-sodium soy
 sauce

½ teaspoon freshly grated
 gingerroot or ¼ teaspoon
 ground ginger
3 drops Tabasco sauce
½ medium-sized navel orange,
 sliced into 4 wedges (garnish)

1. Rinse steaks under cold water and blot dry with paper towel. Place steaks in a single layer in a shallow dish.

2. Place orange rind, juice, soy sauce, ginger, and Tabasco sauce in a small bowl; beat with fork or small whisk to combine marinade. Spoon marinade over fish and turn the steaks once to coat thoroughly. Marinate at room temperature for 30 minutes or cover with plastic wrap and refrigerate up to 2 hours, turning steaks once in marinade.

3. Remove broiler rack and pan from oven and preheat broiler for 15 minutes. Lightly grease broiler rack.

4. Remove steaks from marinade and place 2 inches apart on prepared broiler rack; reserve marinade for basting.

5. Position broiler pan 5 inches from heat source. Broil steaks, basting once with marinade, until surface of steaks is lightly golden, about 4 minutes. Turn steaks with a wide metal spatula and continue broiling, basting once with marinade, until second side is lightly golden, about 4 to 5 minutes. When done, steaks should feel firm to the touch and barely flake when tested with the tip of a knife. Transfer to platter, garnish with orange wedges, and serve.

PER SERVING:	CAL. 219 (26% FROM FAT)	FAT 6 G	SOD. 338 MG
	PROT. 31 G	CARB. 8 G	CHOL. 50 MG

◆ BAKED TROUT WITH SHALLOTS, ORANGE, AND WATERCRESS

The sautéed shallots and orange juice not only keep these tender fillets moist while baking but add to the lovely final presentation.

SERVES 2

2 teaspoons extra virgin olive oil
2 tablespoons minced shallots
3 tablespoons fresh orange juice, strained
2 unskinned fillets of brook or rainbow trout (about 12 ounces total weight)
⅛ teaspoon coarse salt
¼ teaspoon freshly milled black pepper

2 tablespoons minced watercress leaves, tough stems discarded
2 teaspoons grated orange rind
Several watercress leaves, tough stems discarded (garnish)
1 medium navel orange (7 ounces), halved and cut into ½-inch slices (garnish)

1. Adjust rack to upper third of oven and preheat to 375 degrees. Lightly grease a shallow baking pan; set aside.

2. In a small saucepan, heat olive oil over low heat. Add shallots and cook, covered, until they are soft but not brown, about 2 minutes. Remove from heat and stir in 2 tablespoons orange juice. (If shallots start to stick to bottom of pan while cooking, stir in a little of the 2 tablespoons orange juice to loosen.)

3. Wash fillets in cold water and thoroughly blot dry with paper towel. Place fillets in prepared pan, skin side down. Sprinkle surface of fillets with salt and pepper. Spoon shallot mixture over fillets.

4. Bake fillets in preheated oven until fish barely flakes when tested with the tip of a knife, about 8 to 10 minutes. Remove from oven.

5. In a small bowl, combine minced watercress and orange rind.

6. Transfer fillets to platter and spoon remaining 1 tablespoon of orange juice over them. Sprinkle watercress-orange rind mixture over fillets. Garnish platter with an outer border of watercress leaves and orange slices; serve immediately.

PER SERVING:	CAL. 341 (42% FROM FAT)	FAT 16 G	SOD. 92 MG
	PROT. 37 G	CARB. 12 G	CHOL. 99 MG

VEGETABLES

The colorful bounty of local farms during early summer through late fall always presents a challenge to me when I shop for vegetables during their natural seasons. Today, many supermarkets offer a dazzling variety of fresh produce, as do specialty markets. The wide range of vegetables available to us throughout the year provides unending and exciting combinations of color, texture, and taste.

Fresh vegetables are used exclusively in this chapter, with the exception of the tiny green peas available in the frozen food section of most supermarkets.

Vegetables should never be overcooked. The recipes in this chapter do not, of course, cover every possible method of cooking a vegetable, nor do they mention every vegetable you might encounter, but they will provide helpful hints on how to select many vegetables for purchase, and explain how to prepare them in unusual and imaginative ways.

◆ BAKED ACORN SQUASH RINGS

Select a hard acorn squash that has no cracks or blemishes for this late-fall and winter favorite.

SERVES 2

1 large acorn squash (about
   1 pound)
1½ tablespoons dark rum,
   preferably Myers's
2 teaspoons unsalted butter,
   melted

1 tablespoon firmly packed light
   brown sugar
⅛ teaspoon freshly grated
   nutmeg

1. Wash and dry squash. Cut off 1 inch from top and bottom of squash; discard ends. Slice squash into 4 even rounds, each about ½ inch thick. Using a small knife, cut out fiber and seeds from center of rings and discard.

2. Adjust rack to center of oven and preheat to 375 degrees. Lightly grease bottom of a 9-by-13-by-2-inch ovenproof baking dish.

3. Place squash rings in a single layer in prepared pan. With a fork, prick top of each round at ¼-inch intervals. Brush rum over squash and let stand at room temperature for 15 minutes to absorb liquor.

4. Brush each round evenly with melted butter.

5. In a small bowl, combine brown sugar and nutmeg. Carefully sprinkle mixture on top of each round.

6. Bake in preheated oven until tender when tested with fork, about 25 to 30 minutes. Arrange in a slightly overlapping pattern on platter and serve immediately.

PER SERVING:	CAL. 148 (35% FROM FAT)	FAT 6 G	SOD. 8 MG
	PROT. 1 G	CARB. 25 G	CHOL. 10 MG

◆ ASPARAGUS AND TOMATOES

Peeling the asparagus stalks will ensure even cooking.

SERVES 2

1 pound asparagus (about 12 large spears)

2 well-ripened plum tomatoes (4 ounces)

2 teaspoons extra virgin olive oil

2 large scallions, trimmed, sliced lengthwise, washed and then cut crosswise into 1-inch pieces to make ½ cup

1½ teaspoons minced fresh basil or ½ teaspoon crumbled dried basil

⅛ teaspoon coarse salt

⅛ teaspoon freshly milled black pepper

1. Wash asparagus several times in cold water to get rid of sand. Using a sharp knife, cut off woody ends at base of spears. With a vegetable peeler, peel up from base of spears, leaving tips intact. Cut off asparagus tips, leaving about 2 inches of spear, and reserve. Cut asparagus stalks in half lengthwise and then slice crosswise into 2-inch lengths.

2. Plump fresh tomatoes in 1 quart boiling water for 1 minute. Rinse under cold water. When cool enough to handle, core tomatoes and peel skins with a small paring knife. Cut tomatoes in half crosswise. Gently squeeze each half and discard most of the seeds. Place on plate and slice into ½-inch strips.

3. In a 10-inch nonstick skillet, heat oil over medium heat. Add scallions and cook, partially covered, until lightly golden, about 2 minutes. Stir in tomatoes and any accumulated juices from plate. Cook, covered, until barely tender when tested with fork, about 1 minute. Stir in asparagus stalks and cook, covered, stirring once or twice, until barely tender when tested with the tip of a knife, about 3 minutes. Stir in asparagus tips and basil. Continue cooking, covered, stirring once or twice, until tips are tender, about 3 minutes. (If tomato-scallion mixture starts to stick to bottom of pan, stir in 2 teaspoons of water to loosen.) Season with salt and pepper; remove from heat. Transfer to platter and serve immediately.

PER SERVING:	CAL. 100 (40% FROM FAT)	FAT 5 G	SOD. 12 MG
	PROT. 6 G	CARB. 11 G	CHOL. 0 MG

◆ ARTICHOKES WITH GREEN DIPPING SAUCE

Artichokes are now available year-round but are more plentiful February through May. Select large artichokes with tightly packed leaves. Artichokes with open, spreading leaves are tough. During late fall and the early winter months, do not be discouraged from buying artichokes that have bronze-tipped outer petals. This is a result of frost, and growers refer to such artichokes as being "winter-kissed." They may look unattractive, but will have a more intense flavor and I think are the best-tasting artichokes of all. In spring, the leaves should be bright green. Discoloration is a sign of age or damage. Cook artichokes only in an enameled, glass, or stainless-steel-lined pan. They will discolor if cooked in aluminum or cast-iron saucepans.

SERVES 2

2 large artichokes (about 1¼ pounds)	1 tablespoon minced green bell pepper
½ lemon	1 tablespoon minced fresh chives
2 tablespoons lemon juice	1 tablespoon minced Italian parsley leaves
1½ tablespoons low-fat mayonnaise	⅛ teaspoon coarse salt
3 tablespoons low-fat yogurt	⅛ teaspoon freshly milled white pepper
½ teaspoon Dijon mustard	

1. Wash artichokes in cold water. Cut off the stem flush with the base so that the artichokes will stand upright when placed in saucepan. Hold one artichoke in the palm of your hand and snap off any small or discolored leaves at the base. Place the artichoke on a cutting board and cut off about 1 inch from top. Rub the cut edge with cut lemon to prevent discoloration. With a pair of kitchen shears, snip off about ½ inch from tip of each leaf. Rub the cut edges with lemon. Repeat with other artichoke.

2. Place artichokes upright in a 3½-quart saucepan (or one large enough that the two artichokes will fit in snugly when placed in pan). Pour in enough water to reach 3 inches up the sides of the pan. Add lemon juice to water. Cover pan and bring to a boil over high heat. As soon as water reaches a boil, turn heat down to medium and cook artichokes, covered, until a petal near center pulls out easily, about 30 to 45 minutes. Remove from pan, drain artichokes upside down on a platter lined with paper towel, and let cool to room temperature.

3. While artichokes are cooking, make dipping sauce: In a small bowl,

combine remaining ingredients and whisk with a fork to mix well. Transfer sauce to a small bowl for dipping.

4. Place artichokes on individual plates and pull off outer petals one at a time. Dip base of petal into sauce; pull through teeth to remove soft, pulpy portion of petal; discard remaining petal. Continue until all petals have been removed. Spoon out fuzzy center (the choke) at base and discard. The bottom, or heart, of the artichoke is entirely edible, and it happens to be the best part. Cut into small pieces and dip into sauce.

PER SERVING:	CAL. 89 (11% FROM FAT)	FAT 1 G	SOD. 257 MG
	PROT. 5 G	CARB. 17 G	CHOL. 1 MG

◆ BROCCOLI WITH GARLIC AND LEMON

A good vegetable any time of year. When selecting broccoli, make sure the buds are tightly closed. The tips may be tinged with purple but not yellow, which is a sign of age.

SERVES 2

1 small bunch broccoli
(10 ounces)
2 teaspoons olive oil
½ teaspoon minced garlic
1 tablespoon fresh lemon juice, strained

⅛ teaspoon coarse salt
⅛ teaspoon freshly milled black pepper
2 teaspoons grated lemon rind (garnish)

1. Remove florets from broccoli, leaving about ½ inch of stems. Cut or break florets into 1-inch pieces. Wash in cold water, drain, and set aside. Remove and discard the large, coarse leaves from stems and cut off about ½ inch of tough lower part of stalk. Wash thoroughly and peel stalks with a vegetable peeler. Cut stalks in half lengthwise. (If stalks are more than 1 inch in diameter, cut into quarters.) Cut halved or quartered stalks into 1-inch pieces.

2. Bring 2 quarts of water to a boil. Add broccoli and cook until almost tender when tested with a fork, about 3 minutes. Drain thoroughly in a colander. Transfer broccoli to platter.

3. While broccoli is cooking, heat oil in a small saucepan over low heat. Add garlic and sauté until lightly golden, about 1 minute. Remove

from heat and stir in lemon juice. Spoon garlic mixture over broccoli. Season with salt and pepper. Garnish with lemon rind and serve immediately.

PER SERVING:	CAL. 69 (56% FROM FAT)	FAT 5 G	SOD. 24 MG
	PROT. 3 G	CARB. 6 G	CHOL. 0 MG

◆ PARSLEYED BABY CARROTS

Sweet-tasting baby carrots always make a beautiful presentation. I frequently use them as a garnish for broiled chicken, lamb, or fish.

SERVES 2

12 baby carrots (8 ounces)
2 teaspoons unsalted butter
2 teaspoons minced Italian parsley
    leaves

⅛ teaspoon coarse salt
⅛ teaspoon freshly milled white
    pepper

1. Cook carrots in 1 quart lightly salted boiling water until barely tender when tested with fork, about 3 minutes. Transfer to colander and rinse under cold water. Blot dry with paper towel. (Carrots may be prepared up to this point 4 hours in advance, placed in bowl, and covered with plastic wrap.)

2. In a 10-inch nonstick skillet, melt butter over medium-high heat. Add carrots and cook, stirring once or twice with wooden spoon, until heated, about 1½ minutes. Stir in parsley and season with salt and pepper. Transfer to small bowl and serve immediately.

PER SERVING:	CAL. 84 (48% FROM FAT)	FAT 5 G	SOD. 36 MG
	PROT. 1 G	CARB. 10 G	CHOL. 0 MG

◆ MARINATED EGGPLANT

Select a glossy, firm, unblemished eggplant for this tangy marinated vegetable. For best flavor, serve at room temperature. It can also be served as an appetizer on unsalted crackers. Eggplant can be made up to three days before serving and stored, covered, in refrigerator until needed.

SERVES 2

1 small eggplant (12 ounces)
1 tablespoon olive oil
1 large clove garlic, peeled and
　split in half
1½ tablespoons imported white
　wine vinegar or white balsamic
　vinegar

1½ teaspoons minced fresh basil
　or ½ teaspoon crumbled dried
　basil
⅛ teaspoon coarse salt
⅛ teaspoon freshly milled black
　pepper

1. Remove broiler pan and preheat oven at broil setting. Line broiler pan with a single sheet of aluminum foil.

2. Wash eggplant and blot dry with paper towel. Trim both ends of eggplant but do not peel. Slice eggplant crosswise into 1-inch rounds. Cut each round in half and then into ½-inch wedges, like a pie.

3. Lightly brush both sides of each wedge with olive oil. Arrange wedges in single layer in broiler pan.

4. Position broiler pan 3 inches from heat source. Broil until lightly golden on both sides, about 3 minutes on each side. (Watch carefully so wedges do not burn.)

5. Rub a small serving bowl with split garlic clove and leave garlic in bowl. Add eggplant and any accumulated pan juices to bowl. Add vinegar and basil. Season with salt and pepper; toss lightly. Cover with plastic wrap and let cool to room temperature. Remove garlic and toss once again just before serving.

PER SERVING:	CAL. 109 (53% FROM FAT)	FAT 7 G	SOD. 7 MG
	PROT. 2 G	CARB. 12 G	CHOL. 0 MG

◆ ESCAROLE AND SUN-DRIED TOMATOES

A very hearty dish in early fall through the winter months, when escarole is abundant at the market. You can substitute curly endive for the escarole.

SERVES 2

1 medium head escarole (about
   12 ounces)
¼ cup sun-dried tomatoes, not
   packed in oil
2 teaspoons minced garlic

1 tablespoon extra virgin olive oil
⅛ teaspoon coarse salt
⅛ teaspoon freshly milled black
   pepper

1. Discard any wilted or bruised leaves from escarole. Separate leaves and trim off about 2 inches of tough bottom ends of greens. Slice greens into 3-inch lengths and wash several times in tepid water to get rid of grit. Place escarole in a 3-quart pot. Do not add water; the final rinse water clinging to leaves will be sufficient to steam them. Cook, covered, over high heat, pushing leaves down with wooden spoon once or twice, until stems are tender, about 5 minutes. Thoroughly drain in colander.

2. While escarole is cooking, place sun-dried tomatoes in a bowl and pour boiling water over to cover. Let stand 2 minutes to soften; drain thoroughly. When cool enough to handle, finely chop tomatoes and set aside.

3. In a 10-inch nonstick skillet, place garlic and oil. Sauté over medium heat just until garlic is very lightly golden. Add escarole and cook, partially covered, stirring frequently, until extremely soft, about 4 minutes. Stir in sun-dried tomatoes and cook for an additional minute. Season with salt and pepper and serve.

PER SERVING:	CAL. 120 (37% FROM FAT)	FAT 7 G	SOD. 240 MG
	PROT. 6 G	CARB. 16 G	CHOL. 0 MG

◆ GREEN BEANS WITH CARROTS AND TARRAGON

Make this beautiful combination when you can find crisp, tender, young beans about ¼ inch wide and no more than 5 inches in length.

SERVES 2

2 medium-sized carrots (5 ounces)
4 ounces green beans
2 teaspoons extra virgin olive oil
1 tablespoon minced shallots
1½ teaspoons minced fresh

tarragon or ½ teaspoon
crumbled dried tarragon
⅛ teaspoon coarse salt
⅛ teaspoon freshly milled black
pepper

1. Wash carrots, trim, and peel lightly with a vegetable peeler. Cook in 1 quart boiling water until barely tender when tested with a fork, about 4 minutes. Transfer to strainer and rinse under cold water. Blot dry with paper towel and cut into ¼-inch by 4-inch sticks (the same size as green beans).

2. Wash green beans, trim both ends, and cook in 1 quart boiling water until barely tender when tested with a fork, about 4 to 5 minutes. Drain in a strainer, rinse under cold water, and blot dry with paper towel. (Vegetables may be prepared up to this point 3 hours in advance, combined in a bowl, and covered with plastic wrap.)

3. In a 10-inch nonstick skillet, heat oil over medium heat. Add shallots and cook, partially covered, stirring frequently with wooden spoon, until lightly golden, about 2 minutes. Add carrots and green beans and continue cooking, stirring constantly, until vegetables are heated through, about 1 minute. Stir in tarragon and cook for an additional 20 seconds. Season with salt and pepper; remove from heat. Transfer to platter and serve immediately.

PER SERVING:	CAL. 82 (48% FROM FAT)	FAT 5 G	SOD. 22 MG
	PROT. 2 G	CARB. 10 G	CHOL. 0 MG

◆ MINTED GREEN BEANS

Green beans harmonize beautifully with chives or scallions, mint, and extra virgin olive oil. This dish is at its best when served at room temperature.

SERVES 2

6 ounces green beans
1 tablespoon extra virgin olive oil
1 tablespoon snipped fresh chives
   or thinly sliced scallions (green
   part only)
1½ teaspoons minced fresh mint

or ½ teaspoon crumbled dried
   mint
⅛ teaspoon sugar
⅛ teaspoon coarse salt
⅛ teaspoon freshly milled black
   pepper

1. Wash green beans and trim both ends. (If beans are more than 5 inches in length, slice in half diagonally.) Cook green beans in 3 quarts boiling water until tender when tested with a fork, about 5 minutes. Drain in colander, rinse under cold water, and blot dry with paper towel.

2. Transfer to serving bowl, drizzle olive oil over top, and toss lightly. Add chives or scallions, mint, and sugar. Season with salt and pepper; lightly toss again. Cover with plastic wrap and set aside to cool to room temperature. Toss lightly once again just before serving.

PER SERVING:	CAL. 86 (68% FROM FAT)	FAT 7 G	SOD. 5 MG
	PROT. 1 G	CARB. 6 G	CHOL. 0 MG

◆ TWO-MINUTE MUSHROOMS

Select small, white button mushrooms no larger than 1 inch in diameter, with tight-fitting stems, for this very fast sauté.

SERVES 2

8 ounces small, white button
   mushrooms
2 teaspoons olive oil
½ teaspoon minced garlic
⅛ teaspoon coarse salt

⅛ teaspoon freshly milled black
   pepper
2 teaspoons minced Italian parsley
   leaves

1. Wipe mushrooms with a damp cloth. Cut off stems and save for another purpose or discard.

2. In a 10-inch nonstick skillet, heat oil over low heat. Add garlic and sauté, stirring constantly with wooden spoon, until very lightly golden, about 1 minute.

3. Add mushroom caps and turn heat to high; quickly toss with wooden spoon until caps are well coated with oil and garlic. Cook, stirring constantly, just until mushrooms begin to exude their juices, about 1 to 2 minutes. Season with salt and pepper. Stir in parsley and remove from heat. Transfer to platter and serve immediately.

PER SERVING:	CAL. 70 (58% FROM FAT)	FAT 5 G	SOD. 5 MG
	PROT. 2 G	CARB. 6 G	CHOL. 0 MG

◆ STUFFED PORTABELLA MUSHROOMS

These mushrooms make a great side dish or can also be an excellent appetizer. Recipe can easily be doubled if entertaining.

SERVES 2

⅓ cup fresh bread crumbs
1 teaspoon minced garlic
1 tablespoon minced Italian
  parsley leaves
2 teaspoons grated lemon rind
1 tablespoon fresh lemon juice,
  strained

2 large portabella mushrooms,
  each about 4 inches in
  diameter
1 tablespoon extra virgin olive oil
⅛ teaspoon coarse salt
⅛ teaspoon freshly milled black
  pepper

1. Adjust oven rack 4 inches from heat source and preheat on broil setting.

2. In a small bowl, combine bread crumbs, garlic, parsley, lemon rind, and lemon juice.

3. Slice stems off at base of mushrooms and discard. Wipe mushrooms with a damp cloth to remove any grit.

4. Put mushrooms, gill side down, on a baking sheet and brush tops with ½ tablespoon oil. Broil mushrooms until golden, about 3 minutes. Turn mushrooms over and season with salt and pepper. Broil mushrooms for an additional 3 minutes. Mound bread crumb mixture onto

mushroom centers and drizzle with remaining ½ tablespoon oil. Broil stuffed mushrooms until stuffing is golden, about 1 to 2 minutes. (Watch carefully so that stuffing does not burn.) Transfer to plate and serve.

PER SERVING:	CAL. 109 (43% FROM FAT)	FAT 6 G	SOD. 82 MG
	PROT. 5 G	CARB. 12 G	CHOL. 0 MG

◆ GRILLED POTATOES

These potatoes go very well with any of the grilled recipes in this book. After parboiling, they can be grilled at the same time you are barbecuing your meat or fish.

SERVES 2

2 large russet or Yukon
   gold potatoes (about
   1 pound)
2 teaspoons olive oil

⅛ teaspoon coarse salt
⅛ teaspoon freshly milled black
   pepper

1. Scrub potatoes under cold running water with a stiff brush. Place in a 5-quart pot with enough water to cover by 2 inches. Cover pot and bring to a boil. Parboil potatoes, covered, until a fork can penetrate part-way but meets firm resistance toward the center, about 6 minutes. Drain in colander. When potatoes are cool enough to handle, peel. Trim about ½ inch from each end of potato and discard. Slice each potato lengthwise into 3 even pieces. Place potatoes in a single layer on a plate. Lightly brush both surfaces of sliced potatoes with a little oil. (Brushing surfaces with a little oil will prevent them from sticking when placed on heated grill.)

2. Place potato slices on preheated grill about 4 inches from heat source. Cook until lightly golden on underside, about 3 minutes. Using a long spatula, turn potatoes and continue grilling until second side is lightly golden, about 3 minutes. Transfer to platter and season with salt and pepper; serve immediately.

PER SERVING:	CAL. 220 (19% FROM FAT)	FAT 5 G	SOD. 8 MG
	PROT. 4 G	CARB. 42 G	CHOL. 0 MG

◆ HERBED POTATO SALAD

A wonderful salad to make during the summer months or whenever fresh herbs are available. For best flavor, serve warm or at room temperature.

SERVES 2

4 small red-skinned potatoes
  (12 ounces)
1 tablespoon minced red onion
1 tablespoon imported white wine
  vinegar
⅛ teaspoon coarse salt

⅛ teaspoon freshly milled white
  pepper
1 tablespoon extra virgin olive oil
1 tablespoon minced Italian
  parsley leaves

1. Scrub potatoes under cold running water with a vegetable brush. Trim off and discard ends and cut potatoes into 1-inch cubes. In a steamer with 1 inch of water in bottom, cook potatoes, covered, until tender, about 5 to 7 minutes. (Cooking them in a steamer will keep the skins intact better than boiling in water.)

2. While potatoes are cooking, make dressing: In the same bowl in which you are serving salad, place onion, vinegar, salt, pepper, and olive oil. Whisk until dressing is well blended.

3. As soon as potatoes are cooked, transfer to bowl with dressing. This must be done while the potatoes are still hot so that they will absorb the full flavor of the dressing. (Salad can be prepared up to 2 hours before serving. Cover with plastic wrap and let stand at room temperature.) Gently toss again with parsley just before serving.

PER SERVING:	CAL. 187 (35% FROM FAT)	FAT 7 G	SOD. 13 MG
	PROT. 3 G	CARB. 28 G	CHOL. 0 MG

◆ SAUTÉED ROMAINE

If the head of romaine is heavier than 1 pound, cook just the outer leaves and save the tender inner leaves for salad.

SERVES 2

1½ teaspoons minced garlic
4 teaspoons extra virgin olive oil
1 medium-sized head romaine
   lettuce (about 1 pound),
   bottom trimmed, and leaves

washed, spun dry, and sliced
   crosswise into 2-inch lengths
⅛ teaspoon coarse salt
⅛ teaspoon freshly milled black
   pepper

1. In a 3-quart nonstick saucepan, cook the garlic and oil over low heat just until softened, about 30 seconds. Add the romaine and stir well to coat with the oil. Cook romaine, covered, over medium heat, stirring frequently, until wilted and tender, about 10 to 12 minutes. Season with salt and pepper, transfer to small bowl, and serve.

PER SERVING: CAL. 136 (35% FROM FAT)	FAT 5 G	SOD. 275 MG
PROT. 8 G	CARB. 13 G	CHOL. 0 MG

◆ SAVOY CABBAGE AND POTATOES

A great winter combination, especially satisfying when served with Oven-fried Pork Chops [page 98].

1 small head Savoy cabbage
   (about 12 ounces)
1 tablespoon extra virgin olive oil
½ cup thinly sliced yellow onion
2 medium-sized red-skinned
   potatoes (8 ounces), cut into
   1-inch cubes

⅛ teaspoon coarse salt
⅛ teaspoon freshly milled black
   pepper
½ teaspoon sugar
½ teaspoon caraway seeds

1. Discard any bruised outer leaves from cabbage. Wash cabbage and blot dry with paper towel. Quarter, remove center core, and cut cabbage crosswise into ½-inch slices.

2. Drizzle oil in bottom of 3½-quart nonstick saucepan. Place onion, cabbage, and potatoes in pan. Add salt, pepper, sugar, and caraway seeds and stir to combine. Cover pan and cook vegetables over medium-low heat until potatoes are tender when tested with a fork, about 20 to 25 minutes. (This vegetable combination can be cooked up to 2 hours before serving and reheated over low heat.)

3. Transfer to platter and serve immediately.

PER SERVING:	CAL. 151 (26% FROM FAT)	FAT 5 G	SOD. 44 MG
	PROT. 5 G	CARB. 26 G	CHOL. 0 MG

◆ YELLOW SQUASH WITH RED PEPPER

Look for small, firm yellow squash that are no more than 5 inches in length for this versatile combination.

SERVES 2

2 small yellow squash (about 6 ounces)
1 teaspoon olive oil
1 teaspoon unsalted butter
¼ cup thinly sliced red onion
1 medium-sized red bell pepper (5 ounces), halved, cored, seeded, and sliced into ½-inch strips
1½ teaspoons minced fresh basil or ½ teaspoon crumbled dried basil
⅛ teaspoon coarse salt
⅛ teaspoon freshly milled black pepper

1. Scrub squash under cold running water until the skins feel smooth. Blot dry with paper towel and trim off both ends. Starting from bottom end, slice at a 20-degree angle into ½-inch diagonal slices; set aside.

2. In a 10-inch nonstick skillet, heat oil and butter over low heat. Add onion and cook, partially covered, stirring frequently, until soft but not brown, about 3 minutes. Add pepper, cover pan, and cook, stirring once or twice with wooden spoon, until crisp tender, about 3 minutes. Stir in squash and continue cooking, covered, until squash is barely tender when tested with fork, about 3 minutes. Increase heat to high and continue cooking, uncovered, stirring constantly, until squash is tender

when tested with fork, about 2 minutes. Stir in basil. Season with salt and pepper; remove from heat. Transfer to platter and serve immediately.

PER SERVING:	CAL. 77 (49% FROM FAT)	FAT 5 G	SOD. 4 MG
	PROT. 2 G	CARB. 9 G	CHOL. 5 MG

◆ BAKED TOMATOES PROVENÇALE

This is my adaptation of a side dish I was once served at a little French restaurant in New York City.

SERVES 2

2 large firm, ripe tomatoes (about 1 pound)
1½ tablespoons low-fat mayonnaise
1½ tablespoons freshly grated Parmesan cheese

⅛ teaspoon freshly milled black pepper
2 tablespoons dry bread crumbs
2 teaspoons minced Italian parsley leaves

1. Adjust rack to upper third of oven and preheat to 375 degrees. Lightly grease a small baking sheet; set aside.

2. Wash tomatoes and blot dry with paper towel. Core tomatoes; slice off about ½ inch from top and bottom of each tomato and discard. Slice each tomato into 3 even rounds.

3. In a small bowl, combine mayonnaise, Parmesan cheese, and pepper. Using a small metal spatula, spread cheese mixture over each tomato slice.

4. In another small bowl, combine bread crumbs and parsley. Sprinkle bread crumb mixture over tomatoes.

5. Arrange tomatoes in a single layer on prepared baking sheet. Bake in preheated oven until cheese mixture puffs a little and bread crumb mixture is lightly golden, about 20 minutes. Arrange in a single layer on platter and serve immediately.

PER SERVING:	CAL. 129 (35% FROM FAT)	FAT 5 G	SOD. 267 MG
	PROT. 5 G	CARB. 18 G	CHOL. 4 MG

◆ VEGETABLE KEBABS

Take full advantage of your grill and make these vegetable kebabs while barbecuing any of the meat or fish dishes in this book.

SERVES 2

FOR THE VEGETABLES

2 medium-sized yellow
   squash (about 8 ounces),
   trimmed
1 large, firm red bell pepper
(8 ounces), halved, cored,
   and seeded
6 medium-sized mushrooms
   (3 ounces)

FOR THE MARINADE

2 teaspoons fresh lemon juice
1 tablespoon minced fresh
   oregano or 1 teaspoon
   crumbled dried oregano
⅛ teaspoon coarse salt
¼ teaspoon freshly milled black
   pepper
1 tablespoon olive oil

1. Bring 2 quarts of water to a rolling boil. Add squash and cook, partially covered, until barely tender when tested with the tip of a knife, about 3 minutes. Transfer with a skimmer to a colander, refresh under cold running water, and blot dry with paper towel. When cool enough to handle, slice into 1-inch rounds and transfer to a shallow bowl.

2. Bring water in which squash was cooked back to a boil and blanch pepper for 2 minutes. Transfer to colander and refresh under cold running water; blot dry with paper towel. Slice peppers into 1-by-1½-inch pieces and add to bowl with squash.

3. Wipe mushrooms with a damp cloth. Cut off stems and save for another purpose or discard. Place mushrooms in bowl with other vegetables.

4. In a small bowl, combine all the marinade ingredients except olive oil. Add oil a little at a time and whisk with fork or small whisk to combine. Drizzle marinade over vegetables and toss lightly with two forks to combine. Let vegetables marinate at room temperature for 1 hour, turning in marinade once.

5. Beginning and ending each kebab with a piece of red pepper, thread the vegetables alternately onto two 12-inch metal skewers. Push the pieces close together as you thread. Discard any remaining marinade.

6. Place kebabs on preheated grill 4 inches from heat source. Grill the kebabs, turning frequently with long-handled tongs, until peppers are

tender and kebabs are evenly browned on all sides, about 7 minutes. Remove from grill.

7. Grasp the handle of each skewer with a towel and, using a 2-pronged fork, push the vegetable pieces off the skewer onto individual plates and serve.

PER SERVING:	CAL. 121 (50% FROM FAT)	FAT 7 G	SOD. 6 MG
	PROT. 3 G	CARB. 14 G	CHOL. 0 MG

◆ CANDIED YAMS WITH PECANS

Using dark corn syrup for the glaze provides a rich color as well as distinctive flavoring to the candied yams. This dish is an excellent accompaniment to Pork Loin with Herbed Vegetable Sauce (page 104).

SERVES 2

2 medium-sized yams (about 12 ounces)
¼ cup dark corn syrup, preferably Karo
2 teaspoons unsalted butter
¼ teaspoon ground cinnamon
⅛ teaspoon freshly ground nutmeg
1½ tablespoons finely chopped pecans

1. Lightly grease bottom and sides of an 8-by-8-by-2-inch baking dish; set aside.

2. Scrub yams well under cold running water with a vegetable brush. Place in a 5-quart pot with enough water to cover by 2 inches. Cover pot, bring to a boil, and cook until yams are tender when pierced with the tip of a knife, about 25 to 30 minutes. Transfer to a colander and let stand until cool enough to handle. Peel skins with a small paring knife. Slice each yam in half lengthwise and place halves in a single layer, cut sides up, in prepared baking dish.

3. Adjust oven rack to center of oven and preheat to 350 degrees.

4. In a small saucepan, combine syrup with butter. Bring to a boil over medium heat, stirring once or twice with wooden spoon. Reduce heat to low and simmer, stirring constantly, until thick and syrupy, about 2 minutes. Remove from heat and stir in cinnamon and nutmeg.

5. Spoon syrup over yams and bake in preheated oven, basting every

10 minutes, until potatoes are well glazed, about 30 minutes; remove from oven.

6. Turn oven to broil setting. Sprinkle pecans over top of potatoes. Place 6 inches from heat source and broil until nuts are lightly golden, about 2 to 3 minutes. (Watch carefully so that nuts do not burn.) Serve immediately.

PER SERVING:	CAL. 376 (22% FROM FAT)	FAT 10 G	SOD. 77 MG
	PROT. 3 G	CARB. 73 G	CHOL. 10 MG

◆ SHREDDED ZUCCHINI WITH GARLIC

Select firm, medium-sized zucchini with a good deep color and unblemished skin for this dish. Be sure to squeeze out excess moisture from the zucchini shreds so that they will still be crunchy and crispy when served.

SERVES 2

2 medium-sized zucchini
  (12 ounces)
1 tablespoon extra virgin olive oil
1 teaspoon minced garlic

⅛ teaspoon coarse salt
⅛ teaspoon freshly milled black
  pepper

1. Scrub zucchini under cold running water until the skins feel clean and smooth. Trim both ends. Cut into 1-inch lengths, place horizontally in food processor fitted with shredding disk, and use light pressure on pusher to grate. (If you do not have a food processor, leave zucchini whole and shred with the coarse side of a grater.) Place shredded zucchini in the center of a large piece of cheesecloth or a clean dish towel. Thoroughly squeeze out as much moisture as possible.

2. In a 10-inch nonstick skillet, heat oil over medium-high heat. Add garlic and zucchini. Sauté, turning zucchini with a wide metal spatula constantly, until it is barely tender but still crisp, about 2 minutes. Season with salt and pepper; remove from heat. Transfer to a platter and serve immediately.

PER SERVING:	CAL. 77 (76% FROM FAT)	FAT 7 G	SOD. 4 MG
	PROT. 1 G	CARB. 4 G	CHOL. 0 MG

SALADS

My students frequently ask at what point in the meal they should serve the salad. I tell them it is all a matter of preference. I always like a salad with the meal when serving meat, poultry, or fish, and after the main course when serving a pasta dish or good, hearty soup. The one thing I am obsessive about is always serving salad on a separate plate so that the delicate dressing does not mingle with the entrée.

Green salads should not be tossed with dressing until they are ready to be served, since once dressed they rapidly go limp. (Certain other types of salads are mixed ahead of time and refrigerated while their flavors blend.) A good strategy is to prepare your dressing ahead of time.

Salads should always be exactly what they appear to be—bright, tempting, and as fresh as possible. In selecting greens for salads, look for crisp leaves with no signs of brown. The heavier the lettuce, whether it be romaine, Bibb, or iceberg, the more tightly packed it will be, giving you more leaves for your money. All recipes here will give you the measured amounts of greens needed for each salad. However, if purchasing a large head of romaine, you may want to trim off all the large outer leaves to save for Sautéed Romaine (page 172), and use the innermost tender leaves for salad. Salad leaves must be trimmed, washed, and dried either by absorbing the moisture with paper towels or a clean dish towel or by my favorite method—spinning dry in a salad spinner. If the greens are fresh and have been thoroughly dried after washing, you can hardly go wrong. After drying, I usually wrap them between two layers of paper towel, lightly roll into a cylinder, place in a plastic bag, seal tightly, and store them in the refrigerator up to twenty-four hours before using. The leaves should be torn rather than cut to avoid bruising. For salads that require shredded greens, a knife must be used, but postpone shredding until just before the greens are needed, since they wilt quickly after being cut.

Many meals call for nothing more complex than a mixed green salad tossed with a light, refreshing dressing such as a vinaigrette of good imported vinegar and a little extra virgin olive oil. Top-quality, fruity extra virgin olive oil is the best choice as a dressing for simple salads. Just remember to use a ratio of 1 teaspoon vinegar to 1 tablespoon extra virgin olive oil, seasoned with a little salt and pepper, for a simple dressing—no further embellishment is needed.

SALADS

◆ CHICKPEA SALAD

I can still remember sitting at my grandfather's table eating this salad. The onion was actually quartered and used as a scoop for the beans. Both were eaten at the same time, with crusty Italian bread. He always insisted that the skins be removed from the chickpeas. This crispy salad can be varied by using other beans, such as cannellini or red kidney beans. It is an excellent accompaniment to the Tuna and Orange Salad (page 152) or Broiled Flounder with Thyme (page 143).

SERVES 2

1 small red onion (about 4 ounces)
1 16-ounce can chickpeas, rinsed and well drained
1½ teaspoons imported red wine vinegar
1 scant teaspoon minced fresh oregano or ¼ teaspoon crumbled dried oregano

⅛ teaspoon coarse salt
⅛ teaspoon freshly milled black pepper
1 tablespoon extra virgin olive oil
1 tablespoon minced Italian parsley leaves

1. Peel onion and slice in half. Slice into paper-thin slices. Place onion in a bowl, cover with 4 ice cubes and fill bowl with enough cold water to cover onion slices. Let soak for at least 1 hour, or cover with plastic wrap and refrigerate until needed. (Soaking the red onion will ensure crispness.) Just before assembling salad, drain onion slices in strainer and thoroughly blot dry with paper towel.

2. To remove skins from chickpeas, squeeze each one gently between thumb and forefinger to slip off the skin; discard skins.

3. Place vinegar, oregano, salt, and pepper in serving bowl. Stir with fork or small whisk to combine. Add oil, a little at a time, and whisk thoroughly to incorporate.

4. Add onion, chickpeas, and parsley to bowl, toss thoroughly with dressing, and serve. (Salad may be completely assembled, covered with plastic wrap, and stored in refrigerator up to 2 hours. Toss once again before serving.)

PER SERVING: CAL. 237 (40% FROM FAT)   FAT 11 G   SOD. 257 MG
PROT. 9 G   CARB. 28 G   CHOL. 0 MG

◆ CUCUMBER AND RADISH SALAD

Creamy Horseradish Dressing adds zesty excitement to this crispy salad.

SERVES 2

1 small cucumber (about
   6 ounces), trimmed, peeled,
   and thinly sliced to make
   1½ cups
6 large radishes (about 4 ounces),

trimmed and sliced paper-thin
   to make ¾ cup
Creamy Horseradish Dressing
   (page 192)

1. Arrange cucumber slices in a circular outer border, with slices slightly overlapping, on individual salad plates. Arrange radish slices in the same manner in the center of the plates, slightly overlapping cucumber slices. (Salad can be prepared up to 2 hours before serving. Cover plates with plastic wrap and refrigerate until needed.) When ready to serve, spoon dressing over each portion and serve immediately.

PER SERVING:	CAL. 61 (55% FROM FAT)	FAT 4 G	SOD. 45 MG
	PROT. 2 G	CARB. 6 G	CHOL. 1 MG

◆ GRAPEFRUIT SALAD WITH WATERCRESS DRESSING

A superb winter salad to make when firm pink grapefruit are in season. This salad is an excellent accompaniment to any of the fish or seafood recipes in this book.

SERVES 2

2 medium-sized firm pink
   grapefruit (about 1½ pounds)
1 medium-sized bunch watercress
   (6 ounces)
1 tablespoon extra virgin olive oil
¼ cup watercress, cut into 1-inch
   pieces

⅛ teaspoon Dijon mustard
1 teaspoon honey, preferably
   orange blossom
⅛ teaspoon coarse salt
⅛ teaspoon freshly milled black
   pepper

1. With a small, sharp knife, cut a small section from the top and bottom of each grapefruit. With the tip of the knife, divide grapefruit skin into 6 sections. Peel each section, removing most of the white membrane as you peel. With a vegetable peeler, remove all the white membrane from grapefruit.

2. Place a medium-sized strainer over a bowl. Cut out each grapefruit segment, removing its protective membrane over the strainer to catch juice. Let grapefruit drain in strainer for at least 30 minutes; reserve 2 tablespoons juice for dressing.

3. Wash watercress several times in cold water, drain well, and blot dry with paper towel or spin dry in salad spinner. Remove tough lower stems. Measure out ¼ cup watercress and reserve it for dressing.

4. Arrange remaining watercress on two salad plates. Arrange slices of grapefruit in a circular pattern, slightly overlapping, on top of watercress.

5. Place remaining ingredients, including reserved juice and watercress, in a blender or food processor fitted with metal blade. Run machine nonstop until watercress is finely minced and dressing is creamy, about 1 minute; stop machine once to scrape inside work bowl with plastic spatula. (Dressing may be made up to 1 hour before using; transfer to a small jar and refrigerate until needed.)

6. Spoon dressing over each salad and serve immediately.

PER SERVING:	CAL. 140 (43% FROM FAT)	FAT 7 G	SOD. 43 MG
	PROT. 3 G	CARB. 18 G	CHOL. 0 MG

◆ HONEYDEW WALDORF SALAD

A lovely salad for those hot summer days, this is enlivened with the pale pink, delicately flavored Strawberry Yogurt Dressing (page 193). This salad goes extremely well with Broiled Rock Cornish Hen (page 131), Broiled Swordfish Steaks (page 155), or Shrimp and Snow Pea Salad (page 149).

SERVES 2

2 cups bite-sized pieces honeydew melon

1 cup small red seedless grapes

½ cup thinly sliced celery, strings removed

2 tablespoons coarsely chopped pecans

3 tablespoons Strawberry
  Yogurt Dressing (page 193)

4 medium-sized iceberg or Bibb
  lettuce leaves (garnish)

1. Place melon pieces in strainer set over a bowl. Place in refrigerator to drain thoroughly for at least 1 hour; discard liquid.

2. Combine melon, grapes, celery, and pecans in a bowl. Spoon dressing over salad and lightly toss with two spoons. Cover with plastic wrap and refrigerate salad up to 2 hours. (Do not chill any longer than this, because the honeydew may exude more liquid, making for a soggy salad.)

3. When ready to serve, arrange lettuce leaves on two salad plates. Spoon salad on lettuce leaves and serve immediately.

PER SERVING:	CAL. 198 (24% FROM FAT)	FAT 6 G	SOD. 100 MG
	PROT. 3 G	CARB. 38 G	CHOL. 1 MG

♦ GREEN BEAN AND ZUCCHINI SALAD WITH TARRAGON DRESSING

Cooked green beans and crunchy raw zucchini tossed with tarragon dressing give this salad a new dimension in texture as well as flavor.

SERVES 2

4 ounces green beans
1 small zucchini (4 ounces)
1 medium-sized clove garlic,
  peeled and split in half
1 teaspoon white balsamic vinegar
1½ teaspoons minced fresh
  tarragon or ½ teaspoon
  crumbled dried tarragon

⅛ teaspoon sugar
⅛ teaspoon coarse salt
⅛ teaspoon freshly milled black
  pepper
1 tablespoon extra virgin olive oil

1. Wash green beans and trim both ends. If green beans are more than 4 inches in length, slice diagonally in half crosswise. Cook beans in 2 quarts boiling water until tender when tested with fork, about 5 minutes. Drain in colander, rinse under cold water, and blot dry with paper towel.

2. Scrub zucchini and blot dry with paper towel. Trim ends and cut

into 2-inch lengths. Slice each piece in half lengthwise and slice into ¼-inch julienne strips.

3. Thoroughly rub inside of serving bowl with split garlic and leave in bowl. Push garlic to one side and place remaining ingredients except olive oil in serving bowl. Stir with fork or small wire whisk to combine. Add oil a little at a time and whisk to combine thoroughly.

4. Add zucchini to serving bowl and toss with dressing. Add green beans and toss once again. Cover with plastic wrap and refrigerate for at least 1 hour before serving. Remove garlic and toss once again just before serving.

PER SERVING:	CAL. 88 (67% FROM FAT)	FAT 7 G	SOD. 5 MG
	PROT. 3 G	CARB. 6 G	CHOL. 0 MG

◆ MIXED GREEN SALAD WITH MUSTARD VINAIGRETTE

A good salad to serve during the winter months, when Bibb and Boston lettuces are plentiful. Mustard and garlic add a snappy bite to the dressing.

SERVES 2

1 medium-sized head Bibb or Boston lettuce (about 7 ounces)
1 medium-sized head Belgian endive (2 ounces)
4 large radishes (3 ounces), trimmed and thinly sliced
4 medium-sized mushrooms (2 ounces), wiped, stems removed, and thinly sliced
1 teaspoon balsamic vinegar

¼ teaspoon minced garlic
¼ teaspoon Dijon mustard
1½ teaspoons minced fresh basil or ½ teaspoon crumbled dried basil
¼ teaspoon sugar
⅛ teaspoon coarse salt
⅛ teaspoon freshly milled black pepper
1 tablespoon extra virgin olive oil

1. Using a pair of kitchen shears, trim any bruised tips from lettuce. Separate leaves and wash greens several times in cold water. Drain well and gently blot dry with paper towel or spin dry in salad spinner. Break into bite-sized pieces and place in salad bowl.

2. Halve Belgian endive lengthwise. Cut out bitter center core; wipe leaves with a dampened cloth to remove sand. Slice into ½-inch widths and add to salad bowl. Add radishes and mushrooms to bowl. (Salad ingredients can be prepared up to 2 hours before serving. Cover with plastic wrap and refrigerate until needed.)

3. Place remaining ingredients except olive oil in a small bowl and stir with fork or small whisk to combine. Add oil a little at a time and whisk until dressing is well combined. Toss dressing with salad ingredients and serve immediately.

PER SERVING:	CAL. 102 (61% FROM FAT)	FAT 8 G	SOD. 37 MG
	PROT. 3 G	CARB. 8 G	CHOL. 0 MG

◆ LETTUCE AND CARROT SALAD

Easy to prepare and eye-catching. The horseradish dressing gives this salad its special, snappy taste.

SERVES 2

½ medium-sized head iceberg lettuce (about 6 ounces)
2 medium-sized carrots (5 ounces)
2 tablespoons snipped fresh chives
or thinly sliced scallions (green part only)
Creamy Horseradish Dressing (page 192)

1. Remove center core from lettuce. Separate leaves and wash in cold water. Drain well and gently blot dry with paper towel or spin dry in salad spinner. Stack several leaves at a time and slice crosswise into ¼-inch strips. Place a mound of shredded lettuce on each salad plate.

2. Wash carrots, trim, and peel lightly with a vegetable peeler. Cut into 2-inch lengths, place horizontally in food processor fitted with shredding disk, and use firm pressure on pusher to grate. (If you do not have a food processor, leave carrots whole and shred on the coarse side of a grater.) Mound carrots in center of plate and garnish with chives or scallions.

3. Spoon dressing over each portion and serve immediately.

PER SERVING:	CAL. 84 (40% FROM FAT)	FAT 4 G	SOD. 58 MG
	PROT. 3 G	CARB. 11 G	CHOL. 1 MG

◆ ORANGE AND KIWI SALAD

A perfectly delightful highlight when served with either Broiled Rock Cornish Hen (page 131) or Broiled Flounder with Thyme (page 143). This colorful recipe was developed by David Wald, a dear friend and excellent cook.

SERVES 2

2 large navel oranges
  (1¼ pounds)
2 kiwifruit (3 ounces)
2 teaspoons raspberry vinegar
⅛ teaspoon sugar

⅛ teaspoon coarse salt
⅛ teaspoon freshly milled black
  pepper
1 tablespoon extra virgin
  olive oil

1. Cut a slice from top and bottom of oranges to expose the fruit. Peel the oranges and remove all the white membrane with a vegetable peeler. Slice crosswise into ¼-inch rounds. Place in strainer set over a bowl to drain thoroughly for at least 30 minutes; reserve 1 tablespoon juice for dressing.

2. Cut about ¼ inch from top and bottom of kiwifruits. To remove the fuzzy brown skin, peel lengthwise with a vegetable peeler using a zigzag motion. Slice into ¼-inch rounds.

3. Arrange orange slices in a circular outer border, with slices slightly overlapping, on individual salad plates. Arrange kiwi slices in the same manner in center of the plates, slightly overlapping orange slices.

4. Place raspberry vinegar, 1 tablespoon reserved orange juice, sugar, salt, and pepper in a small bowl. Stir with fork or small whisk to combine. Add oil a little at a time and whisk until dressing is well blended.

5. Spoon dressing over fruit and serve immediately.

PER SERVING:	CAL. 173 (35% FROM FAT)	FAT 7 G	SOD. 4 MG
	PROT. 2 G	CARB. 29 G	CHOL. 0 MG

◆ RED ONION AND TOMATO SALAD

Serve this salad during the summer months when tomatoes are at their best and fresh basil is readily available.

SERVES 2

1 small red onion (about
   4 ounces)
2 large, firm, ripe tomatoes (about
   1 pound)
⅛ teaspoon sugar
⅛ teaspoon freshly milled black
   pepper

2 teaspoons freshly grated
   Parmesan cheese
1 tablespoon extra virgin olive oil
6 large basil leaves, sliced into fine
   shreds (see Note)

1. Peel onion and slice into paper-thin rounds. Separate onion rings and place in a bowl. Cover rings with 4 ice cubes and fill with enough cold water to cover. Let soak for at least 1 hour or cover with plastic wrap and refrigerate until needed. (Soaking the red onion will ensure crispness when ready to serve.) Just before assembling salad, drain onion rings in strainer and blot thoroughly dry with paper towel.

2. Wash tomatoes and blot dry with paper towel. Core tomatoes; slice off about ½ inch from top and bottom of each tomato and discard. Slice each tomato into 3 even rounds.

3. Arrange tomato rounds and onion rings in an overlapping pattern on two salad plates.

4. Place sugar, pepper, and Parmesan cheese in a small bowl. Stir with fork or small whisk to combine. Add oil a little at a time and whisk thoroughly to incorporate.

5. Spoon dressing over the tomato and onion slices. Sprinkle basil over the top and serve.

NOTE: To cut basil leaves into fine shreds, known as a chiffonade, stack the leaves one on top of another. Starting from broad end of leaves, roll into a tight cylinder. Place the cylinder on a cutting board. Holding the cylinder tightly to keep its shape, cut crosswise through the roll at ¹⁄₁₆-inch intervals to produce fine shreds. To prevent basil shreds from darkening, slice into chiffonade just before dressing salad.

PER SERVING:	CAL. 136 (50% FROM FAT)	FAT 8 G	SOD. 62 MG
	PROT. 4 G	CARB. 15 G	CHOL. 2 MG

◆ ROMAINE AND STRAWBERRY SALAD

The flavorful, creamy dressing truly enhances this refreshing salad, which can be served with or after the meal. It is an excellent accompaniment to Peachy Drumsticks with Orange Sauce (page 130) or Lamb Shoulder Chops with Mustard and Dill (page 106).

SERVES 2

1 medium-sized head romaine lettuce (about 1 pound)
12 medium-sized ripe strawberries (6 ounces)

3 tablespoons Strawberry Yogurt Dressing (page 193)

1. Discard tough outer leaves from romaine. Break off the tender inner leaves and wash several times in cold water. Drain well and blot thoroughly dry with paper towel or spin dry in salad spinner. Break off the tough bottom ends of each leaf and discard. Place leaves between 2 layers of paper towel; roll up and place in plastic bag and seal tightly. Refrigerate for at least 2 hours to crisp the romaine. (Greens may be refrigerated up to 24 hours before using.)

2. Rinse berries in cold water, drain thoroughly in strainer, and blot dry with paper towel or spin dry in salad spinner. To core the berries, gather up the leaves of each stem cap and with the tip of a small knife cut a ¼-inch circle around the base of the cap. Pull the leaves, and the white core will come out as well. Slice strawberries in half lengthwise. Transfer, cut sides down, to a flat plate lined with paper towel. Cover with plastic wrap and refrigerate until needed. (Berries may be prepared up to 2 hours before assembling salad.)

3. When ready to serve, break greens into bite-sized pieces and place on two salad plates (preferably glass). Mound strawberries in center of each plate, cut sides down. Spoon 1½ tablespoons dressing on top of each salad and serve immediately.

PER SERVING:	CAL. 83 (13% FROM FAT)	FAT 1 G	SOD. 78 MG
	PROT. 5 G	CARB. 15 G	CHOL. 1 MG

◆ SPINACH SALAD

Baby leaf spinach is now available year-round, so this is a perfect salad for any season. The mellow Tomato Shallot Dressing brings out its full flavor.

SERVES 2

8 ounces baby leaf spinach
1 medium-sized cucumber
  (8 ounces)

4 tablespoons Tomato Shallot
  Dressing (page 194)

1. Wash baby spinach in cool water and spin dry in salad spinner.
2. Peel cucumber and halve lengthwise. Remove seeds with a melon baller and slice crosswise into ¼-inch pieces.
3. Place a mound of spinach leaves on each salad plate. Mound sliced cucumber on top of spinach. Spoon 1½ tablespoons of dressing on top of each salad and serve.

PER SERVING:	CAL. 85 (43% FROM FAT)	FAT 5 G	SOD. 98 MG
	PROT. 4 G	CARB. 10 G	CHOL. 0 MG

◆ ZUCCHINI SALAD

This salad is best when you can find small, firm zucchini at the market.

SERVES 2

3 small zucchini (12 ounces)
4 tablespoons Tomato Shallot
  Dressing (page 194)

4 large Bibb lettuce leaves
1 teaspoon minced Italian parsley
  leaves (garnish)

1. Scrub zucchini under cold running water until the skins feel clean and smooth. Bring 1 quart of water to a rolling boil and add zucchini. When water returns to a boil, cook, uncovered, until barely tender when tested with the tip of a knife, about 3 minutes. Transfer to a colander and refresh under cold water. Blot dry with paper towel and cool to room

temperature. Trim both ends of zucchini. Slice into ½-inch rounds and place in a small bowl. Toss with dressing. Cover with plastic wrap and refrigerate for at least 2 hours.

2. Wash lettuce leaves in cold water. Drain well; place between 2 layers of paper towel and gently blot dry.

3. Place 2 lettuce leaves on each salad plate. Toss zucchini again with dressing and spoon on top of greens. Garnish each with minced parsley and serve.

PER SERVING:	CAL. 76 (48% FROM FAT)	FAT 5 G	SOD. 11 MG
	PROT. 3 G	CARB. 8 G	CHOL. O MG

DRESSINGS

◆ CREAMY HORSERADISH DRESSING

This tangy, creamy dressing is alive with the flavor of horseradish. Besides using it on the two salads in this chapter for which it is recommended, you will find that it also makes an extraordinary contribution when spooned over cold poached chicken breast or chilled cooked shrimp.

YIELDS ¼ CUP
SERVES 2

3 tablespoons low-fat yogurt
1½ teaspoons bottled horseradish, well drained
1 teaspoon apple cider vinegar
¼ teaspoon Dijon mustard
¼ teaspoon freshly milled black pepper
2 teaspoons extra virgin olive oil

1. Place all of the above ingredients except oil in a small bowl and beat with a fork or small whisk to combine. Add oil a little at a time, beating constantly with fork or whisk until dressing is creamy. (Dressing may be made up to 4 hours before serving; transfer to a small jar and refrigerate until needed. Whisk dressing once again before using.)

PER TABLESPOON:	CAL. 21 (77% FROM FAT)	FAT 2 G	SOD. 14 MG
	PROT. .40 G	CARB. 1 G	CHOL. .42 MG

◆ STRAWBERRY YOGURT DRESSING

Commercial yogurt tends to be watery, so it is very important that the yogurt be thoroughly drained before making dressing. In addition to the recipes for which it is specified, this dressing is also excellent spooned over any combination of the following fruits cut into bite-sized pieces: nectarines, cantaloupe, watermelon, or pineapple. Serve on a bed of Bibb or iceberg lettuce and garnish with thin slices of lime. Dressing can be stored in refrigerator in an airtight jar up to eight days. Whisk with fork before spooning or tossing with different salads.

YIELDS ½ CUP

SERVES 4

½ cup low-fat yogurt
6 medium-sized ripe strawberries
   (3 ounces), hulled and
   quartered, to make ⅓ cup, well
   packed
2 tablespoons low-fat mayonnaise
1 teaspoon fresh lemon juice

1 teaspoon honey, preferably
   orange blossom
1½ teaspoons snipped fresh mint
   or ½ teaspoon crumbled dried
   mint
¼ teaspoon coarse salt

1. Line a fine mesh strainer with a double thickness of dampened cheesecloth. Spoon yogurt into lined strainer set over a bowl. Place, uncovered, in refrigerator to drain thoroughly for at least 1½ hours. (Yogurt will exude as much as 2 tablespoons of liquid, and after draining, it should be the consistency of whipped heavy cream.) Discard liquid. Using a rubber spatula, scrape yogurt from cheesecloth into food processor fitted with metal blade.

2. Add remaining ingredients to food processor. Run machine nonstop for 30 seconds. Remove cover and scrape down sides of work bowl with plastic spatula. Run for an additional 30 seconds, until dressing is pale pink, with a smooth consistency. Transfer to airtight jar and refrigerate for at least 3 hours before using so that all the flavors meld together.

PER TABLESPOON:	CAL. 19 (19% FROM FAT)	FAT .41 G	SOD. 36 MG
	PROT. 1 G	CARB. 3 G	CHOL. 1 MG

◆ TOMATO SHALLOT DRESSING

Make sure you select an extremely well-ripened tomato to bring out the full mellow flavoring of this dressing. Not only does it go well with spinach and zucchini, it also harmonizes very nicely when tossed with bite-sized salad greens such as Bibb or romaine lettuce. Dressing can be stored in the refrigerator in an airtight jar for up to ten days. Whisk with fork before spooning or tossing with various salads.

YIELDS ½ CUP

SERVES 4

1 medium-sized very ripe tomato (about 4 ounces)

1 tablespoon imported white wine vinegar

2 tablespoons extra virgin olive oil

1 tablespoon snipped fresh basil or 1 teaspoon crumbled dried basil

¼ teaspoon sugar

¼ teaspoon coarse salt

¼ teaspoon freshly milled black pepper

1 large shallot (2 ounces), peeled and quartered

1. Plump tomato in 1 quart boiling water for 1 minute. Rinse under cold water. When cool enough to handle, core tomato and peel skin with a small paring knife. Cut in half crosswise and squeeze gently to discard most of the seeds. Place tomato on a plate and cut into 1-inch cubes.

2. Put tomato and any accumulated juices from plate in food processor fitted with metal blade. Add all the remaining ingredients except shallot to work bowl. Turn machine on and drop quartered shallot, one piece at a time, through the feed tube. Stop machine once and scrape down inside work bowl with plastic spatula. Run machine nonstop until shallot is finely minced and dressing is a smooth, creamy consistency, about 1 minute. Transfer dressing to airtight jar and refrigerate until needed.

PER TABLESPOON:	CAL. 32 (76% FROM FAT)	FAT 3 G	SOD. 2 MG
	PROT. .26 G	CARB. 2 G	CHOL. 0 MG

QUICK BREADS

The simplest baked goods to prepare are quick breads. They range from fruity, cakelike loaves to tender, moist muffins. What distinguishes this variety of baked goods is that no yeast is used in their preparation. Quick breads are referred to by a wide assortment of names: batter breads, sweet breads, fruity breads, breakfast or dessert breads. The distinct advantage they all possess is that they can be served interchangeably for breakfast, brunch, lunch, dinner, dessert, or just plain snacking.

For tender, well-shaped loaves or muffins, it is important to beat (or fold) mixture just until the flour is moistened and barely disappears into the batter. After incorporating all the ingredients, the batter should be lumpy, without any streaks of unincorporated flour. Do not overbeat or the loaves will be tough.

The following pages contain family favorites and adaptations of classic quick-bread recipes. Directions and baking times are given for large loaves as well as smaller loaves. I make the 9-inch loaves if entertaining or during the holiday season. During the rest of the year, I prefer making three of the smaller 5-inch loaves, as they freeze very well. After the loaves are baked and cooled, wrap in plastic wrap and then in foil. They can be kept in the freezer up to two months. To defrost, unwrap and let stand at room temperature for 2 hours. These fruit breads are wonderful to have on hand for unexpected guests and always make welcome, inexpensive hostess gifts.

For storing or freezing muffins, cool to room temperature, place in plastic bag, and seal tightly. Store in refrigerator up to three days or freeze up to two months. If freezing, remove from plastic bag ½ hour before serving. Muffins can be warmed in a preheated 300-degree oven (or toaster oven) for 10 minutes.

QUICK BREADS

◆ GLAZED APPLE LOAF

Everyone from youngsters to oldsters likes this moist, old-fashioned apple loaf, which is especially good as a dessert. You may want to top it with a scoop of frozen yogurt for an extra-special treat.

MAKES ONE 9-INCH LOAF OR THREE 5-INCH LOAVES
YIELDS 12 SLICES

2¼ cups unbleached all-purpose flour
1½ teaspoons baking powder
½ teaspoon baking soda
½ teaspoon ground cinnamon
¼ cup (½ stick) unsalted butter, at room temperature
⅓ cup sugar
2 large eggs

1 teaspoon pure vanilla extract
½ cup low-fat sour cream, at room temperature
2 medium-sized Golden Delicious apples (10 ounces), peeled, halved, cored, and sliced into ¼-inch wedges
½ cup apricot preserves, heated and strained

1. Adjust rack to bottom third of oven and preheat to 350 degrees. Grease and flour the bottom and sides of a 9-by-5-by-3-inch loaf pan or three 5½-by-3¼-by-2¼-inch loaf pans; set aside.

2. In a medium-sized bowl, whisk flour, baking powder, baking soda, and cinnamon; set dry ingredients aside.

3. In a large bowl, cream butter and sugar until the mixture is light and fluffy. Beat in eggs, one at a time, beating until the mixture is smooth. Stir in vanilla. Stir dry ingredients into the batter alternately with sour cream, beginning and ending with dry ingredients, just until combined and batter looks thick and chunky.

4. Turn batter into prepared pan(s) and smooth top(s) with a narrow metal spatula. For single loaf, press flat sides of apple slices into batter, leaving about ¼ inch of each slice showing. For small loaves, press apple slices right down to bottom of pan. Bake in preheated oven until golden on top and cake tester inserted in center comes out clean, about 60 minutes for large loaf or 30 to 35 minutes for small loaves. Let loaf or loaves cool in pan(s) on a rack for 10 minutes. Invert onto rack, remove pan(s) and invert again onto second rack.

5. While loaf or loaves are still warm, brush warm apricot glaze over top and sides. Serve warm or at room temperature.

| PER SLICE: | CAL. 219 (20% FROM FAT) | FAT 5 G | SOD. 172 MG |
| | PROT. 4 G | CARB. 41 G | CHOL. 32 MG |

◆ APPLESAUCE RAISIN LOAF

The raisins and applesauce make this an especially moist, flavorful bread. It is fine at breakfast, lunch, or snack time, and it goes extremely well with Poached Chicken with Apricot Sauce (page 125).

MAKES ONE 9-INCH LOAF OR THREE 5-INCH LOAVES

YIELDS 12 SLICES

1 cup dark seedless raisins
2 cups unbleached all-purpose flour
2 teaspoons baking powder
¼ teaspoon baking soda
¼ teaspoon salt
1 teaspoon ground cinnamon
½ teaspoon freshly grated nutmeg

¼ cup (½ stick) unsalted butter, at room temperature
⅓ cup lightly packed light brown sugar
2 large eggs
1¼ cups applesauce, preferably unsweetened

1. Adjust rack to bottom third of oven and preheat to 350 degrees. Grease and flour the bottom and sides of a 9-by-5-by-3-inch loaf pan or three 5½-by-3¼-by-2¼-inch loaf pans; set aside.

2. Place raisins in a small bowl and cover with boiling water until plumped, about 1 minute. Transfer to strainer, cool to room temperature, and set aside.

3. In a medium-sized bowl, whisk flour, baking powder, baking soda, salt, cinnamon, and nutmeg; set dry ingredients aside.

4. In a large bowl, cream butter and light brown sugar until the mixture is light and fluffy. Beat in eggs, one at a time, beating until the mixture is smooth. Stir dry ingredients into the batter alternately with applesauce in two batches, just until ingredients are blended; batter should be lumpy. Fold raisins into batter with spatula.

5. Turn batter into prepared pan(s) and smooth top with a narrow metal spatula. Bake in preheated oven until golden on top and cake

tester inserted in center comes out clean, about 50 minutes for large loaf or 35 minutes for small loaves. Let loaf or loaves cool in pan(s) on a rack for 10 minutes. Invert onto rack, remove pan(s) and invert again onto second rack. Cool completely on rack before serving.

PER SERVING:	CAL. 223 (19% FROM FAT)	FAT 5 G	SOD. 194 MG
	PROT. 4 G	CARB. 42 G	CHOL. 31 MG

◆ APRICOT PINEAPPLE LOAF

The apricots give this loaf an unusual, tangy flavor, while the pineapple adds moist texture. This fruit loaf makes a welcome, inexpensive hostess gift or a popular dessert when served with lemon sorbet or vanilla frozen yogurt.

MAKES ONE 9-INCH LOAF OR THREE 5-INCH LOAVES
YIELDS 12 SLICES

1 8-ounce can crushed
    pineapple
2½ cups unbleached all-purpose
    flour
2 teaspoons baking powder
½ teaspoon baking soda
¼ teaspoon salt

¼ cup (½ stick) unsalted butter, at
    room temperature
¾ cup sugar
2 large eggs
2 teaspoons pure vanilla extract
1 cup dried apricots, cut into
    ½-inch pieces

1. Adjust rack to bottom third of oven and preheat to 350 degrees. Grease and flour the bottom and sides of a 9-by-5-by-3-inch loaf pan or three 5½-by-3¼-by-2¼-inch loaf pans; set aside.

2. Drain pineapple in a strainer set over a bowl. Using the back of a wooden spoon, firmly press pineapple to extract juice. You should have ½ cup after draining pineapple. If you don't, make up the difference in liquid by adding a little water; reserve juice. Set aside.

3. In a medium-sized bowl, whisk flour, baking powder, baking soda, and salt; set dry ingredients aside.

4. In a large bowl, cream butter and sugar until the mixture is light and fluffy. Beat in eggs, one at a time, beating until the mixture is smooth. Stir in vanilla. Stir dry ingredients into the batter alternately with pineapple juice in two batches, just until ingredients are blended;

batter should be lumpy. Fold pineapple and apricots into batter with rubber spatula.

5. Turn batter into prepared pan(s) and smooth top(s) with a narrow metal spatula. Bake until golden on top and a cake tester inserted in center comes out clean, about 1 hour for large loaf or 35 to 40 minutes for small loaves. Let loaf or loaves cool in pan(s) on a rack for 10 minutes. Invert onto rack, remove pan(s), and invert again onto second rack. Cool to room temperature before serving.

PER SLICE:	CAL. 175 (19% FROM FAT)	FAT 4 G	SOD. 145 MG
	PROT. 3 G	CARB. 32 G	CHOL. 21 MG

◆ BANANA PECAN LOAF

The bananas should be well ripened to add a sweet, moist texture to this tempting loaf. For a quick dessert, try serving thin slices of this golden-hued bread with a scoop of vanilla or chocolate frozen yogurt.

MAKES ONE 9-INCH LOAF OR THREE 5-INCH LOAVES
YIELDS 12 SLICES

2 cups unbleached all-purpose flour
¾ cup sugar
¾ teaspoon baking soda
¼ teaspoon salt
¼ teaspoon freshly grated nutmeg
1⅓ cups lightly toasted pecans, coarsely chopped
3 large, very ripe, speckled bananas, mashed well with fork (1½ cups)
¼ cup low-fat yogurt, at room temperature
2 large eggs, lightly beaten
5 tablespoons unsalted butter, melted and cooled to room temperature
2 teaspoons pure vanilla extract

1. Adjust rack to bottom third of oven and preheat to 350 degrees. Grease and flour the bottom and sides of a 9-by-5-by-3-inch loaf pan or three 5½-by-3¼-by-2¼-inch loaf pans; set aside.

2. In a large bowl, combine flour, sugar, baking soda, salt, nutmeg, and pecans; set aside.

3. In a medium-sized bowl, stir mashed bananas, yogurt, beaten eggs, melted butter, and vanilla with a wooden spoon. Lightly fold banana

mixture into dry ingredients with rubber spatula in three batches just until combined and batter looks thick and chunky.

4. Turn batter into prepared pan(s) and smooth top(s) with a narrow metal spatula. Bake in preheated oven until golden and cake tester inserted in center comes out clean, about 55 to 60 minutes for large loaf or 35 to 40 minutes for small loaves. Let loaf or loaves cool in pan(s) on a rack for 10 minutes. Invert onto rack, remove pan(s), and invert again onto second rack. Cool to room temperature before serving.

PER SLICE:	CAL. 236 (36% FROM FAT)	FAT 10 G	SOD. 109 MG
	PROT. 5 G	CARB. 34 G	CHOL. 30 MG

◆ CRANBERRY NUT BREAD

Cranberries, orange, pecans, and whole wheat flour flavor this holiday favorite. For easier slicing, bake one day before serving. This bread is an excellent accompaniment to Peachy Drumsticks with Orange Sauce (page 130) or Glazed Rock Cornish Hen (page 132).

MAKES ONE 9-INCH LOAF OR THREE 5-INCH LOAVES
YIELDS 12 SLICES

2 cups fresh whole cranberries
2¼ cups unbleached all-purpose
    flour
1½ teaspoons baking powder
½ teaspoon baking soda
¼ teaspoon salt
1 cup sugar
1 tablespoon grated orange rind

½ cup fresh orange juice
¼ cup water
3 tablespoons canola or vegetable oil
2 large eggs, lightly beaten
1 cup lightly toasted walnuts, coarsely chopped

1. Adjust rack to bottom third of oven and preheat to 360 degrees. Grease and flour the bottom and sides of a 9-by-5-by-3-inch loaf pan or three 5½-by-3¼-by-2¼-inch loaf pans; set aside.

2. Pick over cranberries, discarding any bits of stem and bruised berries; wash berries in cold water. Thoroughly drain in strainer and blot dry with paper towel. Coarsely chop cranberries and set aside.

3. In a medium-sized bowl, combine flour, baking powder, baking soda, and salt; set aside.

4. In a large bowl, stir sugar, orange rind, orange juice, water, oil, and beaten eggs with a wooden spoon until well combined. Stir in dry ingredients, just until moistened and batter looks lumpy. Stir in cranberries and nuts.

5. Turn batter into prepared pan(s) and smooth top(s) with a narrow metal spatula. Bake in preheated oven until a dark golden color and cake tester inserted in center comes out clean, about 50 to 60 minutes for large loaf or 40 to 45 minutes for small loaves. Let loaf or loaves cool in pan(s) on a rack for 10 minutes. Invert onto rack, remove pan(s), and invert again onto second rack. Cool completely; wrap tightly in plastic wrap and store in refrigerator overnight before serving.

PER SLICE:	CAL. 175 (34% FROM FAT)	FAT 7 G	SOD. 200 MG
	PROT. 3 G	CARB. 21 G	CHOL. 20 MG

◆ LEMON-GLAZED PRUNE LOAF

For brunch, tea, luncheon, or just snacking, this tangy loaf always disappears as quickly as it is baked in my household. For easier slicing, bake one day before serving. This is an adaptation of one of the many recipes developed by my cousin Lorraine Mullen. No Christmas would be complete without a visit from Lorraine and a gift of no less than six different types of bread.

MAKES ONE 9-INCH LOAF OR THREE 5-INCH LOAVES
YIELDS 12 SLICES

1¼ cups unbleached all-purpose flour
¾ cup old-fashioned oats, preferably Quaker
1½ teaspoons baking powder
½ teaspoon baking soda
¾ cup sugar
¼ cup canola or vegetable oil
2 large eggs, lightly beaten

1½ teaspoons grated lemon rind
1 teaspoon pure lemon extract
½ cup low-fat buttermilk, at room temperature (see Note)
1 cup large pitted prunes, cut into ½-inch pieces
¼ cup fresh lemon juice, strained
¼ cup sugar

1. Adjust rack to bottom third of oven and preheat to 350 degrees. Grease and flour the bottom and sides of a 9-by-5-by-3-inch loaf pan or three 5½-by-3¼-by-2¼-inch loaf pans; set aside.

2. In medium-sized bowl, combine flour, oats, baking powder, and baking soda; set aside.

3. In a large bowl, stir sugar, oil, beaten eggs, lemon rind, and lemon extract with a wooden spoon until well combined. Stir in dry ingredients alternately with buttermilk in two batches, just until moistened and batter looks lumpy. Fold prunes into batter with spatula.

4. Turn batter into prepared pan(s) and smooth top(s) with a narrow metal spatula. Bake in preheated oven until lightly golden on top and cake tester inserted in center comes out clean, about 55 minutes for large loaf or 35 to 40 minutes for small loaves. Let loaf or loaves cool in pan(s) on rack for 10 minutes. Invert onto rack, remove pan(s), and invert again onto second rack placed over a large piece of aluminum foil.

5. Prepare glaze: In a small saucepan, combine lemon juice and sugar. Cook over low heat, stirring once or twice, until sugar is completely dissolved, about 1 minute.

6. While loaf or loaves are still warm, pierce top(s) and sides thoroughly with toothpick. Brush glaze over pierced surfaces several times until completely absorbed. Cool loaf or loaves completely before serving. (This bread is best made one day in advance, covered loosely with foil, and refrigerated overnight. Return to room temperature before serving.)

NOTE: If you do not have buttermilk on hand, mix 1 tablespoon lemon juice with ½ cup low-fat milk and let stand until curdled, approximately 5 minutes.

PER SLICE:	CAL. 161 (22% FROM FAT)	FAT 4 G	SOD. 131 MG
	PROT. 3 G	CARB. 30 G	CHOL. 13 MG

MUFFINS

◆ BASIC MUFFINS

Homemade muffins fresh from the oven are always a special treat on their own or when served as part of the meal. I usually make batches and freeze them. For storing or freezing, cool muffins to room temperature, place in plastic bag, and seal tightly. Store in refrigerator up to three days or freeze up to two months. If freezing, remove from plastic bag ½ hour before serv-

ing. Muffins may be warmed in a preheated 300-degree oven (or toaster oven) for 10 minutes.

MAKES 8 LARGE MUFFINS

1¾ cups unbleached all-purpose
   flour
1½ teaspoons baking powder
¼ teaspoon baking soda
¼ teaspoon salt
¼ cup (½ stick) unsalted butter, at
   room temperature

⅓ cup sugar
1 large egg
1 teaspoon pure vanilla extract
¾ cup plain low-fat yogurt, at
   room temperature
Vegetable oil cooking spray

1. Adjust rack to center of oven and preheat to 375 degrees.

2. In a medium-sized bowl, whisk together flour, baking powder, baking soda, and salt; set aside.

3. In a large bowl, cream butter and sugar until light and fluffy. Add egg and beat well. Stir in vanilla extract. Beat in dry ingredients alternately with yogurt, starting and ending with dry ingredients.

4. Spray bottom and sides of an 8-cup muffin pan with vegetable oil cooking spray.

5. Spoon batter into prepared cups, dividing evenly. Bake in preheated oven until muffins are golden brown, about 25 to 30 minutes. Set pan on wire rack to cool slightly, about 6 minutes. Remove muffins from pan and serve warm.

PER MUFFIN:	CAL. 178 (23% FROM FAT)	FAT 5 G	SOD. 140 MG
	PROT. 4 G	CARB. 31 G	CHOL. 37 MG

VARIATIONS

APPLESAUCE MUFFINS

Basic Muffin batter   4 tablespoons applesauce

1. Prepare batter as directed for Basic Muffins and spoon into prepared muffin cups. Using the back of a teaspoon, make a well in center of batter in each muffin cup about 1 inch wide by ½ inch deep. Spoon 1½ teaspoons applesauce into each cavity. Bake as directed for Basic Muffins.

2. Transfer muffins onto cooling rack by lifting out with a pair of metal tongs or two forks so that applesauce will not spill out of cavities after baking.

PER MUFFIN:	CAL. 181 (22% FROM FAT)	FAT 3 G	SOD. 139 MG
	PROT. 4 G	CARB. 31 G	CHOL. 36 MG

BLUEBERRY MUFFINS

Basic Muffin batter   1 cup fresh blueberries

1. Prepare batter as directed for Basic Muffins. Using a rubber spatula, gently fold blueberries into batter. Bake and cool as directed for Basic Muffins.

PER MUFFIN:	CAL. 188 (22% FROM FAT)	FAT 5 G	SOD. 142 MG
	PROT. 4 G	CARB. 33 G	CHOL. 37 MG

CRANBERRY MUFFINS

Basic Muffin batter
2 teaspoons finely grated orange
   rind
1 cup fresh whole cranberries,

picked over, washed,
thoroughly drained, and
coarsely chopped

1. Prepare batter as directed for Basic Muffins. Using a rubber spatula, gently fold orange rind and cranberries into batter. Bake and cool as directed for Basic Muffins.

PER MUFFIN:	CAL. 185 (21% FROM FAT)	FAT 4 G	SOD. 138 MG
	PROT. 4 G	CARB. 32 G	CHOL. 36 MG

ORANGE DATE MUFFINS

Basic Muffin batter
2 teaspoons grated orange rind

1 cup pitted dates, cut into ¼-inch
   cubes

1. Prepare batter as directed for Basic Muffins. Using a rubber spatula, gently fold orange rind and dates into batter. Bake and cool as directed for Basic Muffins.

PER MUFFIN:	CAL. 239 (16% FROM FAT)	FAT 5 G	SOD. 140 MG
	PROT. 5 G	CARB. 47 G	CHOL. 37 MG

STRAWBERRY SURPRISE MUFFINS

Basic Muffin batter   8 teaspoons strawberry preserves

1. Prepare batter as directed for Basic Muffins. Spoon 1½ tablespoons batter into each prepared muffin cup. With the back of a teaspoon, make an indentation in center of batter in each muffin cup. Spoon 1 teaspoon strawberry preserves into each cavity. Cover with remaining batter. Bake and cool as directed for Basic Muffins.

PER MUFFIN:	CAL. 194 (20% FROM FAT)	FAT 4 G	SOD. 141 MG
	PROT. 4 G	CARB. 35 G	CHOL. 36 MG

◆ CORN MUFFINS

Incredibly easy to prepare. Especially good when served for breakfast or with any of the hearty soup recipes in this book. Wrap any leftovers muffins individually with plastic wrap and refrigerate up to four days. Can be reheated in 300-degree oven or sliced in half and toasted in toaster oven.

MAKES 8 LARGE MUFFINS

¾ cup yellow cornmeal, preferably Indian Head brand
¾ cup unbleached all-purpose flour
3 tablespoons sugar
1½ teaspoons baking powder
¼ teaspoon salt

3 tablespoons unsalted butter, melted and cooled to room temperature
¾ cup low-fat milk, at room temperature
1 large egg, lightly beaten
Vegetable oil cooking spray

1. Adjust rack to center of oven and preheat to 425 degrees.

2. In a large bowl, whisk together cornmeal, flour, sugar, baking powder, and salt. Make a well in center and add melted butter, milk, and beaten egg. Stir just until dry ingredients are moistened.

3. Spray bottom and sides of an 8-cup muffin pan with vegetable oil cooking spray.

4. Spoon batter into prepared cups, dividing evenly. Bake in preheated oven until muffins are golden brown, about 15 to 20 minutes. Set pan on wire rack to cool slightly, about 3 minutes. Remove muffins from pan and serve warm.

PER MUFFIN:	CAL. 174 (23% FROM FAT)	FAT 5 G	SOD. 156 MG
	PROT. 5 G	CARB. 30 G	CHOL. 37 MG

◆ RAISIN BRAN MUFFINS

These classic muffins have been a favorite on my breakfast table for years. They are so easy to make that I am sure you will want to serve them as often as I do.

MAKES 8 LARGE MUFFINS

1 cup shredded 100% bran cereal
¾ cup low-fat milk, at room
  temperature
¾ cup unbleached all-purpose
  flour
⅓ cup firmly packed light brown
  sugar
2 teaspoons baking powder

¼ teaspoon salt
½ teaspoon ground cinnamon
1 large egg, lightly beaten
3½ tablespoons canola or
  vegetable oil
½ cup dark seedless raisins
Vegetable oil cooking spray

1. Adjust rack to center of oven and preheat to 400 degrees.

2. Place bran in a large bowl. Add milk and mix thoroughly to moisten cereal. Let mixture stand until bran is softened, about 10 minutes.

3. In a medium-sized bowl, whisk together flour, brown sugar, baking powder, salt, and cinnamon; set dry ingredients aside.

4. Add beaten egg and oil to softened bran mixture and stir until

blended. Add dry ingredients and stir just until combined; do not over-mix (batter will be lumpy). With a rubber spatula, fold raisins into batter.

5. Spray bottom and sides of an 8-cup muffin pan with vegetable oil cooking spray.

6. Spoon batter into prepared cups, dividing evenly. Bake in pre-heated oven until muffins are a deep golden brown, about 18 to 20 minutes. Set pan on wire rack to cool slightly, about 5 minutes. Remove muffins from pan and serve warm.

PER MUFFIN:	CAL. 197 (22% FROM FAT)	FAT 5 G	SOD. 220 MG
	PROT. 5 G	CARB. 35 G	CHOL. 29 MG

SPREADS

◆ RAISIN SPREAD

Use this spread for Basic Muffins (page 204) or any of the muffin variations that do not contain fruit. See variations at bottom of recipe.

YIELDS ¼ CUP

1 cup golden raisins
¼ cup applesauce
½ teaspoon finely grated
　lemon rind

1 teaspoon fresh
　lemon juice

1. In a 1½-quart saucepan, combine raisins with 1 cup water. Cover pan and bring to a boil over high heat. Cook just until raisins are plumped, about 30 seconds. Transfer to a strainer and refresh under cold water. Set strainer over a bowl and with the back of a wooden spoon press raisins to get rid of excess liquid; discard liquid.

2. Place raisins and remaining ingredients in blender or food processor fitted with metal blade. Run machine nonstop until you have a smooth paste. Stop machine once and scrape down inside work-bowl with plastic spatula. Transfer to a small jar and refrigerate for at least

3 hours or until needed. (Raisin spread may be stored in refrigerator up to 1 month.)

PER TABLESPOON:	CAL. 39 (1% FROM FAT)	FAT .05 G	SOD. 2 MG
	PROT. .40 G	CARB. 10 G	CHOL. 0 MG

VARIATIONS

APRICOT OR PRUNE SPREAD

Substitute 1 cup dried apricots or prunes (well packed) for the raisins. Cook apricots or prunes for 2 minutes before draining. Follow same procedure as directed for Raisin Spread.

PER TABLESPOON:	CAL. 28 (1% FROM FAT)	FAT .04 G	SOD. 1 MG
	PROT. .39 G	CARB. 7 G	CHOL. 0 MG

DESSERTS

DESSERTS

APPLE MERINGUE   215

APRICOT CUSTARD   216

BANANA FLAMBÉ   217

CRUNCHY BLUEBERRY CUPS   218

   CRUNCHY APPLE CUPS   219

   CRUNCHY PEACH CUPS   219

POACHED NECTARINES WITH BLUEBERRY SAUCE   219

NECTARINE CLAFOUTI   220

   APRICOT CLAFOUTI   221

   PEACH CLAFOUTI   221

ORANGE COMPOTE WITH LIQUEUR   222

PEACH CREAM   222

DESSERT PANCAKES WITH VARIOUS FILLINGS AND
   TOPPINGS   224

   PEACH FILLING   225

   APPLE FILLING   225

   STRAWBERRY FILLING   226

   BLUEBERRY SAUCE TOPPING   226

   STRAWBERRY SAUCE TOPPING   226

POACHED SLICED PEARS WITH MARMALADE SAUCE   227

PINEAPPLE SORBET WITH SAMBUCA   228

PLUM CRISP   228

   APPLE CRISP   229

SAUCES

I can still remember the old icebox we had when I was a child. The iceman came down our street every day; if we wanted ice, we put a sign in our window and he would stop. The ice was a huge block, covered with a large piece of burlap. I was always amazed at how deftly he used an ice pick to chisel away from the block a piece of ice that always fit perfectly into our ice compartment. During the summer months it was always fun to get some of the ice shavings as he chipped away. I am sure many of you can still remember the drip tray at the bottom of the icebox, which had to be emptied daily.

Chilled desserts were very limited in those days because of refrigeration. Although desserts were never the highlight of a meal, I never failed to ask as I was sliding into my chair at the dinner table, "What's for dessert?" The answer was always the same: "Fruit," or occasionally "Jell-O." When company was coming, desserts were usually very special, but there were also times when a variation of one or another of the quick breads in this book was made for simple entertaining.

I vividly recall the first dessert I ever made. I was six years old, and it was Jell-O. This could be made only once a week—when the iceman delivered the ice—because only then would the Jell-O chill properly. The day our first electric refrigerator was delivered will stay in my memory forever. I can still see my mother, my sister Louisa, and myself with our hands clasped as we danced around the sparkling new G.E. My biggest thrill was not having to wait for a special day each week to prepare my famous culinary creation—I made Jell-O every day for two weeks straight.

Today I rarely serve any dessert for my husband and myself other than fresh fruit or an impromptu fruit salad—how history repeats itself. But I refuse to make Jell-O!

Most human beings have an irrepressible appetite for something sweet at the end of a meal. Taking today's tastes into consideration, I have developed recipes that are not only delicious but use sugar sparingly and substitute part-skim ricotta cheese and low-fat yogurt for heavy cream. As you read through the following pages, you will find that while my desserts are all fruit based, they provide a wide variety of selections, including crisps, custard, clafoutis, meringue, parfaits, dessert pancakes, and others. Simple recipes for fruit sauces that can be served with sorbets for a quick dessert, variations on crunchy fruit cups, and of course the quick breads in the previous chapter will expand your repertoire of final sweet touches to your perfect meal.

DESSERTS

◆ APPLE MERINGUE

For best flavor, serve this dessert warm or at room temperature.

SERVES 2

2 large Golden Delicious
   apples (12 ounces),
   peeled, quartered, cored,
   and sliced crosswise into
   ½-inch pieces to make
   2 cups, well packed
⅓ cup unsweetened apple juice

2 large egg whites, at room
   temperature
Pinch of salt
Pinch of cream of tartar
3 tablespoons sugar
¼ teaspoon pure vanilla extract

1. In a 10-inch nonstick skillet, combine sliced apples and apple juice. Cover pan and bring to a boil over high heat. As soon as juice reaches a boil, turn heat down to medium. Cook, uncovered, spooning juice over apples, until they are barely tender when tested with a fork, about 3 minutes. Transfer apples to a strainer set over a bowl; reserve juice. Spoon drained apples into two 6-ounce ovenproof custard cups. Spoon 1 tablespoon of the reserved juice over each; set aside.

2. Adjust rack to center of oven and preheat to 375 degrees.

3. Beat egg whites until foamy. Add salt and cream of tartar and continue beating until whites hold soft peaks. Gradually add sugar; continue beating until stiff and glossy. Add vanilla and beat just until blended. Spoon meringue over apples. Using a rubber spatula, spread meringue to the inside edges of cups.

4. Place baking cups on a small baking sheet (the oven tray from a toaster oven works well). Bake in preheated oven until meringue is lightly golden, about 8 to 10 minutes. Transfer to cooling rack and cool for at least 30 minutes before serving, or serve at room temperature.

PER SERVING:	CAL. 169 (2% FROM FAT)	FAT .48 G	SOD. 102 MG
	PROT. 2 G	CARB. 41 G	CHOL. 0 MG

◆ APRICOT CUSTARD

An excellent do-ahead winter dessert. The texture of this dessert is more like a light cheesecake than a custard. It can be served either at room temperature or well chilled.

SERVES 2

2 tablespoons diced dried apricots, cut into ½-inch cubes

2 cups low-fat yogurt, well drained in strainer

1 extra large egg, lightly beaten

3 tablespoons sugar

½ teaspoon pure vanilla extract

1. Adjust rack to center of oven and preheat to 350 degrees. Lightly grease two 6-ounce ovenproof custard cups; set aside.

2. Place apricots in a small bowl. Add enough boiling water to cover and let stand for 10 minutes to soften. Transfer to strainer and drain thoroughly. Place 1 tablespoon diced apricots in bottom of each prepared custard cup.

3. Place yogurt, beaten egg, and sugar in a deep bowl. Beat with a wire whisk until smooth and creamy. Stir in vanilla. Pour mixture into cups over apricots. Place custard cups in a deep ovenproof baking dish. Add enough boiling water to baking dish to reach two-thirds of the way up the sides of cups.

4. Bake in preheated oven until slightly puffed, very lightly golden around edges, and a cake tester inserted in center comes out clean, about 35 to 40 minutes. Immediately remove from water bath and place on a rack to cool to room temperature. This dessert can be served at room temperature or well chilled (chill in refrigerator for at least 3 hours before serving).

PER SERVING:	CAL. 224 (25% FROM FAT)	FAT 6 G	SOD. 152 MG
	PROT. 12 G	CARB. 30 G	CHOL. 119 MG

◆ BANANA FLAMBÉ

Select a perfect, unblemished yellow banana that is slightly tinged with green for this spectacular dessert.

SERVES 2

½ pint vanilla frozen yogurt
1 large yellow banana (6 ounces), tipped with green
2 teaspoons unsalted butter, cut into ½-inch cubes

2 tablespoons honey, preferably orange blossom
1 tablespoon crème de cacao liqueur
3 tablespoons cognac, warmed

1. Scoop frozen yogurt onto individual serving plates and place in freezer until needed.

2. Peel banana and cut in half lengthwise, then crosswise.

3. In a 10-inch nonstick skillet, melt butter over medium-high heat; add honey and swirl pan so that it is evenly coated. Continue cooking and swirling pan until mixture is a light caramel color, about 30 seconds. Add liqueur and swirl in pan to combine.

4. Add banana quarters to sauce and turn heat up to high. Using a serving fork and spoon, keep turning and basting quarters in sauce until lightly glazed, about 30 seconds. Add warmed cognac, shake pan, and ignite. Remove from heat and keep basting until the flame goes out.

5. To serve, place two sections of banana, curved side up, on either side of frozen yogurt. Spoon sauce over each portion and serve immediately.

PER SERVING:	CAL. 289 (23% FROM FAT)	FAT 7 G	SOD. 58 MG
	PROT. 3 G	CARB. 48 G	CHOL. 20 MG

◆ CRUNCHY BLUEBERRY CUPS

A satisfying finale for lunch or dinner when fresh blueberries are in season. This dessert is best served lukewarm while the streusel topping is still crisp. See variations at bottom of recipe.

SERVES 2

1¼ cups fresh blueberries
½ teaspoon finely grated lemon rind
2 teaspoons fresh lemon juice, strained
2 teaspoons sugar
½ teaspoon cornstarch
2 tablespoons light brown sugar, firmly packed

2 tablespoons unbleached all-purpose flour
1½ tablespoons wheat germ
¼ teaspoon ground cinnamon
1½ tablespoons unsalted butter, well chilled and cut into 12 pieces
½ teaspoon sifted confectioners' sugar (for dusting)

1. Adjust rack to center of oven and preheat to 350 degrees. Lightly grease two 6-ounce ovenproof custard cups; set aside.

2. Pick over blueberries to remove any stems. Place blueberries in a strainer and wash thoroughly under cold water. Blot dry with paper towel and transfer to a deep bowl.

3. In a small bowl, combine lemon rind, lemon juice, sugar, and cornstarch; stir with a spoon until cornstarch is completely dissolved. Pour lemon mixture over blueberries. Toss berries to coat thoroughly with lemon mixture. Spoon blueberry mixture into prepared custard cups; set aside.

4. Place brown sugar, flour, wheat germ, and cinnamon in a small bowl. Stir with fork to combine thoroughly. Add butter and blend with your fingertips until mixture resembles coarse (pea-sized) crumbs. Spoon crumb mixture over blueberries.

5. Place custard cups on a small baking sheet (the oven tray from a toaster oven works well). Bake in preheated oven until the blueberry mixture is bubbling around the edges of the custard cups and the crumbs are golden, about 20 minutes.

6. Transfer to rack and cool to lukewarm, about 25 minutes. Dust with confectioners' sugar just before serving.

PER SERVING:	CAL. 209 (24% FROM FAT)	FAT 6 G	SOD. 13 MG
	PROT. 3 G	CARB. 40 G	CHOL. 13 MG

VARIATIONS

CRUNCHY APPLE CUPS

For a winter dessert, substitute 1½ cups peeled and diced Golden Delicious apples (½-inch cubes) for the blueberries. Bake as directed for Crunchy Blueberry Cups, increasing baking time to about 25 minutes.

PER SERVING:	CAL. 198 (25% FROM FAT)	FAT 6 G	SOD. 8 MG
	PROT. 2 G	CARB. 37 G	CHOL. 13 MG

CRUNCHY PEACH CUPS

For another summer dessert, you can substitute 1½ cups well-packed peeled and diced ripened peaches (½-inch cubes) for the blueberries. Bake as directed for Crunchy Blueberry Cups.

PER SERVING:	CAL. 204 (23% FROM FAT)	FAT 5 G	SOD. 8 MG
	PROT. 3 G	CARB. 38 G	CHOL. 13 MG

◆ POACHED NECTARINES WITH BLUEBERRY SAUCE

One of the great, all-time favorite desserts to serve during the summer months.

SERVES 2

2 large, unblemished nectarines
   (12 ounces)
¾ cup water
½ cup sugar

1½ tablespoons fresh lemon juice
4 tablespoons Blueberry Sauce
   (page 234)

1. Wash and dry nectarines. Using a small knife, halve one nectarine lengthwise through stem end. Grasp both halves firmly and twist in opposite directions until one side pulls free of the pit. If you cannot easily pry the pit from the other half with your fingers, cut the pit out neatly with a serrated knife. Repeat with other nectarine.

2. Place water, sugar, and lemon juice in a heavy 2½-quart saucepan. Bring to a boil over medium heat, stirring constantly with a wooden

spoon until all the sugar is dissolved. Turn heat to low and cook syrup for 5 minutes.

3. Place nectarine halves skin side down in syrup. Cover pan and simmer until the nectarines are barely tender when tested with a cake tester, about 3 minutes. Using two spoons, gently turn each nectarine half skin side up in syrup. Continue simmering, covered, until the fruit is slightly softened when tested again with cake tester, about 2 minutes.

4. Using a slotted spoon, transfer nectarines to a large, flat plate, skin sides up, to cool a little. When cool enough to handle, carefully peel the skin from each half with a small knife. Place peeled halves back on same plate, cut sides down.

5. Spoon 1 tablespoon of syrup over each half; cover with plastic wrap and refrigerate until ready to serve. (Nectarines may be poached up to 4 hours before serving.) Discard remaining syrup.

6. When ready to serve, drain nectarines and discard any remaining syrup on plate.

7. Place two nectarine halves on each dessert plate, cut sides down. Carefully spoon 2 tablespoons of Blueberry Sauce around nectarine halves on each plate and serve.

PER SERVING:	CAL. 170 (4% FROM FAT)	FAT 1 G	SOD. 2 MG
	PROT. 2 G	CARB. 43 G	CHOL. 0 MG

◆ NECTARINE CLAFOUTI

This quick-to-prepare homestyle dessert looks like a puffed fruit pancake when finished and is best served lukewarm. See variations at bottom of recipe.

SERVES 2

2 medium-sized ripe nectarines (8 ounces), halved, pitted, and sliced lengthwise into ¼-inch slices to make 1½ cups
1 5½-ounce can apricot nectar

1 large egg, lightly beaten
3 tablespoons sugar
¼ teaspoon ground cinnamon
3½ tablespoons unbleached all-purpose flour
½ teaspoon sifted confectioners' sugar (for dusting)

1. Adjust rack to center of oven and preheat to 350 degrees. Lightly grease a shallow 2½-cup ovenproof baking dish.

2. Arrange nectarine slices in a slightly overlapping pattern in two layers in prepared dish.

3. Place apricot nectar, beaten egg, sugar, cinnamon, and flour in blender or food processor fitted with metal blade. Run machine nonstop until batter is smooth, about 1 to 1½ minutes. (It is important that machine runs for at least one minute so that clafouti will puff during baking.) Slowly pour batter over nectarines.

4. Bake in preheated oven until surface is golden and slightly puffed, about 30 to 35 minutes. The clafouti is done when the batter has set into a custardlike mass on surface and a cake tester comes out clean when inserted in center.

5. Remove from oven and transfer to a cooling rack. Let clafouti cool on rack until lukewarm, about 35 minutes. Dust surface of lukewarm clafouti with confectioners' sugar. Spoon onto individual dessert plates and serve.

PER SERVING:	CAL. 245 (15% FROM FAT)	FAT 4 G	SOD. 36 MG
	PROT. 6 G	CARB. 49 G	CHOL. 108 MG

VARIATIONS

APRICOT CLAFOUTI

Substitute 4 ripe apricots (about 8 ounces), halved, pitted, and sliced lengthwise into ¼-inch slices to make 1½ cups, for the nectarines. Prepare and bake as directed for Nectarine Clafouti.

PER SERVING:	CAL. 245 (14% FROM FAT)	FAT 4 G	SOD. 36 MG
	PROT. 6 G	CARB. 48 G	CHOL. 109 MG

PEACH CLAFOUTI

Substitute 2 medium-sized ripe peaches (10 ounces), blanched, peeled, halved, pitted, and sliced lengthwise into ½-inch slices to make 1½ cups, for the nectarines. Prepare and bake as directed for Nectarine Clafouti, decreasing baking time to 25 to 30 minutes.

PER SERVING:	CAL. 241 (14% FROM FAT)	FAT 4 G	SOD. 35 MG
	PROT. 5 G	CARB. 48 G	CHOL. 109 MG

◆ ORANGE COMPOTE WITH LIQUEUR

A light, sweet finale to any meal; particularly good after a fish or seafood dinner.

SERVES 2

2 large navel oranges (1¼ pounds)   2 tablespoons Grand Marnier or
1 tablespoon confectioners' sugar   mandarin liqueur

   1. Cut a slice from top and bottom of oranges to expose the fruit. Peel the oranges and remove all the white membrane with a vegetable peeler. Cut out each orange segment, removing its protective membrane as you cut. Place orange sections in strainer set over a bowl to drain thoroughly. Place in refrigerator to chill for at least 1 hour or until ready to serve.

   2. When ready to serve, place orange sections in a bowl and toss with confectioners' sugar. Spoon sections into two dessert dishes, preferably glass. Sprinkle 1 tablespoon liqueur over each dessert and serve.

PER SERVING:	CAL. 144 (1% FROM FAT)	FAT .17 G	SOD. 2 MG
	PROT. 2 G	CARB. 31 G	CHOL. 0 MG

◆ PEACH CREAM

Select clingstone peaches for this dessert; they have a firmer flesh adhering to the stone and are better for cooking than the freestone variety, which have a juicier pulp and are better for eating fresh.

SERVES 2

2 large, ripe cling peaches   ½ cup whipped part-skim ricotta
  (14 ounces)   cheese (page 9)
2 tablespoons granulated sugar   2 teaspoons confectioners' sugar
2 teaspoons fresh lemon juice,   ⅛ teaspoon pure almond extract
  strained   2 teaspoons toasted slivered
1 tablespoon dark rum, preferably   almonds
  Myers's

1. Blanch peaches in 4 cups boiling water for 2 minutes. Transfer to a strainer and rinse under cold water. When cool enough to handle, peel skins, cut peaches in half, discard stones, and coarsely chop fruit. (You can chop peaches in the food processor fitted with metal blade. For an even chop, quarter peaches before placing in processor and chop with 3 to 4 quick on-off turns.)

2. In a 1½-quart saucepan, combine peaches, granulated sugar, and lemon juice. Bring to a boil over high heat. As soon as mixture reaches a boil, turn heat down to medium-low. Cook, stirring frequently with wooden spoon, until very little liquid is left in pan and peaches just start to stick to bottom of pan when stirred with spoon, about 10 to 12 minutes. Transfer to bowl. Cool to almost room temperature and stir in rum. Cover with plastic wrap and refrigerate until well chilled, about 1½ hours.

3. In a small bowl, combine whipped ricotta, confectioners' sugar, and almond extract. Blend thoroughly with fork or small whisk. Using a rubber spatula, fold ricotta mixture into peach mixture.

4. Spoon peach cream into two 8-ounce wine glasses and chill for at least 2 hours before serving. Garnish with toasted almonds just before serving.

PER SERVING:	CAL. 226 (20% FROM FAT)	FAT 5 G	SOD. 77 MG
	PROT. 8 G	CARB. 35 G	CHOL. 19 MG

◆ DESSERT PANCAKES WITH VARIOUS FILLINGS AND TOPPINGS

Part-skim ricotta cheese and whole wheat flour contribute a light texture to the batter, adding a delicate flavor to these crepelike pancakes. This is also an excellent light breakfast pancake. I usually double the batter if serving them for breakfast. The batter can also be made the night before and refrigerated. Stir with whisk to combine once again before cooking.

PANCAKES

SERVES 2

¼ cup part-skim ricotta cheese
1 large egg
1 teaspoon sugar

1½ teaspoons canola oil
2 tablespoons whole wheat flour
Vegetable oil cooking spray

1. Place ricotta cheese, egg, sugar, and oil in a deep bowl. Beat with a whisk until thick and creamy, about 30 seconds. Add flour and beat until well combined. (Batter should be made at least 2 hours before cooking pancakes. Cover with plastic wrap and leave at room temperature. Stir with whisk to combine before spooning batter onto hot skillet.)

2. Lightly grease a 12-inch nonstick skillet with cooking spray. Heat skillet over medium-high heat. Pour 2 tablespoons (use ¼-cup measure just half full) batter into skillet. Repeat with remaining batter to make a total of 4 pancakes, leaving 2-inch spaces between pancakes. When pancakes are lightly golden on the underside and bubbles appear on the surface, turn and brown lightly on second side. Transfer pancakes to plate and serve with various fillings and toppings.

PER SERVING:	CAL. 156 (55% FROM FAT)	FAT 10 G	SOD. 75 MG
	PROT. 8 G	CARB. 9 G	CHOL. 132 MG

◆ VARIOUS FILLINGS AND TOPPINGS

PEACH FILLING

2 medium-sized ripe peaches
(10 ounces), peeled, halved,
pitted, and coarsely chopped
3 tablespoons dark seedless raisins

1 tablespoon light brown sugar,
firmly packed
1 tablespoon fresh orange juice

1. In a 1½-quart saucepan, combine all of the filling ingredients. Bring to a boil over high heat. Turn heat to low and cook, stirring frequently, until peaches are soft and filling is slightly thickened, about 8 minutes. Transfer to bowl and cool to room temperature. (Filling can be made 1 day ahead, covered with plastic wrap, and refrigerated. Return to room temperature 1 hour before making pancakes.) To serve, spread filling in between and on top of pancakes.

PER SERVING:	CAL. 273 (31% FROM FAT)	FAT 10 G	SOD. 80 MG
	PROT. 9 G	CARB. 40 G	CHOL. 133 MG

APPLE FILLING

Substitute 2 medium Golden Delicious apples (10 ounces), peeled, halved, cored, and coarsely chopped to make 1 cup, well packed, for the peaches. Substitute 2 teaspoons fresh lemon juice for the orange juice. Cook and serve as directed for Peach Filling. (Filling may be made 1 day ahead, covered with plastic wrap, and refrigerated. Return to room temperature 1 hour before making pancakes.)

PER SERVING:	CAL. 280 (31% FROM FAT)	FAT 10 G	SOD. 81 MG
	PROT. 9 G	CARB. 40 G	CHOL. 133 MG

STRAWBERRY FILLING

1 cup thinly sliced strawberries   ½ teaspoon grated lemon rind
1 tablespoon confectioners' sugar   1 tablespoon Grand Marnier

1. Place strawberries in a small bowl. Lightly toss berries with confectioners' sugar, lemon rind, and Grand Marnier. Cover bowl and leave at room temperature for ½ hour before making pancakes.
2. To serve, spread filling between and on top of pancakes.

PER SERVING:	CAL. 215 (43% FROM FAT)	FAT 10 G	SOD. 76 MG
	PROT. 9 G	CARB. 21 G	CHOL. 132 MG

BLUEBERRY SAUCE TOPPING

4 tablespoons Blueberry Sauce
(page 234)

1. Stack pancakes, spoon 2 tablespoons sauce over each portion, and serve.

PER SERVING:	CAL. 185 (47% FROM FAT)	FAT 10 G	SOD. 76 MG
	PROT. 8 G	CARB. 17 G	CHOL. 132 MG

STRAWBERRY SAUCE TOPPING

4 tablespoons Strawberry Sauce
(page 235)

1. Stack pancakes, spoon 2 tablespoons sauce over each portion, and serve.

PER SERVING:	CAL. 208 (42% FROM FAT)	FAT 10 G	SOD. 78 MG
	PROT. 8 G	CARB. 23 G	CHOL. 132 MG

◆ POACHED SLICED PEARS WITH MARMALADE SAUCE

Especially good for late fall or during the winter months, when Bosc pears are abundant.

SERVES 2

2 cups water
1 cup sugar
¼ cup fresh lemon juice
2 large, firm, unblemished Bosc
    pears (about 14 ounces)

¼ cup orange marmalade
1 tablespoon Grand Marnier

1. In a 3-quart saucepan, combine water, sugar, and lemon juice. Bring to a boil over high heat, stirring frequently until sugar is completely dissolved. Turn heat down to low, cover pan, and cook syrup for about 8 minutes while preparing pears.

2. Remove core and stem from each end of pears. Peel fruit with a vegetable peeler. Cut the pears in half lengthwise. Using a melon baller, remove the center core. Cut away the fibrous line leading from the core to the stem end. Slice each halved pear lengthwise into 3 even pieces.

3. Place pear slices in syrup. Simmer, uncovered, spooning syrup over slices until they are tender when tested with a fork, about 5 minutes (time will vary depending on ripeness of pears). Remove from heat, cover pan, and let pears cool in syrup to room temperature or until ready to serve.

4. Put marmalade in a small saucepan. Stir in about 1 to 1½ tablespoons of the pear syrup, or just enough to barely loosen marmalade (amount will depend on how thick marmalade is). Cook over low heat, stirring constantly, just until marmalade has melted. Remove from heat and stir in liqueur.

5. Using a pair of tongs, lift pear slices from syrup. With narrow ends facing inward, arrange 6 pear slices on each dessert plate in a circular pattern. (Syrup may be reserved for additional poaching or discarded.) Spoon warm sauce over pears and serve immediately.

PER SERVING:	CAL. 325 (2% FROM FAT)	FAT 1 G	SOD. 23 MG
	PROT. 1 G	CARB. 82 G	CHOL. 0 MG

◆ PINEAPPLE SORBET WITH SAMBUCA

This quick and easy dessert is delectable for any occasion. A thin slice of zesty Lemon-glazed Prune Loaf (page 203) would prove a perfect partner.

SERVES 2

½ pint pineapple sorbet, preferably   2 tablespoons Sambuca
  Dole (see Note)

1. Place one scoop of sorbet in each dessert bowl, preferably glass, or in 8-ounce wine glasses. Drizzle 1 tablespoon liqueur over each portion and serve immediately.

N O T E : If pineapple sorbet is unavailable, substitute pineapple sherbet.

PER SERVING: CAL. 151 (.81% FROM FAT)	FAT .12 G	SOD. 11 MG
PROT. 1 G	CARB. 32 G	CHOL. O MG

◆ PLUM CRISP

A great-tasting dessert whenever you can find any type of well-ripened plums, from Italian purple prune plums to large red Santa Rosa plums. For a special treat, serve with a scoop of vanilla frozen yogurt. This crisp can be baked ahead of time and placed in a 300-degree oven ½ hour before serving. See variations at bottom of recipe.

SERVES 2

1½ tablespoons unsalted butter
1½ teaspoons honey, preferably
  orange blossom
¼ cup unbleached all-purpose
  flour
2 tablespoons firmly packed dark
  brown sugar
3 tablespoons lightly toasted
  walnuts, coarsely chopped

10 well-ripened Italian purple
  prune plums or 3 large red
  plums (about 12 ounces),
  halved, pitted, and sliced into
  ½-inch pieces
½ teaspoon sifted confectioners'
  sugar (for dusting)

1. Adjust rack to center of oven and preheat to 400 degrees. Lightly grease bottom and sides of a 3-cup shallow baking dish; set aside.

2. In a small saucepan, heat butter and honey over low heat, stirring, until the butter is melted.

3. In a medium-sized bowl, whisk together flour and brown sugar. Stir in butter mixture and stir until well combined. Stir in walnuts.

4. Layer plums in baking dish. Crumble the walnut topping over the plums and bake the crisp until the top is golden brown and juices from the plums start to surface, about 15 to 20 minutes. Transfer to rack and cool to lukewarm, about 20 minutes. Dust with confectioners' sugar just before serving.

PER SERVING:	CAL. 285 (21% FROM FAT)	FAT 7 G	SOD. 15 MG
	PROT. 2 G	CARB. 56 G	CHOL. 18 MG

VARIATIONS

APPLE CRISP

Substitute 2 large Golden Delicious apples (12 ounces) for the plums. Peel, halve, and core apples, and slice into ½-inch pieces. Prepare and bake as directed for Plum Crisp.

PER SERVING:	CAL. 274 (23% FROM FAT)	FAT 7 G	SOD. 14 MG
	PROT. 1 G	CARB. 53 G	CHOL. 18 MG

PEACH CRISP

Substitute 3 large, ripe peaches (about 1¼ pounds) for the plums. Blanch peaches in boiling water, drain, and peel when cool enough to handle. Halve peaches, remove pits, and slice into ½-inch pieces. Prepare and bake as directed for Plum Crisp.

PER SERVING:	CAL. 261 (23% FROM FAT)	FAT 7 G	SOD. 14 MG
	PROT. 2 G	CARB. 50 G	CHOL. 18 MG

◆ STAR-SPANGLED PARFAIT

Since so many of the commercial low-fat yogurts tend to be watery, drain thoroughly before assembling this distinctive red-white-and-blue dessert.

SERVES 2

1½ cups low-fat yogurt
2 teaspoons grated lemon rind
8 large, ripe strawberries
  (4 ounces), hulled and thinly
  sliced to make 1 cup
1 cup fresh blueberries

2 tablespoons honey, preferably
  orange blossom
2 whole strawberries, hulled
  (garnish)

1. Line a fine mesh strainer with a double thickness of dampened cheesecloth and set it over a bowl. Spoon yogurt into lined strainer and place, uncovered, in refrigerator to drain thoroughly for at least 2 hours. (Yogurt will exude as much as 6 tablespoons of liquid, and after draining, it should be the consistency of whipped heavy cream.) Discard liquid. Using a rubber spatula, scrape yogurt from cheesecloth into a small bowl and stir in lemon rind.

2. Put the sliced strawberries and the blueberries in separate bowls. Drizzle 1 tablespoon honey over each and toss gently with a rubber spatula.

3. Spoon sweetened strawberries into two 8-ounce parfait glasses or 8-ounce wine glasses. Carefully spoon 3 tablespoons of yogurt mixture into each glass over strawberries; spread evenly with a rubber spatula. Carefully spoon sweetened blueberries over yogurt mixture. Place a dollop of the remaining yogurt mixture on top of each dessert and chill for 2 hours before serving. (Do not chill any longer or berries will start to exude their juices.) Garnish with whole strawberries just before serving.

PER SERVING:	CAL. 242 (11% FROM FAT)	FAT 3 G	SOD. 125 MG
	PROT. 10 G	CARB. 47 G	CHOL. 10 MG

◆ FROZEN STRAWBERRY CREAM PARFAIT

It is essential to work quickly when preparing this easy, fast dessert. When served, the strawberry cream will still be partially frozen. See Note for variations.

SERVES 2

1 10-ounce package frozen
   sliced strawberries in syrup,
   unthawed
1 tablespoon Grand Marnier

¼ cup plus 2 teaspoons whipped
   part-skim ricotta cheese
   (page 9)
2 sprigs fresh mint leaves (garnish)

1. Working quickly, cut the block of frozen strawberries into 1½-inch pieces.

2. In blender or food processor fitted with metal blade, place strawberries and liqueur. Run machine nonstop until mixture appears slushy, about 30 seconds. Scrape down inside work bowl with plastic spatula. Evenly distribute ¼ cup ricotta over strawberries. Process until ricotta is well incorporated and strawberry cream is a smooth consistency, about 30 seconds.

3. Spoon into 8-ounce glass goblets and garnish each with 1 teaspoon of ricotta and a sprig of fresh mint; serve immediately.

NOTE: You may substitute a 10-ounce package of frozen raspberries or mixed fruit in syrup for the strawberries.

PER SERVING:	CAL. 206 (13% FROM FAT)	FAT 3 G	SOD. 49 MG
	PROT. 5 G	CARB. 41 G	CHOL. 11 MG

◆ PRUNE WHIP

Light and nearly effortless to make, this creamy dessert makes a fine conclusion to dinner for anyone who loves prunes.

8 ounces large pitted prunes, cut
   into ½-inch cubes
1 teaspoon finely grated
   lemon rind

1 cup whipped part-skim ricotta
   cheese (page 9)
2 tablespoons confectioners' sugar

1. Place prunes in a 1½-quart saucepan and cover with 1 cup water. Bring to a boil and cook just until prunes are softened. Transfer to strainer and drain thoroughly. Place prunes in small bowl, add lemon rind, and cool to room temperature. Cover with plastic wrap and refrigerate until well chilled, about 1 hour.

2. Beat ricotta with confectioners' sugar and fold gently but thoroughly into prune mixture. Ladle into two 8-ounce wine glasses and refrigerate until well chilled, about 2 hours, before serving.

PER SERVING:	CAL. 398 (10% FROM FAT)	FAT 5 G	SOD. 91 MG
	PROT. 10 G	CARB. 84 G	CHOL. 19 MG

◆ LEMON SHERBET WITH FRUIT AND STRAWBERRY SAUCE

A spectacular, light dessert to make whenever you can find fresh strawberries and kiwifruits at the market.

SERVES 2

6 medium-sized ripe strawberries (3 ounces)
1 large kiwifruit (about 2 ounces)
1 tablespoon sugar
½ teaspoon grated lemon rind

1 tablespoon Grand Marnier
½ pint lemon sherbet (preferably tangy, if available)
4 tablespoons Strawberry Sauce (page 235)

1. Rinse berries in cold water, thoroughly drain in strainer, and blot dry with paper towel. To core the berries, gather up the leaves of each stem cap and with the tip of a small knife cut a ¼-inch circle around the base of the cap. Pull the leaves, and the white core will come out as well. Quarter berries and transfer to a small bowl.

2. Cut about ¼ inch from top and bottom of kiwifruit. To remove the fuzzy brown skin, peel lengthwise with a vegetable peeler using a zigzag motion. Slice into ¼-inch rounds; slice each round in half crosswise.

3. Transfer kiwi to bowl with berries; combine with sugar and lemon rind. Cover with plastic wrap; refrigerate for 2 hours.

4. When ready to serve, remove fruit from refrigerator; combine with Grand Marnier. (Strawberries will get too soggy if marinated with liqueur in advance.)

5. Place one scoop of sherbet into individual bowls, preferably glass. Arrange fruit around sherbet. Spoon 2 tablespoons strawberry sauce over each portion; serve immediately.

PER SERVING:	CAL. 256 (7% FROM FAT)	FAT 2 G	SOD. 49 MG
	PROT. 2 G	CARB. 75 G	CHOL. 5 MG

SAUCES

◆ BLUEBERRY SAUCE

One of summer's most tantalizing treats is the sauce made from fresh blue-berries. An excellent sauce for Poached Nectarines (page 219) or Dessert Pancakes (page 224), it also adds a regal touch to lemon sherbet, pineapple sorbet, or vanilla frozen yogurt. Blueberry Sauce will keep up to one month in refrigerator. This sauce also freezes very well, so you may want to double the recipe. If doubling recipe, increase cooking time to 3 minutes. Watch carefully so sauce does not boil over. For freezing, place in freezer containers, removing cinnamon stick. Blueberry Sauce can be frozen for up to six months.

YIELDS 2½ CUPS

2 cups fresh blueberries
½ cup plus 2 tablespoons water
½ cup sugar
1 cinnamon stick about 2 inches
  long

2 tablespoons fresh lemon juice,
  strained
1½ teaspoons cornstarch

1. Pick over blueberries, wash thoroughly, and drain in colander.

2. In a 5-quart saucepan, combine ½ cup water, sugar, and cinnamon stick. Bring to a boil and cook, stirring constantly, until sugar is completely dissolved, about 4 minutes.

3. Add blueberries and lemon juice. Cook, stirring constantly over high heat, just until blueberries start to pop, about 2 minutes.

4. Place cornstarch and 2 tablespoons water in a small cup; stir with spoon until cornstarch is completely dissolved. Turn heat down to medium and stir cornstarch mixture into blueberries. Cook, stirring constantly, until sauce is thickened, about 2 minutes. Transfer sauce and cinnamon stick to a 1½-pint jar and cool to room temperature. Store in refrigerator until needed.

PER TABLESPOON:	CAL. 14 (1% FROM FAT)	FAT .02 G	SOD. .45 MG
	PROT. .04 G	CARB. 4 G	CHOL. 0 MG

◆ STRAWBERRY SAUCE

This sauce may be prepared up to one week before using. Leftover sauce enhances any combination of fresh fruits and is equally delicious when spooned over pineapple or lemon sorbet. Also, it makes a crowning topping for Dessert Pancakes (page 224).

YIELDS 1 CUP

1 10-ounce package Birds Eye
  frozen strawberry halves in
  syrup
2 tablespoons seedless red
  raspberry jam

1 tablespoon fresh lemon juice,
  strained
1 tablespoon Grand Marnier

1. Thaw berries in strainer set over a bowl; reserve juice.

2. Put berries in blender or food processor fitted with metal blade. Run machine nonstop until you have a smooth purée, about 30 seconds. Transfer to a small bowl.

3. Place reserved juice in a 1½-quart saucepan. Add jam and lemon juice; stir to combine. Bring to a boil over high heat, stirring constantly with wire whisk until jam is dissolved. Turn heat to low and cook syrup for 6 minutes. At this point syrup will still be thin. Pour hot syrup over the puréed berries and whisk to combine. Cool to room temperature and stir in Grand Marnier. Transfer sauce to a 10-ounce jar and refrigerate until well chilled and slightly thickened, about 3 hours.

PER TABLESPOON:	CAL. 26 (1% FROM FAT)	FAT .02 G	SOD. 2 MG
	PROT. .10 G	CARB. 7 G	CHOL. 0 MG

Index

Anne Casale began teaching cooking in 1963 when she founded Annie's Kitchen. She served as president of the New York Association of Cooking Teachers for two terms. She has taught in cooking schools throughout the United States and has appeared on numerous television and radio programs. The James Beard Foundation selected her as one of the Best American Cooking Teachers in 1988. Ms. Casale has worked in sales and marketing and as a lecturer, consultant, and designer for restaurants, gourmet shops, and cooking schools. Ms. Casale is the author of *Italian Family Cooking*, *Lean Italian Cooking*, and *Lean Italian Meatless Meals*.